By the same authors

MARIE-HELENE MATHIEU

Plus jamais seuls, Presses de la Renaissance, 2011
La Lumière d'une rencontre, Edifa/Mame, 2008
The story of Faith and Light, DVD, 2006 (English, French,
    Spanish, Italian)
Dieu m'aime comme je suis, Edition Saint Paul, 2002
Mieux vaut allumer une lampe que maudire l'obscurité,
    OCH, 1981

JEAN VANIER

Signs of the Times: Seven Paths of Hope for a Troubled World,
    Darton, Longman & Todd, 2013
Befriending the Stranger, Paulist Press, 2010
Essential Writings, Novalis, 2008
Becoming Human, House of Anansi Press, 2008
Our Life Together. A Memoir in Letters, HarperCollins
    Publishers Ltd, 2007
Community and Growth, Darton Longman & Todd Ltd, 2006
Man and Woman, God Made Them, Paulist Press, 2006
Made for Happiness: Discovering the Meaning of Life with
    Aristotle, House of Anansi Press, 2005
Drawn into the Mystery of Jesus through the Gospel of John,
    Darton, Longman & Todd Ltd, 2004
Finding Peace, House of Anansi Press, 2003
Seeing Beyond Depression, Paulist Press, 2001

Never Again Alone!

THE ADVENTURE OF FAITH AND LIGHT
from 1971 until today

MARIE-HÉLÈNE MATHIEU
with JEAN VANIER

WESTBOW PRESS
A DIVISION OF THOMAS NELSON
& ZONDERVAN

Translation
Maria Cecília de Freitas Cardoso Buckley
Timothy Stephen Buckley

Review of Text
Maureen O'Reilly
Judith Lanier

Illustrations for the covers: Ballade du dimanche (Sunday Ballad), oil on canvas 50 x 50 © Eric Chomis.
Logo of Faith and Light © Meb. Photo Marie-Hélène Mathieu © Stéphane Ouzanoff / Ciric. Photo Jean Vanier © Elodie Perriot.

WestBow Press books may be ordered through booksellers or by contacting:
WestBow Press
A Division of Thomas Nelson & Zondervan
1663 Liberty Drive
Bloomington, IN 47403
www.westbowpress.com
1 (866) 928-1240

ISBN: 978-1-4908-4607-1 (sc)
ISBN: 978-1-4908-4608-8 (hc)
ISBN: 978-1-4908-4606-4 (e)

Library of Congress Control Number: 2014913410

Printed in the United States of America.

WestBow Press rev. date: 09/23/2014

Contents

Acknowledgements

I thank with all my heart those who have helped me to write this book, and in a special way:

Jean Vanier, for encouraging me throughout process of its coming to birth;

Emmanuel Belluteau, for his personal investment in a collaboration nourished by his conviction, competence, listening and patience;

Thérèse de Longcamp, for her commitment in an often difficult and demanding secretarial situation;

the international team of Faith and Light and the team of the OCH for the warm environment surrounding the project everyday.

I would also like to recognize those women and men who worked on very diverse tasks: keyboarding, searching through archives, finding photos, giving personal witness, reviewing the text, etc., and all those countless people who carried the telling of this sacred story in their prayer.

Special acknowledgments for the English version

I wholeheartedly thank Maria Cecília de Freitas Cardoso Buckley and her husband Timothy Stephen Buckley for translating this book from French to English. This was a huge endeavour on their part made possible because of their love for Faith and Light and their wonder for its sacred history.

A tremendous thanks to Maureen O'Reilly and Judith Lanier for the time and effort it took to proofread this book. Their trust in Faith and Light and for Maureen, her experience of responsibility on so many levels have been a priceless gift.

I also genuinely thank Pastor Pamela Landis and Céline Doudelle, who, overcoming all obstacles, invested themselves to make it possible to publish this book.

Finally, thank you to all those who have written this story in their daily life: people with disabilities, parents, brothers, sisters, friends and priests...and all the English-speaking members of Faith and Light, whom by their desire, managed to have its release in English.

May the treasure of this little book radiate now and be known all over the world.

Foreword

Called to Joy
By Jean Vanier

In 2011 Faith and Light celebrated its fortieth anniversary. It remembered its origins: the first pilgrimage organized to Lourdes in 1971 for persons with an intellectual disability[1] and those close to them, to respond to the great isolation of their families.

The conditions in which we started this movement, with Marie-Hélène Mathieu, make for an exceptional adventure. We did not know what would happen next. There was the faltering at the beginning, the obstacles that were overcome, the immense graces received, the discoveries...This adventure continues each

---

1. How to call those who are at the heart of Faith and Light: our children, our sons, our daughters, our brothers, our sisters, our friends who are "different"? The language concerning the person who has intellectual or mental limitations is constantly evolving. We have used the words, "weak," "deficient" and then "maladjusted." Today, the term "handicapped" is still most often used in France. We have chosen to always precede it by the designation "person". In this way, we indicate our respect for each one's unique and irreplaceable dignity. We have strived to replace the verb, "to be" by the verb "to have". François is not a trisomic or a "Down." He is first of all François, a person who has trisomy. We also have used the terms: "touched," "wounded," "affected by" or "suffering" an intellectual disability. In these pages, when we use the expression, "person with a disability" it means a person with an intellectual disability.

month and grows in the heart of the 1500 communities spread throughout the world today.

This mysterious and wonderful story needed to be told. In accepting to share these memories about what guided and motivated us, Marie-Hélène witnesses for the first time what we dealt with in this adventure. She writes about what the families touched by a disability lived, about what the littlest ones brought to us, or the way that the Church welcomed our initiative. Marie-Hélène also witnesses to what is lived in Faith and Light and to its forty years in the service of love for the most fragile. She does it alternating the account with anecdotes and frequently moving reflection, full of truth and of gentleness.

I have in mind each one of the adults or young people who have accompanied me on the way, sometimes over the course of many years, and who have helped me/taught me about themselves, about me and...about God: Raphael, Philippe, Dany, Jacques, Pierrot and all the others....

A pilgrimage for persons who are excluded

As the leader of the community of l'Arche (the Ark) in Trosly[1] in l'Oise, I had already organized pilgrimages for people with disabilities, their families and the assistants to Lourdes, to Rome, to La Salette, to Fatima and to other places. Marie-Hélène, through the OCH[2] which she founded in 1963, was in contact with numerous families with vulnerable persons, many of whom felt excluded from the Church.

---

1. A village about 100 km northeast of Paris - Translator note
2. *Office Chrétien des Personnes Handicapées* - Christian Office of Persons with Disabilities

I met Marie-Hélène in November of 1966, when she came to see me at l'Arche. She had heard about a philosophy professor, "a little idealistic," who lived with people with intellectual disabilities and she had many questions. But, in this community, viewed as "a little strange," she was struck by the joy, the simplicity and the faith that prevailed. That's when, little by little, profound links were woven between us. We had the same vision of faith and love for persons with disabilities. And we were united in the same love of Jesus.

In 1967 in Paris, I participated in a congress organized by Marie-Hélène, president of l'UNAEDE[1], for Christian educators and parents on the topic of the sexual and affective life of persons with a disability. After that Marie-Hélène joined the Board of Directors of l'Arche. Through the OCH she was able to help by directing financial aid to various communities that were being born. Eventually she became coordinator of the communities of l'Arche in France and a member of the International Council. Therefore, over the course of many years, l'Arche was able to benefit from the vision, wisdom and assistance of Marie-Hélène.

At this time, people with an intellectual disability had difficulty finding their place in society and even in the Church. Special religious education was just beginning. Numerous priests refused to give them communion: "Their disability," they would say, "prevented them from understanding this sacrament." Father Bissonnier was beginning to make his voice heard through the teachings that he gave about pedagogy for persons with intellectual disabilities. There were few schools for these children, and even fewer residences or workshops for adults. The parents of these children would often feel lost faced with their child so different

1. *Union Nationale des Assistants et Éducateurs de l'Enfance* - National Union of Assistants and Educators of Infancy

from others. The question that pierced them, consciously or not, was "Whose fault is it? Is this a punishment from God?" The suffering of the parents was not only to see their children suffer physically and psychologically but also to see that their children had been rejected.

In this context it is not surprising that the families and their children were excluded from a good number of pilgrimages, and it is not surprising that there was a lot of resistance among the wise and prudent to the idea of a big pilgrimage that we were preparing for 1971.

Marie-Hélène marvelously describes the birth of a project and how it grew. Why not an international pilgrimage? Little by little our feeling was confirmed. There was the hand of God in all of this. What looked truly impossible became possible. We overcame insurmountable difficulties. Being in Paris, Marie-Hélène was at the heart of the preparation. She was on the front line. I came when I could to the preparation meetings because, at this time, I also had trips in France and even to India for the birth of new l'Arche communities. I also went to Canada where I gave retreats and conferences that would attract people to serve as assistants in l'Arche in France. It was Marie-Hélène who, courageously and with a lot of lucidity, bore the difficulties and the challenges of this preparation.

Our societies and often families looked at the birth of a person with a disability as a tragedy, sometimes even as a punishment from God. However in l'Arche, as in Faith and Light, little by little we have discovered that to meet, to welcome and to enter into relationship with such a person can become a source of life, of becoming more fully human and of a meeting with Jesus. This discovery of the person with disabilities as a source of life and presence of Jesus was mine in l'Arche, but it took me time, a lot of time to become aware of it, to live it and to put adequate spiritual and theological words to it.

My path before the pilgrimage

I started l'Arche in 1964, without knowing anything about persons with disabilities, or the necessary pedagogy to help them to grow. Humanly speaking, nothing had prepared me for the adventure of l'Arche and of Faith and Light. In 1942, during the war, I entered the Naval School that prepared future British Naval officers. Eight years of formation and service on battle ships followed. Little by little, the desire was born in me to better know Jesus and his Gospel. In 1950, the naval authorities accepted my resignation.

I then looked for a place to be prepared for a commitment in the priesthood. This brought me to l'Eau Vive (living water), a community founded by Father Thomas Philippe, close to Paris. It is there that my heart and my mind were opened to the Gospels with the help and friendship of Father Thomas. He became my spiritual father and introduced me to a life of prayer consisting of presence, of communion, of listening and of silence.

In April 1952, Father Thomas had to leave the community he had founded. As he left, he asked me to take on responsibility for l'Eau Vive. With my scant experience, my naivety and my good will, I accepted. At the same time, I began studies in philosophy at the Institut Catholique de Paris. When the community l'Eau Vive closed its doors in 1956, I continued to work on my doctoral thesis and I defended it. In 1964 I started to teach philosophy at the University of Toronto.

About that time, Father Thomas became the chaplain of a small center, the Val Fleuri (flowered valley) in Trosly-Breuil. In Val Fleuri there were around thirty men with intellectual disabilities, many of whom had been locked up in the psychiatric hospital of Clermont for a long time. He invited me to come to meet these men who had suffered the absence of their family and of society. Because, as he told me then, it is the persons who are marginalized and set apart from life in a society who can better reveal to us the meaning of human life.

I was astonished by this visit to Val Fleuri. Before going, I was afraid. How to initiate a conversation with persons like them? What could we talk about? My anxiety was quickly transformed into surprise when I felt in each of the men a call to friendship: "Will you come back to visit us?" Their cry for relationship profoundly touched me.

After this visit, Father Thomas encouraged me to visit psychiatric hospitals, institutions and families who had a child with disabilities. I discovered then the terrible suffering of families and of men and women with an intellectual disability, locked up in institutions, deprived of freedom, of work, and often of respect and of love.

By visiting Father Thomas in Trosly, I became aware that it was possible for me, with the support of Doctor Préaut an eminent psychiatrist well known in the Oise area, to create a small community with persons in need. I would also be able to stay close to Father Thomas. He could help me, as well as help the community, to grow in the love and wisdom of Jesus. The local governmental authorities at this time were looking for volunteers to create centers for adults with disabilities and they were offering financial support. So, why not do something here in Trosly with Father Thomas?

It was this desire to ease suffering and come to the aid of those living with disabilities, often crushed by life but created by God and chosen by Him, that moved me to act. "God has raised up the humiliated from the dust and removed the poor from the dung-heap to sit in the ranks of princes."[1] God said, through the prophet Isaiah, "He stays close to those who are humiliated and

---

1. Psalm 113: 7-8

abandoned,"[1] and Paul reveals to us that God chooses that which is foolish and weak in the world and that which is most despised.[2] "God has brought down the powerful from their thrones and has lifted up the humiliated,"[3] Mary also sings in her Magnificat.

For me, to be Christian is to place oneself at the side of the weak and the poor. To announce the Good News to the poor does not consist only in saying "God loves you", but even more "I, myself, love you and I commit myself to you in the name of Jesus." I had been impressed by Dorothy Day in the United States, who lived with street people, by Tony Walsh, who had lived on a Native-American reservation in Canada to help them to rediscover their language and their culture, and by the community "Friendship House", where people inspired by their Christian faith came to share a life of prayer and friendship with African-American residents in Harlem, in New York. For a long time, I felt close to the spirituality of Charles de Foucauld, of the Little Sisters and Little Brothers of Jesus, whose purpose is to live in fraternities, in the midst of the most excluded and most marginalized. Fundamentally, I wanted to live in the company of poor people.

Everything happened very fast. After finishing my teaching in Toronto in April 1964, and having refused a placement as a permanent professor, I decided with Father Thomas to find a small house in Trosly or nearby, and to take two or three persons from a center that I had visited in the region around Paris, that was overcrowded, violent and difficult. I could start a partnership with Doctor Préaut, find the necessary finances with friends, buy a somewhat ramshackle house – without bathroom and toilet, but adequate – and look for some furniture at an Emmaüs community. Within a few months, everything was ready!

---

1. Isaiah 57: 15
2. 1 Corinthians 1: 18-28
3. Luke 1: 52

This is how, on August 5, the director of this overcrowded center arrived with Raphaël Simi, Philippe Seux and Dany, bringing the lunch that the center had prepared for us. Father Thomas was there with Doctor Préaut and Jacqueline d'Halluin; Louis Pretty and Jean-Louis Coïc came to help me. After lunch and washing the dishes, the visitors left, and I found myself with three men with a disability and my two friends. What to do? Each one went to his bedroom and unpacked his suitcase. Philippe and Raphaël both had a certain human balance beyond their intellectual and physical disabilities. On the other hand, Dany, who was deaf and mute, showed intense anguish and ran out of the house gesticulating and shouting. I was lost in front of him! After some rest, we set the table and shared a meal. Then we prayed around the table before going to bed. These beginnings of l'Arche were so poor, so "crazy"; so impossible! In fact, that night was catastrophic with Dany who got up every hour, crying out. In the morning, I called the director of the center asking her to come immediately to get him. Already I couldn't stand it. Everything began with a failure!

Then, everyday life began. We washed ourselves with water warmed up on the stove; for showers, it was necessary to walk down to Val Fleuri, two hundred meters from the house. There was a sort of "outhouse" in the garden. Friends like Raymond came to help me. They cooked and we worked in the garden. Little by little a sort of routine was established. Everyday, at 7:30am, we participated in Mass with Father Thomas; then we had breakfast, worked in the garden, cleaned up and cooked. Often I did not know what I could or should do. I was so ignorant about the needs of people with disabilities. I adapted myself to each event and to each instant. What was important was to live with Raphaël and Philippe with joy, to listen to them, to prepare and to share meals. I lived in trust that l'Arche was the work of God and that Jesus would help me. I wanted to live the Gospels and to become a friend of the poor, and this implied some measure of insecurity; an abandonment to the present moment.

Deep in my heart I had much peace, and I lived the beginning of l'Arche as a solace. I left the Navy in 1950. Then, I believed that l'Eau Vive would be the place for my final stability. But no, I had to leave this community in 1956. Between 1956 and 1964, I was seeking, on pilgrimage. I had my doctorate in philosophy to write and to defend, and I taught for several months in Toronto. During these years, above all, I maintained my links of heart, spirit and mind with Father Thomas, and the rare contacts I had with him. I looked forward to the time when I could meet him again. Where would all this take me?

L'Arche seemed to me, consciously or unconsciously, as "my home", my dwelling. Finally I had arrived "at home", because before, I only had a little apartment in Paris that Doctor Préaut had lent to me. It was the end of a long path of confident searching. I finally had a place, my whole being was engaged; I was committed to some persons who were poor and this was for all my life. My dream was accomplished. It was the end of a long journey, but, without my knowing, it was certainly the beginning of another very long journey, which I had no idea where it would take me. Finally, I could live the Gospels, close to Father Thomas.

The name "l'Arche" was decided during a meeting with Jacqueline, Father Thomas's secretary, whom I had met at l'Eau Vive in 1950. By creating l'Arche I had done what I believed to be just and true, what I thought God wanted, without too much reflection or planning. Going along with and welcoming what happens day after day, I was assuming my responsibility towards Raphaël and Philippe. By welcoming them as they left the center where they had lived until then, which was a place of oppression, I wanted to do something good for them, to give them a place of freedom and of life, a new family.

Little by little, l'Arche grew. A month after the opening, in the middle of September 1964, I welcomed Jacques Dudouit, then Pierrot Crepieux in December. Other people came to help me, particularly Henri Wambergue who arrived on August 22nd. Sister Marie Benoît arrived at the end of October and took charge of the house with the cooking, the shopping and the cleaning. In March 1965 I also took on the difficult responsibility of the large Val Fleuri, with its thirty men who were more or less disturbed, after the director and almost all the staff resigned. In July, we all went in pilgrimage to Lourdes. Then, in 1966, we went in pilgrimage to Rome: eighty persons in seventeen automobiles! We had a wonderful private audience with Pope Paul VI who, in his message, invited us to holiness. Between 1967 and 1970 we did other pilgrimages to Lourdes, Fatima and La Salette.

The "foolish" foundation of l'Arche and all that subsequently happened to it shows my level of trust and of "naivety" in the face of life. Out of this same spirit came the idea of organizing a big pilgrimage with Marie-Hélène. I did not try to reflect too much on the difficulties in organizing such an event. I gave my word. I already had a little experience of persons with a disability and of pilgrimages. If this was the work of God, then I would take on the responsibility with Marie-Hélène.

The founding pilgrimage

Although I was not always present in Paris for the preparation of the pilgrimage, I participated nevertheless by mobilizing future pilgrims from Canada and the United States, without always being aware of it at the time. During the years 1968 to 1971, I gave conferences and animated many retreats in Canada; a new l'Arche community was born near Cognac, France, another in Toronto, and finally (a true miracle of Providence) in India.

During these conferences, I talked about the Gospels as a source of life, and of Jesus hidden in the poor who transforms us. I perceived, during this eventful period in the Church, a great attraction, especially among the youth, for a profound sense of the Gospels and the place of the poor. At the same time, l'Arche in Trosly and surrounding areas was developing with new homes.

By coordinating the pilgrimage to Lourdes with Marie-Hélène, I had the feeling that a new era began where persons with an intellectual disability would have their rightful place in the Church and in society. In the United States, a big movement took shape to close the doors of the enormous institutions and to create group homes in the cities. My words at the opening, in front of 12,000 pilgrims in the plaza before the Basilica of the Rosary, on Good Friday 1971, gave witness to my interior state: "We will all create, in all the towns and villages, small communities where persons with a disability will find their place."

In spite of all this vast work of coordination and all the activities of the pilgrimage that I guided with Marie-Hélène, my heart was in great peace. I was filled with confidence, this confidence that all that happened in l'Arche, all that I had lived in Canada and in India, and also this big pilgrimage, was the work of God. It was as if Jesus had chosen l'Arche and Faith and Light so that something new might be brought about in the world and in the Church.

The official goal that we had fixed for the pilgrimage was to facilitate the inclusion of persons with intellectual disabilities in diocesan pilgrimages. In reality, the real objective that Marie-Hélène and I were unaware of at the beginning, was hidden in the heart of God: it was the creation of a huge movement for persons with disabilities, their families and their friends, that would spread throughout the world.

In the beginning of l'Arche, as in the beginning of Faith and Light, I had the desire to come to the aid of persons with a disability, so often put aside, including in the Church, and to come to the aid of their families who also felt themselves, not well included by the Church. The success and the fruits of the pilgrimage, the growth of l'Arche and the life in the homes made me discover that these persons had a particular role to play in the world and in the Church.

Persons with disabilities are not only favored by God; it is as if they have a mysterious power to transform hearts and to reveal Jesus, if only we accept to live a relationship with them as friends. Their simplicity, their interior freedom when facing cultural norms, their ability to welcome and their love for each person call forth a true transformation of hearts. They bring down the walls of protection around our hearts in order to awaken what is most beautiful in each one of us.

Cardinal Rylko, president of the Pontifical Council of the Laity in Rome, a number of years after getting to know us, was able to say, "You in l'Arche and in Faith and Light, you have created a true Copernican revolution, it is no longer you who have done good things to persons with disabilities, but you say that it is they who have done good things for you!"

The discovery of the parents

Certainly, before the birth of l'Arche and during its beginnings, I met with many parents of persons with disabilities. Thanks to Faith and Light I was able to become aware of the sufferings, the concerns, but also of the unconditional love of so many parents who marvelously give themselves to their children. My experience in l'Arche at first was in the service of men, and later of women with disabilities, many of whom had been separated from their parents at a very young age and placed in institutions. I personally had extensive experience of community life through l'Arche. On her side, Marie-Hélène had extensive experience with parents. We were, from this point of view, very complementary and I had much to learn.

In all meetings of Faith and Light, I heard the cry of the anxiety of the parents: "What will become of our children when we are no longer here?" L'Arche appeared, to many, like the perfect solution. However, to create a community of l'Arche implies many elements: to find suitable houses, money for investment and for operations, but above all it is necessary to find local people willing to carry the project and a considerable number of assistants who commit themselves to community life.

The advantage of Faith and Light is that it is much easier to begin. To create a community is not first a question of money, but of the desire to meet, to create a group where the people commit themselves to each other. Highly important also is the commitment of friends. In fact, it is the friends, touched and moved by persons with disabilities, who help us to discover the profound sense of Faith and Light. If it is natural that parents are delighted with and commit themselves to Faith and Light, it is marvelous that their children are able to find young friends who love them and want to do things with them.

This has made it possible for youth from all countries to discover the mystery of the person with a disability! Those who, until then, represented a burden or a curse in the eyes of the world were very quickly revealed as a blessing. These young people lived a true transformation of their heart and of their spirit. In the 1970s, there were not many Christian movements that attracted youth; by contrast, Faith and Light was like a magnet. In this way the "movement" – this word was not chosen by chance – developed very rapidly.

In fact, we see today that in order for Faith and Light and l'Arche to continue to be dynamic, alive and missionary, it is necessary not only that young people but also the parents discover a true call from God who transforms hearts and opens them to the Gospel, as a way of peace and of union with Jesus.

It is the very simplicity of Faith and Light that permits its communities to shine even more in the Church. When a community is linked to a parish and can animate the Eucharistic celebration or simply participate in it, it becomes visible. Many parishioners are then able to discover that people with a disability are important and that the essential is not in success, work, knowledge, sports or a beautiful wedding.

I remember the witness of a woman who had left the Church because she found it to be too serious and ritualistic: "I entered a church one afternoon, and I saw a group of persons of different ages and disabilities who sang and danced. They all seemed to be so happy! I went to talk with them. And one day I committed to the community!" It is the simplicity of people with disabilities who reveal God's love and Jesus' vision for the whole world.

The spirituality of l'Arche and of Faith and Light

Life in the homes of l'Arche is very simple. Together we create a sort of a new culture, where communication consists of joy and laughter, and certainly, there is also work, a pedagogy and therapy guided by professionals. The meals are at the heart and the center of life, as a place of beatitude. The words of Jesus are foundational for these communities: "When you give a meal, do not invite the members of your family, nor your friends, nor your rich neighbors; when you give a banquet, invite the poor, the crippled, the sick and the blind. Then you will be happy!"[1]

To eat at the same table as the excluded ones is an evangelical beatitude.

---

1. Luke 14: 12-14

L'Arche developed in this communion with persons excluded from social and ecclesial life; these persons are the center and the source of unity. To live with the poor is to live with Jesus. This spirituality, for Catholics and all Christians, implies a life of prayer, a sacramental life and a true interior life. The daily Eucharist is, for me and for many, necessary so that our hearts open up more in true love.

This simple life of communion with persons with a disability is, in reality, a spirituality. It is a life inspired and directed by the Gospel and by the Word of Jesus to the chosen of the Kingdom. Even if they have not recognized Jesus himself, they have served Jesus without necessarily being aware of it: "All that you do to the least of mine, it is to me that you have done this."[1] In this way l'Arche wanted to live the kingdom of God.

This same spirituality is at the heart of Faith and Light. It is a way of union with Jesus, through life. The social doctrine of the Church, so well developed in the papal encyclicals, especially after Leo XIII, is not first of all a spirituality. It is a theological and sociological work that teaches Christians the duty to be at the service of the poor in society and in the world, with intelligence and generosity. Christians cannot distance themselves from the cry of suffering when it bursts forth in the world. Ordinarily, this service of justice flows from a desire to help the poor, which implies a certain feeling of superiority in relation to the one for whom good is done.

Certainly, in creating l'Arche, I wanted to do good for some people who had been oppressed in a closed and violent institution. Raphaël and Philippe did not have any desire to live all their lives with professionals who wanted to do good for them. Persons with an intellectual disability have been terribly humiliated by our society. They have not always been recognized

---

1. Matthew 25: 40

as having true value, with the right to speak and the possibility to develop personal awareness and to walk a path towards human maturity.

To eat at the same table as persons who are marginalized is not only to give them something to eat; it is to live a relationship of friendship with them, to live in communion with them. To create a relationship, to listen to them, to understand their sufferings and their needs takes time, a lot of time. In fact, to help Raphaël and Philippe regain trust in themselves, to consider themselves as important and valuable persons, took a lot of time!

If in the beginning I committed with Raphaël and Philippe to help them, progressively I discovered that the essential was to live a relationship of mutual trust with each one. It was to create a community in which this life of relationship could be celebrated, lived and deepened. It is a way of humility, of listening, and I would say, of poverty. I was formed to command in the Navy, then to teach philosophy; it was then necessary that I pass from my head – the center of knowledge – to my heart. This way of the heart consists in revealing to the other and the others, humiliated and excluded, their value as persons. They really are messengers of light, of life, of God.

In the many cases where people with an intellectual disability have been viewed by their own parents as a disappointment, and humiliated throughout the years, much time is necessary for persons to rediscover a meaning for their life. I also needed time to renounce my ambitions to be among the best in knowledge and power, and to rediscover the true meaning of my life: to live in communion with Jesus and with people who are different, to bring down the walls of prejudices and fears that were in me, and that separated me from others.

Yes, the communities of Faith and Light and of l'Arche are schools of love; "Love is of God and those who love are born of

God and know God."[1] To love is a way towards God; Jesus leads us to love one another, especially the excluded and the poorest.

To live with and especially to have a loving relationship, simple and trusting, with the poor is to live a covenant. Friendship with the poor is different from the one we live between "equal" persons, who are united by the same activities. Communion with the poor, with the person with a disability, is an end in itself, because he or she is the place where we find God.

The spirituality of Faith and Light is the same as in l'Arche, but it cannot be lived out in the same way. This spirituality is entered into in a community that lives together as l'Arche, or that meets regularly as Faith and Light. Even before the pilgrimage of 1971, families from the same city or region met with one another to prepare for it. This is how the bonds of affection and fraternal support between the members started to grow. These links were truly woven during the pilgrimage. The charism of Faith and Light, as that of l'Arche, is this communitarian life structured around persons who are the weakest. They are the ones who set the tone. Even if, in Faith and Light, the community time is reduced to one or more gatherings per month, summer camps, retreats, pilgrimages, nevertheless their members draw in a strong dynamism, great hope and a profound sense of life. It is true for parents who are no longer isolated, as well as for persons with disabilities who can find meaning for their life in the love of Jesus, and for friends who discover a new vision for society through this friendship with these persons who are the weakest.

This spirituality finds its roots in the deep human need of the parents to move out of their isolation and for their children to have friends and places where they are able to celebrate. This communitarian relationship, with its life of prayer, its moments of celebration and of sharing, becomes a privileged place for all.

---

1. John 4: 7

The tight links woven between the spiritual life and human needs explain the extraordinary development of Faith and Light throughout the world.

Deeply human communities rooted in the Gospel

In Rwanda, where I animated a retreat for families of Faith and Light, I asked this question: "What does Faith and Light bring to you?" Almost all the mothers who were there with their children told me: "Faith and Light has revealed to me that my child is truly a person, and even that he/she is loved by God." Many mothers had, until then, the feeling that their children were a punishment from God and that they were not truly human.

It is because Faith and Light is deeply human that the movement needs this breath of the Spirit that was manifested so strongly during the first pilgrimage to Lourdes. The suffering known to people with disabilities and their parents obviously is not reserved to Catholics. It is the same in all families, whether they are believers or not. Marie-Hélène recounts in this book that Anglicans and Protestants of different confessions were present in this first pilgrimage. It is the same breath that inspired all these families, so happy to discover how God welcomes and loves their children.

The vision of the communities of Faith and Light is centered in the Gospels, and in the teachings of Paul according to which God has chosen the foolish and the weak, the most despised to confound the intellectuals and the powerful of the earth. The charism of Faith and Light is truly in this spiritual and community life inspired by the Gospel, but it is limited to meetings, whereas many parents also aspire to find the necessary services, specialized schools and workshops that their children need. The Faith and Light community helps families to get out of their isolation, and sometimes out of the shame that they might experience, and reveals to them the essential: their child is fully human, is precious and is called to live in communion with Jesus.

This is how persons with a disability become a call and a way toward unity among Christians. The mystery of Jesus' cross is at the heart of Christian life, and of every community, and it enlightens this mystery of human suffering that Jesus assumed. He did not abolish suffering but he gives strength to live it.

For me, it was evident from the beginning that Faith and Light was meant for all Christians coming from different churches, even if this movement was born in the heart of the Catholic Church in Lourdes. I had already had experience, as an officer in the British Navy, of a common life with Christians of different confessions, and in my retreats in Canada we had lived times of deep communion together. L'Arche in Toronto was founded in 1969 by a couple from the Anglican Church that welcomed many persons with a disability from this Church – and they all came to the pilgrimage of 1971.

The desire for communion with other religions

I went to India, in November of 1969, to answer a call from Mahatma Gandhi's disciples to start a l'Arche community there. During my visit to this country, I met with his disciples, who efficiently helped in the creation of this new community. The encounter with the spirit and the thoughts of Gandhi; his love for all people, especially the most excluded, and his life of prayer, have deeply changed my heart. I lived a true conversion. I could verify signs of the presence of God in this culture so different from the one I knew in the West. I discovered a dimension and a deepening of my own faith in Jesus by verifying the work of God in others, in another religion. Isn't this what the Second

Vatican Council brought to light in its decrees *Lumen Gentium* and *Gaudium et Spes*?

This deepening of my heart and of my faith continued the following year, when the l'Arche community opened in Bangalore with the name, Asha Niketan, and under the leadership of Gabriele Einsle. In Hinduism, there is a whole current of spirituality according to which God is seen in the poor, the rejected and the leper. The five communities of l'Arche in India have become more profound by a common life between persons with a disability and assistants from Hindu, Muslim and Christian faiths. A true witness of unity in everyday life, with and through the presence of people with a disability!

In one of his poems, Tagore talks about the feast in a village that prepares itself to welcome the god. This will be a beautiful and grand display! All the important people are there, very well dressed for the occasion, the streets are all decked out; the municipal band is in place. The chief of the village, going here and there to confirm if everything is in order and clean, stops in front of a dilapidated little hut. The poor woman who lived there is preparing everything; she hurriedly cleans the dirt floor of her poor little dwelling. "What are you doing there? Come, the god will arrive", cries the chief to this woman who answers: "I clean up my house because God will come here." The chief bursts out in scornful laughter: "What! Do you truly believe that the god will come to the home of a poor person like you?" She exclaims: "But who, except God, visits a poor person?"

These meetings with the spirituality of the poor in India have given me a great desire to make the spirit of Faith and Light known to Hindu, Muslim, Buddhist, etc. families, who live great suffering with their son or daughter with a disability. Faith and Light, born in Lourdes, has a profound Christian dimension that does not permit its development in other religions, but we can hope that, one day, a similar movement could be born in other religions, and that it could bring new hope to parents faced with the presence of their children with disabilities. I believe that this desire in me is the reflection of a desire of God who loves all His children of all cultures and religions. Already today Muslim mothers, supported by members of Faith and Light, have tried an experiment. They have begun, under another name, groups filled with life, strongly inspired by the spirit of Faith and Light and by its activities.

Because people with intellectual disabilities have a capacity to open up and attract the heart of each person (this is part of their mystery), they can sometimes be seen in certain cultures as a blessing and not only as a curse. I remember an old Muslim grandfather who came with his grandson to a conference I gave in Burkina Faso. He told me: "Nobody, until now, has told us that God loves our children." The littleness and the beauty of some of these children can be a source of unity between persons of different cultures and religions. Isn't the mission of l'Arche and Faith and Light to reveal the beauty and capacity for relationship of these persons, often banished from society, and in this way to work for peace and for unity among all human beings?

The brothers of Taizé, with others, organized a pilgrimage in Bangladesh, in which a significant number of persons with disabilities belonging to different religions participated. Following the pilgrimage, Brother Franz wrote this:

"We discover more and more that those who are rejected by society because of their weakness and of their apparent uselessness are in reality a presence of God. If we welcome them, they progressively lead us out of a world of competition and of the need to do big things, to steer us towards a world of communication of hearts, towards a life, simple and full of joy, where we accomplish little things with love. [...]

The challenge that confronts us today impels us to point out that the service that we give to our brothers and sisters who are weak and vulnerable signifies the opening of a way of peace and of unity: to welcome each one in the rich diversity of religions and of cultures, to serve the poor, prepares a future of peace."

The holy story of Faith and Light

The story of Faith and Light is a "holy" story. This story is holy because it tells us something about God, about humanity and about the relationship between God and humanity. The Bible is a story where God reveals himself through the story of specific people and concrete facts. The four Gospels are the story of Jesus, and they reveal who this man was and his mission of God's love for all human beings. It is also a story of suffering. Jesus proved to be dangerous for the "religious establishment" of the time because he questioned their way of interpreting the Scriptures and exercising religious power. He was therefore rejected and in the end sentenced to death as a criminal. The person who came to reveal love and change our hearts is brought down, tortured and killed.

Through the story of concrete facts and specific people, we see the birth and growth of the Church. We are then better able to understand who God is, who the Holy Spirit is, and how this Spirit inspired the newborn Church. The story of the Church sprang forth from Jesus' extreme poverty and degradation, weakened and excluded. It also sprang forth from the truth of his words, his life given over, from his deeds and his resurrection from the dead. And, progressively, a vision of the human person emerged, which spread across the earth. We need to read and understand the story of God's action in the world and then enter into the vision of God that is revealed.

The story of Faith and Light is also a sign from God. Out of the suffering of Gérard and Camille and their two children, and out of the conversation and the communion between Marie-Hélène and me, was born this great pilgrimage. Out of the pilgrimage, communities were born, which continue to spread to all the continents and which are transforming broken hearts into hearts of thanksgiving. What might have seemed to some to be a curse became a blessing, that is, a place from which we can draw forth good.

The 1971 pilgrimage was not an ordinary pilgrimage; it was organized for and with people with intellectual disabilities who, until then, had generally been excluded from diocesan pilgrimages and sometimes from the Church. This explosion of joy and life in Lourdes revealed the importance of people with intellectual disabilities for the Church, for humanity and for our societies. The weakest, the most foolish, the most despised are really important for humanity and for the Church - that is the message of Faith and Light and l'Arche.

The human family can only find peace if we all turn ourselves toward the weakest to recognize them and to lift them up. Not only are these persons important, really human, but they also have the power to transform hearts if we really want to live in relationship and in communion with them. The one who is the most despised becomes then a source of life and of hope. Isn't this why St Paul says that the parts of the body that are the weakest are indispensable to the body of the Church?[1]

The danger, for our societies, is the hardening of hearts because of fear that spreads among so many people: fear of failure, fear of losing a standard of life, fear of losing money, fear of catastrophes and of accidents. It is exactly those who have lived fears and humiliations, and who are fragile, who can become a source of a new hope.

---

1. Corinthians 12: 22-23 (and following)

The growth of Faith and Light did not happen without opposition. All that is new awakens resistance. The pilgrimage of 1971 unfolded with lots of enthusiasm, but there were also those who could not see in the blossoming and development of this movement a sign of the Holy Spirit acting in hearts. After the Council, at least in France, there were tensions in the Church, a certain opposition between social action and piety. Resistances at the birth of Faith and Light almost turned into a battle. Marie-Hélène describes these tensions with much discretion, with the support of facts and the documents in the archives of Faith and Light. Isn't it the same resistance that every new movement finds in the Church?

The Holy Spirit guides with firmness and gentleness, and sometimes even with a burst of light. This is how Faith and Light was able to grow and spread throughout the world. It is necessary to add that its deep human aspect, the joy of the parents and of their children with a disability in finding friends and in having places of meeting were like soil, very human soil, in which the Holy Spirit could take root.

The joy that springs today from 1,500 Faith and Light communities in 80 countries is meant to become a joy for all humanity. God, being at the source of this grand development throughout the world, reveals that He is close to all of us with our poverties and our richness.

In this, Faith and Light is prophetic. Prophecy is not a vision of the future but a vision of salvation for human beings today imprisoned in a world of division, of injustice, of violence, of egoism and sometimes hatred, a world where so many people feel alone and isolated. Faith and Light shows a way that is not primarily economic, but a way of opening hearts to people who are fragile. It is no longer to seek the first place, nor to win by force in a spirit of rivalry, but to open up together with persons who are weaker; to come together to create communities of encounter where there is more love and peace. Isn't this what John-Paul II said in January of 2004:

"This is why it was said, very rightly, that people with disabilities are privileged witnesses of humanity. They can teach everyone what is the love that saves and they can become messengers of a new world, no longer dominated by force, by violence and by aggression, but by love, solidarity, welcome, a new world transfigured by the light of Christ, the Son of God incarnated, crucified and raised up for us."[1]

---

1. Message from Pope John-Paul II to the participants of the international symposium: "Dignity and rights of the person with an intellectual disability", in the Vatican, January 5, 2004.

Prologue

Francesco Gammarelli had everything necessary for happiness: a prestigious profession as the Pope's tailor; a beloved wife, Olga; an older son, Max, and then a little daughter, Sabina. They did not notice immediately that Sabina had "problems". By the end of the first month, they had discovered that she did not see, that she did not communicate, and that she had a profound disability. Francesco then closed himself up in revolt and despair. He avoided his home, his friends and cut himself off from God.

In his world without hope, one day, in 1977, he receives a phone call from Gwenda, a young woman who invites Sabina to a meeting of her Faith and Light community. Francesco is enraged: Sabina is incapable of participating in any type of meeting! Gwenda gently insists and, for the sake of peace, he gives in. When Gwenda welcomes them, she pays attention first of all to the small girl in the arms of her father: "How are you, Sabina?" For the first time, someone talks to Sabina as if she is a person. Francesco did not show it, but he was deeply moved. At first, the community welcomed Sabina alone. Later, her parents joined her.

It was in Rome, in 1979, that I met Francesco. A group of us were sitting in a circle, singing and playing. Suddenly, I saw Sabina get up, and with stumbling steps, pass from one person to another, touching each face. When she arrived at her father, she gave a joyful cry and threw herself into his arms. What an unforgettable vision of this little girl and her daddy, united in an exchange of love through trust.

Francesco, later international vice-coordinator for Faith and Light, one day accompanied me to a meeting in Rome with the director of a charitable association that could give us financial aid for a new international pilgrimage. After listening to me, the director showed an almost shocking surprise: "You ask for financial help! But you do not do anything, no school, no workshops, no homes…" With passion, it was Francesco's turn to exclaim, filled with emotion: "Nothing?! I will tell you what we do." He told the story of Sabina, her broken life, his divided home, and then the coming of Faith and Light, the discovery of the beauty hidden in his daughter, the welcome of a community with people with intellectual disabilities, their parents and their young friends that had given life to him again. "Only one person with a disability, such as Sabina, that we discover all her value, only one family that finds hope again, forgets its ordeal, shares the suffering of others, this has no price. This is worth much more than all the supersonic airplanes on earth. Well, there are thousands of families like mine in the world. This is what Faith and Light does!"

The director was visibly moved, and so was I. In my heart, this cry: "Never again naked. Never again alone. Saved!"[1] Suddenly I had the brilliant vision of what, in an invisible way, Faith and Light was starting to accomplish and a great desire that all of this not be lost. This story – a sacred story – needed to be told.

To tell these forty years of the movement's history at first seemed to me an enormous challenge. But it is a beautiful challenge. There is only one thing to do, said little Theresa of the Infant-Jesus, as she began the story of her life: "to sing the mercies of the Lord." Here is a key for us: to sing the marvelous deeds of God through the littlest ones, through Faith and Light.

---

1. Jean Giono, French writer – 1895-1970

In a completely different way, I was helped by Father Gerald Arbuckle, a priest-theologian from New Zealand, who has dedicated himself to the history of associations and religious communities. He has discovered that in order for them to survive through the years, the essential thing is to return to the roots of their foundation. How were they born, what was their goal, the first inspirations? How have they developed, spread? This is what needed to be put together and brought to light for our movement, to make its roots accessible for all.

Even if we had the grace, Jean Vanier and myself, to be the artisans of its foundation, the history of Faith and Light belongs to each one of its members, parents, friends, to each person with an intellectual disability. All have written it and continue to write it daily. It also belongs to all who are waiting for a friendly hand, a voice that tells them: "I love you as you are. God loves you as you are."

I hope that the wonderful story of Faith and Light, this mysterious adventure, with its ups, its downs and its joys, gives witness to the effective and delicate manner, humble and simple, by which our Heavenly Father takes care of those who are dearest to His heart, so many Sabinas and so many families throughout the world. It is for them that God entrusted Faith and Light to us.

CHAPTER 1

The Beginnings

Faith and Light is not the fruit of long hours of reflection and deep thought, and neither was there a pre-established plan. The Lord and His mother gave us Faith and Light at Easter 1971. It came as their response to the suffering of persons with intellectual disabilities and their families. The Lord, I am convinced, wanted to make the words of St. Paul more alive, more present: "God has chosen that which is weak to shame the strong, that which is foolish to shame the wise."

To accomplish His work, as is His custom, God made use of circumstances and of encounters. Over a long period of time, He prepared several persons: Jean Vanier, Camille and Gérard Proffit, and me, and afterward many others. From a human perspective, we never ought to have met and even less, be linked through a common mission. It is God's surprising action that all of a sudden appeared in our lives.

My encounter with persons with disabilities

Like Jean Vanier, I did not know anyone in my family who had a disability. Then why, when I was ten years old, was I touched by Anne and Emmanuel, two children with profound disabilities,

1

who were surrounded by tenderness in their families? Why did Alice, seventeen years old and, held back in our middle school class, touch my heart one day with her secret suffering? I do not know. But I am certain that Anne, Emmanuel, and above all Alice were not there by chance because once I discovered the existence of a School for Special Education Teachers, I knew immediately that this was the direction for my life.

After my studies, Father Henri Bissonier, who was our professor in orthopedagogy, invited me to work with him at the *Secrétariat Catholique des Enfants Malades*[1] and at the *Bureau International Catholique de l'Enfance* (BICE)[2].

In this context, and later at the *Office Chrétien des Personnes Handicapées* (OCH)[3], I frequently met parents. Their sharing revealed their loneliness, their anguish about the future of their children, and for many of them a crushing feeling of guilt and the suffering of being so misunderstood by the Church. For some, the discovery of their child's disability was synonymous with their break with or alienation from God. How can one believe in the love of an all-powerful God who permits such injustices to happen? Many found a place of support in the *Union Nationale des Associations de Parents d'Enfants Inadaptés* (UNAPEI)[4] that had taken on the creation of specialized establishments and worked closely with public authorities. Many parents also longed for spiritual support, for help to live their trials in the light of the Gospel.

Already in 1962, with several parents who had a child with disabilities, we on the staff of BICE had the rough draft of a plan for a pilgrimage to Lourdes. The suggestion came from

---

1. Catholic Secretariat for Sick Children - Translator note
2. International Catholic Secretariat for Children - Translator note
3. Christian Office for Persons with Disabilities - Translator note
4. National union of associations of parents of children with disabilities

Geneviève Hourdin, the wife of Georges, founder and director of *La Vie catholique*[1]. They had eight children, the last of which, Marie-Anne, had Down syndrome. We had thought, at that time, of a pilgrimage that would be uniquely fashioned for parents of children with intellectual disabilities, but without the presence of their children. This would be a combination of symposium and pilgrimage, bringing together between two hundred and three hundred people. In addition to a spiritual program, there would be conferences and workshops to provide formation and to shed light, from a Christian perspective, on the difficulties these parents faced. *La Vie catholique* was ready to furnish financial support. There were two or three meetings of parents and friends, including the wife of Marshal Leclerc de Hautecloque. This project did not succeed. It lacked a team that was sufficiently solid and motivated, and it lacked someone to carry it forward and I was not able to be that person.

In a certain sense, the hour had not yet come. It was necessary for these meetings to happen. Trust was born and grew among those involved, and especially we saw, as a priority the participation of persons with disabilities themselves in order to mobilize hearts and forces.

During that same time period (1963), the Christian Office of Persons with Disabilities (OCH) was created. As I came to say, in reality, my meetings with parents of children with disabilities were daily. Their suffering touched me profoundly, particularly their pain when given the news of the disability or illness of a child who had been awaited with so much joy.

Having witnessed this marked me deeply. As the person responsible for supervising the internship of three special educators at the Hôpital des Enfants Malades[2], I was able to participate in

---

1. *The Catholic Life* a Catholic news magazine - Translator note
2. A pediatric hospital in Paris - Translator note

some consultations. One day a young couple came. The father carried a little boy in his arms who was about eighteen months old, all curled up, and he manifested no apparent interaction or connection with his parents. The doctor made a very long examination without saying a word. Afterward he placed the child back in the arms of his father with only these words: "Nothing can be done. He is beyond medical help. It is necessary to place him in an institution and think about having another child." The pain of the parents was immeasurable; the mother completely fell apart, not able to hold back her tears, and the father, livid, forced himself to remain stoic.

"Nothing can be done." I was desolate and revolted. By these words, the child was more irremediably condemned than by his disability. There is always something to do! The child with the greatest limitations is able to sense if it is loved or rejected, if it is a source of tears or of joy. That morning I understood that in order to help a child to grow, it is necessary to first connect with the child's parents and give them assurance of the hidden beauty of the one who has been entrusted to them. The child's intelligence might be very limited but not his or her capacity to love. In order to live, the child only desires one thing: to be loved and to love in return. The essential elements in my eyes were: not to leave the parents in their isolation but, to accompany them through the years, to help them to meet other families, and if they absolutely need to be separated from their child, to try to find a solution that is most suitable and does not sever the bonds of love.

A current event that also profoundly marked me at the time was what we called "the Liège process."

In this town in Belgium, little Corinne, born without arms and legs, was killed by her parents. Both were acquitted of any crime and carried in triumph by a joyous crowd. According to public opinion it was a shock. In Belgium, in France and in many other countries, famous personalities as well as ordinary people were alarmed at the prospect of becoming a society where respect for life was so manifestly ridiculed. Many voices were raised in all the media to call to mind the unique and sacred character of each human being.

At the same time, it was obvious that the parents, facing this terrible drama, were left in an unimaginable isolation. The question becomes, "Is it possible to affirm the dignity of every human life without, at the same time, accompanying, supporting and helping the families that find themselves faced with the double responsibility to welcome and to raise a child like little Corinne..."

Radio Luxembourg (RTL) decided to create a center for children with dysmelia (a congenital malformation of the limbs that resulted from taking thalidomide, a medication that was prescribed to pregnant women before knowing its horrible side effects). The fundraising started by RTL, beyond all expectations, reached and surpassed its goal of four million francs. The directors of the radio network then thought of starting an association at the service of persons with disabilities and their families, and invited me to take on this responsibility. Before agreeing definitively, I decided to meet Marthe Robin[1] to entrust the project to her. Her silence surprised me. Then she asked: "Could you, in this responsibility, pursue a work with a spiritual and religious dimension?" It was obvious that it was not possible. Inside of me the decision reversed. Marthe, by closing one door, opened another: "Don't we need an association with goals similar to

---

1. Marthe Robin (1901-1981), with Father Finet, began the Foyers de Charité, spiritual retreat centers animated by a community of faithful. A small countrywoman, she lived in Châteaneuf-de-Galaure (Drôme, in southeast France). She became completely paralyzed at the age of eighteen and could not tolerate light. She offered her life to Jesus, and received thousands of people who came to ask her for counsel and for the support of her prayer. The cause of her beatification has been opened.

these that you told me about, to give support to parents, to create centers of welcome, to bring awareness to others, and all this in the light of the Gospel?"

The following year, in October 1963, the OCH was born.

The families and their children with disabilities

In the years 1950 to 1970 there were very few possibilities offered to parents, after the brutal announcement or the progressive discovery of the intellectual disability of their child. Often a medical doctor would recommend that parents separate themselves from their child.

Those who had enough financial resources placed their child in an expensive institution in Switzerland or Belgium. Others searched for a welcoming family in the countryside. The quality of the material care and the emotional environment depended at the time solely on know-how, good will and on the moral values of the caregivers. Others looked for asylums and, in certain areas, psychiatric hospitals, where persons with all types of mental illnesses were left. In the absence of suitable places, the "mentally deficient" were placed there, although they did not need any psychiatric treatment. What they needed was a warm and loving place where they would receive help to do what they were capable of doing. And especially, they needed to discover their unique gift to be loved and to be able to love, a gift they are called to develop and to radiate exactly as we are.

Asylums offered collective room and board, but they lacked the dimension of personal concern for the other. This dimension, with tenderness, recognition, and simple respect, would be the basis for the OCH, and later, for Faith and Light. It was in one of these institutions that Jean Vanier discovered, with horror, the disorder, violence and despair that encompassed the life of those who were not like others. It was there that he had the prophetic notion of l'Arche.

In the majority of cases, the child stayed at home, either because the parents were faced with refusals everywhere, or because they were not able to "put their child away." So, the child stayed, sometimes hidden in the back of the apartment. To have a child with an intellectual disability, "an idiot", as they were called at the time, was a shame for all the family.

I knew a couple that lived in the countryside, Pierre and Marie-Jo, who had a child with disabilities. After the pilgrimage of 1971, which changed their life, Pierre heard of many families in their region that hid their children with disabilities. He then asked his employer, the PTT[1] that he be downgraded to a mail carrier, which would make it possible for him to visit the different families daily. During these visits, he would sometimes talk about his own son, his difficulties and his joys. In this way, he succeeded in gaining the trust of those families. His personal sharing frequently elicited sharing in response, and the acknowledgement of the presence of a child with disabilities - so carefully hidden until then. A little light in the darkness! A new phase opened up for these families, because voicing the truth already frees us from a very heavy weight to carry. This sometimes helped them to find their way to a community.

At that time there also existed another possibility for welcoming children with disabilities: institutions created and managed by religious orders. These were often criticized due to the large number of children that they welcomed and for their sometimes outdated, educational methods. However, it is necessary to do them justice. These communities were always the pioneers in caring for persons with disabilities rejected by society:

---

1. Postes, télégraphes et telephones (post office, telegraph and telephone) - Translator note

those who were deaf, blind, lepers, persons with psychiatric disorders; persons with multiple disabilities... And many of these institutions were not content just to keep those they cared for alive. They made efforts to surround those they welcomed with love and to innovate in all areas, particularly in pedagogy. We can think of Saint John Eudes, Saint Camillus de Lellis, Saint John of God, Abbot de l'Épée, Pierre-François Jamet, John Bost and so many others.

And then, in the 1950s, there was a group of parents who, with immense love for their children and enormous faith and courage, faced the problem. They started to create small educational centers and joined together to form a very important and efficient association, the UNAPEI[1]. Today it brings together sixty thousand families and manages three thousand institutions and social-medical services.

Those whom Providence had prepared

The history of Faith and Light is the story of several encounters. The first was the one with Camille and Gérard Proffit. With their two children, Thaddée and Loïc, they were the first inspiration for the pilgrimage that led to the birth of the Faith and Light movement. Farmers in the Somme region of France, they had married ten years earlier and hoped for a large family in which perhaps one of the children would receive a vocation to the priesthood. How could they have imagined that two boys would be born with profound disabilities? Two boys who could neither walk or talk, and who were totally dependent. Camille even said, "I scarcely know if they recognize us!"

---

1. National union of associations of parents of children with disabilities - Translator note

When Thaddée became too heavy for his mom to care for him full-time, he was placed in a large center in Lozère. Every month, Camille spent a day with him. This meant she would spend two nights on the train each visit. Loïc stayed at home. I met him when he was eight years old, frequently looking up in the air, seemingly lost in incomprehensible thoughts. He loved music and was overjoyed when his dad helped him dance.

In the summer of 1967, Camille and Gérard wanted to travel to Lourdes as a family. However, the pilgrimage sponsored by their diocese was closed to them. The organizers cited common sense and practical reasons, which were customary at the time: "Your children wouldn't understand anything about all that goes on in Lourdes. Furthermore, they might run the risk of disturbing the other pilgrims." Camille and Gérard nevertheless persisted in their plan and decided to go to Lourdes on their own. Once they arrived in the holy city, they unfortunately were unable to find any room, at least not for the children. "Put them in the Accueil Notre-Dame[1], that's the place for them," was the response they got.

But people certainly were not taking into account Gérard and Camille's determination. They finally convinced a hotelkeeper to take them in, but only if they would agree that all meals would be served in their room! For three days, Camille and Gérard deeply felt the rejection of their children, whether in their comings and goings throughout the city, or in the liturgies. They were hurt by the looks, the comments of pity or disapproval. "When you have children like that, you should stay at home!" Being excluded from the pilgrimage made them feel a bit as if they were being excluded by the Church.

---

1. A center in Lourdes for welcoming persons who were ill or with physical disabilities - Translator note

There were also Dr. Paul Biérent and his wife, Marcelle, among the first to participate in this adventure. They had known much suffering: their daughter, Anne-Joëlle, had encephalitis when she was five years old. She had very serious after-effects and died when she was only fifteen. For her parents, the pain of her death was even greater than the pain related to her disability. They had dreamed of going to Lourdes with her, and could not forgive themselves for having postponed it.

And there was Jean Vanier. Regarding Jean, his journey is well known and impressive. Son of General Georges Vanier, Governor-General of Canada, he studied in the Royal Navy and was a naval officer. Then he met Father Thomas Philippe, a Dominican, and studied philosophy and theology with him. Later Jean was a Professor of Philosophy in Toronto.

In 1963, Father Thomas was living in Trosly-Breuil, a village ten kilometers from Compiègne. He was the chaplain for Val Fleuri, an institution that welcomed about thirty men with intellectual and developmental disabilities. When Jean went to visit Father Thomas, he was astonished by the quality of heart of the residents. Jean also had the opportunity to visit psychiatric asylums in the region that sheltered persons with an intellectual disability. Their thirst for relationships and friendship resounded in him as a call. In 1964 he moved to a house in Trosly-Breuil to live there with Raphaël and Philippe, two men with intellectual disabilities who had been abandoned by their families. On August 4, 1964, with the support of Father Thomas, he founded the first l'Arche community, with the intention of sharing his life with these two men and with another assistant. But things unfolded very differently when he accepted to be director of Val Fleuri in December of the same year. The Val Fleuri was integrated into the community of l'Arche.

In July 1965 the community made its first pilgrimage to Lourdes. Jean says he immediately saw the fruits. He noticed how even the persons with a profound disability were sensitive to the symbols of the water, the fountains, the pool, the procession with candles, the prayers with the crowd... He marveled at the faith of the people who were sick and the most fragile, who identified themselves with little Bernadette. She had been one of the poorest and most despised person in Lourdes, but also the one who most trusted in Mary's tenderness. The heart of each one from l'Arche was somehow renewed and the unity in the community was reinforced. After this, each year, the whole community went on a journey to a "holy place".

On November 7, 1966, I went to visit l'Arche and I met Jean for the first time. I was more than reserved. In my circle, we found it suspicious that a naval officer studied philosophy, became a professor, and after that had the idea of setting himself up, without any experience, in a village close to Compiègne as director of a house for adults with intellectual disabilities. I must say that I shared this prejudice.

However, Marie-Madaleine Revon, a good friend of Mrs. Vainer, Jean's mother, was the president of an association for delinquent youth of which I was administrator. She had a deep admiration for l'Arche and its founder. At the end of each Board meeting she insisted that we go together to visit this community.

Worn out by her insistence, I finally gave in. One fine afternoon we took the train to arrive in Trosly-Breuil for supper. Jean Vanier came to pick us up at the train station in Compiègne. Going through the forest and arriving in the small village under the pelting rain and the cold at the end of the afternoon, all seemed sinister. In the chapel, Mass had already begun, and there were about fifteen people who sang at the top of their lungs... out of tune! However, this was the first shock: to see the sureness of their hearts and the fervor of their faith. Those who were there seemed to drink in the words of Father Thomas Philippe, words that were totally inaccessible to their level of intelligence, but whose hearts seemed to perceive the faith and the love behind the words.

Afterwards we went to have supper in the small home of l'Arche and I was welcomed like an old friend. They all asked me questions. People joyfully teased one another, and each one told what happened to them during the day. In the simplicity and freedom of the exchanges I hardly distinguished who had a disability and who did not. At the end of the meal, Pierrot, one of the persons with disabilities, declared: "The visitors do the dishes!" In reality, Jean Vanier washed the dishes, while everybody dried them and put things away. Then some candles were lit to indicate time for prayer. Everyone who wanted gathered again around the table. We shared about Jesus. We talked to him. We entrusted to him our countless intentions: for someone's godmother who had just died as well as for the neighbor's little cat that was lost.

In the train back to Paris, neither Marie-Madeleine nor myself had any desire to talk. Personally, I was very touched. Because of my profession and my activities, I had visited many institutions that welcomed persons with a disability in France as well as in other countries. But what touched me that day was something I had never felt in any other place. This was not a simple institution; it was a family, a family of brothers and sisters who shared life together. It was a family of God's children who shared the same faith in friendship and communion, where each one gave and received, just as naturally, as we breathe, without even thinking about it. It knocked down my prejudices!

When Jean drove us back to the train station, I ventured to talk with him about the UNAEDE National Congress[1] that we

---

1. (Union Nationale des Assistants et Éducateurs de l'Enfance) National Union of Assistants and Educators of Children of which I was the president.

were organizing for April with the theme: "Psycho-pedagogic techniques at the service of the person". Since he seemed to be interested, I asked him if he could collaborate. Some days later he came to the OCH and accepted my invitation. He even accepted to give a presentation on "homes for the feeble minded", according to the expression used at the time. The following year Jean committed himself again and became a member of the team planning the large congress around a topic that was very hot: "The affective and sexual life of maladjusted children and youth". During 1967 we worked together and also met at the Board meetings for SIPSA, the association that administered the l'Arche community, in which Jean had invited me to participate.

An idea springs up!

From time to time I also took part in the days that the members of l'Arche and their friends spent together at the Abbey d'Ourscamp, close to Trosly. These were occasions of weaving bonds of trust. It was in the evening of one of these days, when Camile Proffit, the Biérents and Jean Vanier were present that the idea of a pilgrimage to Lourdes suddenly sprang up. This would be a pilgrimage with and for persons with intellectual and developmental disabilities. Camille had continued to carry the suffering of what her family had experienced in Bernadette's village.

There are dreams that die as soon as they form: we call these chimeras. Others, on the other hand, seem to be able to become reality. In their origin, there is a sort of "inspiration". We asked ourselves at the time: "Why not try? If God wants it, everything is possible."

And everything moved very quickly. On the following day, I met Jean at a professional meeting. He asked me: "To move forward it is important to know if you commit yourself to such a project." In that moment I had a crushing vision of what that represented. My professional responsibilities were heavy. I was the general secretary for the OCH and for BICE's[1] medical-pedagogical and psychosocial commission. I was the adjunct general delegate for the SCEJI[2]. In the OCH we were preparing to launch a new publication, *Ombres et Lumière*[3], a Christian magazine for parents and friends of persons with disabilities, and I had accepted to be its director. Besides all that, most of my free time was occupied by the presidency of the UNAEDE. How could I, besides all of this, add a project as ambitious as this pilgrimage? It was true that, for his part, Jean carried at least as many responsibilities as I did.

We were a few months away from the events of 1968[4]. I could imagine the lack of support from the people I worked with, largely influenced by the ideology of the moment. This pilgrimage did not match the current thinking of the times at all. I risked becoming caught in a trap. From a human point of view to say "yes" and to commit to this project was totally crazy. However that was exactly what I answered! I believed so much in the graces of Lourdes and in the desire of God that the weakest not be excluded and that they find their place in the Church. It also seemed important to me that the parents could come out of their isolation and discover new hope in the capacities of their children. Finally, the perspective of collaborating with Jean Vanier gave me

1. Translator's Note: "Bureau International Catholique de l'Enfance" - International Catholic Office for Children
2. Secrétariat catholique de l'enfance et de la jeunesse inadaptés - Catholic Secretariat for maladjusted children and youth
3. *Shadows and Light* – Translator note
4. In May 1968 French students and workers went on strike and confronted the government. This movement profoundly changed the relationships between races, sexes and generations in France - Translator note

much peace. I give thanks for the mutual unity and trust - gifts of Jesus - that grew between us. When our opinions differed, a deep communion was always present to accomplish the mission placed in our hands. Close links were woven between a small group of persons sharing the same vision, who knew that they could totally depend on each other. Besides Camile Proffit I think of Pierre Leborgne, general director of a bank in Compiègne, vice-president of the Secours Catholique[1], who would later become international treasurer of Faith and Light, I also think of Father Hviid[2] who would be our international chaplain from 1970 to 1982. The unity among us was vital, especially during the times of great difficulty. And they were many!

On the evening of January 16, 1968 Jean Vanier and myself met at the home of the Biérents to evaluate this idea with Geneviève and Georges Hourdin, and with Paul Vernon, president of UNAPEI[3], who came not as an official, but as a parent (his fourth and last son had Down syndrome). With the exception of Georges Hourdin, who had doubts (he "confessed" later in the newspaper *Le Monde!*), we can say that we had an "enthusiastic" unanimity. Nevertheless, it was wise to enlarge the number of people consulted. We would only advance if we had enough signs that this project came from God. We were ready to stop everything if this was not the case.

It was necessary, first of all, to assure that the Church was in agreement. Jean Vanier immediately contacted Bishop Desmazières, bishop of Beauvais and reference bishop for l'Arche.

---

1. Non-profit organization created by Jean Rhodain in 1946; affiliated with Caritas International, it seeks to promote social justice and is attentive to poverty and exclusion - Translator note

2. *Cf.* pages 43-44

3. Union nationale des associations de parents d'enfants inadaptés - National union of associations of parents of maladjusted children

He was quick to show his support for the idea and to write a word of approval and encouragement.

On her side, Camille, the mother of Thaddée and Loïc, kept contact with Canon Caffarel, founder of the Équipes Notre-Dame[1]. He had organized many large gatherings in Lourdes. We were able to present our project to him during an informal meeting. Father Caffarel immediately told us that the project seemed to him to be very rooted in the Gospels, and that it looked like the way God works. He assured us of his moral support and prayers. How much encouragement this was for us, coming from such a rock of faith, such a great man of action!

Very soon I also asked to meet with Marthe Robin who had, as I have already mentioned, inspired the founding of the OCH. I had signed up for a retreat at Châteauneuf-de-Galaure. On March 21st, I had the joy of having a conversation with her about the project of Faith and Light. Her agreement was total: "It must go on. I will pray for you..." She knew the weight that parents of children with disabilities carry. She was the godmother of a little Canadian boy, Georges-Michel, born with Down syndrome and called by God when he was three years old. She saw that he, and other children like him, were rejected, and therefore close to the heart of Jesus. I met with Marthe each year. How can we, today, not think about how much we owe her for the profusion of graces that we received in Lourdes in 1971, as well as for the spreading of the movement throughout the world, well beyond what we could ever have imagined?

It seemed to us that the moment had arrived to contact Bishop Théas, bishop of Tarbes and Lourdes, and Bishop Viscaro, rector of the sanctuaries. They seemed to ignore the fears of the city of Lourdes and gave Jean Vanier a very favorable welcome.

---

1. Teams of Our Lady – an international Catholic movement for married couples - Translator note

On another front, Father Henri Bissonier received Paul and Marcelle Biérent on January 24, 1968, and I was present. He was not very enthusiastic about this daring enterprise. However, he advised us to seek out Father Martin Hillairet, a Dominican in charge of the SCEJI in the diocese of Nantes, who he thought could be a good chaplain for our project. He also suggested that in the team that was being formed, it would be good that I would participate as a delegate from the BICE for the Faith and Light pilgrimage. This is what happened.

Fears and resistances

In our numerous contacts we recognized three types of attitudes. There were those who encouraged our initiative: first of all the parents, and the friends who were convinced of its importance. Many were ready to commit themselves and would remain faithful to the movement well after the pilgrimage. Others would not "show their hand" and it seemed as if they were waiting to see which way the wind would blow, given the great risk of the project.

Finally, a certain number of people were obviously against our initiative: some of them because of their ignorance about the situation of persons with disabilities (this was the case with the apostolic nuncio at the time); others because of the current ideology (such as the fear of large, triumphalist public manifestations or that the idea of an event organized around a disability could stir up painful reactions). There were also other reasons that we will mention later.

In a general way at that time, the city of Lourdes had prejudices towards persons with intellectual and developmental disabilities. For many years this was a real question for me. Soon after the apparitions, sick people or people with a physical or a sensory disability were welcome in Lourdes. It became, in a sense, their city. The first seven recognized cases of healing were people who were hemiplegic, paraplegic or blind. Why, then, this "exclusion" of persons with intellectual and developmental disabilities? There are two possible reasons. First of all, at the time of Bernadette, intellectual disability was not well known and frequently it was confused with mental illness, which generated fear. In Lourdes, at the moment of the apparitions, the mayor nominated a commission of three medical doctors to examine the "case" of Bernadette. They did not find any illness in her. The apparitions could not be explained by a nervous disorder or hallucinations, as had been proposed hypothetically by some. Still, those in charge of the sanctuaries and the medical doctors were very careful to limit the recognition of miracles to people who were sick or with a physical disability. As Bishop Jacques Perrier, bishop of Tarbes and Lourdes, later wrote "until recently pilgrimages were asked to not bring persons with mental illnesses[1]".

Regarding persons with intellectual disabilities in the 1960s, if they were frequently ignored, rejected and refused in Lourdes, this also happened in almost all other places. The reasons given to Camille and Gérard, as well as to other parents, for excluding their children was "their incapacity to benefit from a pilgrimage and the risk of disturbing other participants". If parents ignored this advice and arrived in Lourdes with their child with an intellectual disability, they would find themselves isolated and disillusioned. This was the case of Friquette Hendryx, who came to Lourdes with her daughter, Sophie, who has a profound disability. After a solemn Mass, where the child had been placed in the front row with some other young ladies with disabilities like herself, Friquette was obliged to go back up to the city all by herself, in the middle of the crowd, pushing Sophie's wheelchair: "I cried, carrying my pain, but I also thought of the pain of others."

---

1. Lourdes aujourd'hui. Et demain?, Nouvelle Cité, 2008.

On the bridge over the River Gave, another mother approached her with her son in a wheelchair. Soon a third mother joined them "It is not normal that we remain so isolated! It is necessary to bring together all parents." The Dominican priests welcomed the idea of organizing a meeting. Around thirty parents, with their children, participated in this gathering and met again before their departure.

A first, little door was open and gave birth to the Service for Maladjusted Children. Today it is known as the Service for the Children of the Immaculate (SEI). Since then this organization is present every year during the pilgrimage of the Rosary, in October, to welcome children with intellectual disabilities and their parents. It was a precious contribution, but unfortunately limited to five days per year and for only about thirty families. However, many parents of children with disabilities were waiting to be able to go to Lourdes, like dry soil thirsting for life-giving water.

Reactions from the Church

After the kind agreement by Bishops Théas and Viscaro at the end of July 1968, the new bishop, Bishop Donze, who had been informed about the project, responded eighteen months later: "I assure you of all my sympathy and dedication, as Bishop de La Chanonie and Bishop Théas did."

Reservation came chiefly from the SCEJI, from whom we had expected active support. The project left this service anxious and fearful that the suffering, multiplied by hundreds of pilgrims, would be unbearable. They also feared that the parents would come hoping for a miraculous cure and would go back home frustrated with their expectations. These remarks opened up questions asked of us: "Would not the gathering of such a large number of men and women wounded in their intelligence risk provoking all kinds of serious accidents and a sort of chaos?" And especially this question: "Wouldn't this big gathering risk to awaken hopes that have no future and leave the pilgrims in a state of even greater isolation after the pilgrimage?"

As I feared since the beginning, I found myself "between a rock and a hard place", since I was the general delegate from the SCEJI. Obviously an uncomfortable situation! I was 100% committed to the pilgrimage, but initially I was obliged to officially limit myself to the role of delegate of the BICE[1].

It was even more embarrassing that these rumors and fears were spreading among dioceses within and outside of France. In a letter written after an informal meeting of French and Belgian priests in Brussels, Father André Delpierre[2], a priest from the Belgian team for Faith and Light, wrote: "I see in this gathering of the poor of God, the people with disabilities, a lack of respect for their poverty." He added: "With all the love and the kindness that I have for them, I cannot help thinking that we are placing them in the perfect situation for them to appear "like a bunch of fools" and we do not have the right, out of respect for them, to do this." He continued, giving the argument that persons with disabilities would understand nothing as the pilgrimage went on and that we would therefore "painfully aggravate their feeling of not being like other people, unduly adding to their personal suffering..."

Besides that, the priest affirmed: "We have no right to hope for any spiritual enrichment, because all their natural, psychological and sensorial environment is twisted. It would be a presumption.

---

1. (Bureau International Catholique de l'Enfance) International Catholic Office for Children

2. This priest later became very devoted to Faith and Light and was a faithful friend and collaborator with *Ombres et Lumière*.

It is simply to tempt God. It is to ask the Virgin for a massive, global miracle that we have no right to ask, because we do not offer the necessary conditions." He then reminded us that our project risked having "considerable costs that would require the generosity of Christians for a hypothetical, if not negative, spiritual outcome," Father Delpierre concluded that "especially after being aware of so many reasons against the project, and not one visibly in favor", he could not make his inscription.

The same type of opinion came from Spain. The National Secretariat for Special Education, which was part of the Bishops' Education Commission, thought it was impossible to collaborate with us. It wrote this: "The idea would be welcomed by traditionalist groups that would ask for cures or would exult in suffering. On the other hand, the more progressive groups would see it as a triumphalist manifestation. When we factored in the enormous economical problems, we decided to substitute a day at Montserrat for the pilgrimage. We will call it a "meeting", because the word "pilgrimage" is outdated. This initiative will be addressed more to the parents than to the handicapped." In spite of this, we kept contact with them. In the end, three hundred Spanish pilgrims participated in the pilgrimage. Among the requests they made afterward, was "the realization of a national project in Spain in 1972 similar to the one in Lourdes."

We were very aware of the "cultural revolution" of 1968 that attacked more or less all society. It also impacted the Church in its theological, moral, spiritual, pastoral, liturgical foundations ... It was like a tidal wave that shook everything. All of us in Faith and Light were jolted to some degree by the aftershocks.

We also had the grace of being close to persons with disabilities. Their simple faith was lived essentially through the heart and through meeting the person of Jesus.

A decisive lunch

In spite of these reactions, the contacts continued and an outline for the pilgrimage began to take shape. The decision was made on April 9, 1968, at the home of Paul and Marcelle Biérent, during a working lunch. Father Caffarel, Father Hillairet, Paul Vernon, Geneviève Hourdin, Camille Proffit, Jean Vanier and I were present. This meeting, which took place exactly three years before the opening of the pilgrimage in Lourdes, marked the true launching of the project.

In order that this pilgrimage not immediately be called a "pilgrimage for the mentally handicapped", it was good that we give it a name. The first name given was Light and Faith[1]. It was immediately adopted. Someone brought up the concern that it risked being confused with the magazine *Ombres et Lumière*, but the objection was quickly swept aside because the pilgrimage was a one-time event, while we hoped the magazine would have a long life. We also needed to determine a date. We agreed on the time we needed for preparation and this led us to schedule the pilgrimage for the dates of September 2-6 1971.

This same day we determined, from Jean Vanier's proposition, what the three main ideas of the pilgrimage would be. First of all, to help the persons with disabilities to discover that they are specially loved by God, capable of an authentic relationship with Him, even capable of true holiness, and to enable them to find their true place in the Church.

Next, to respond to the suffering of the parents, often in revolt and despair, to help them to discover the hidden beauty of their child, to find a meaning for their suffering and to live it in the light of faith.

---

1. This name was kept until October, when some people remarked that it is faith first that brings light into our lives.

Finally, to recall the belief of the Church in the dignity of the person with intellectual and developmental disabilities, the need for their prayer for the unity of Christians and for peace in the world.

These are still basic ideas of Faith and Light today.

After this launching meeting, in April of 1968, we focused on preparations for a first international meeting. We needed to make many contacts. This included meeting with the religious authorities of Lourdes, searching for links with friends from other countries, and identifying key persons in the different regions of France to create a national network. All of this led to the first international meeting.

CHAPTER 2

The Time of Decisions
(1968-1969)

This first international meeting took place on December 8, 1968. For us this date has a providential meaning, but we did not choose it. The meeting had first been scheduled for September, then for October. This date was imposed on us by the time it took to advance the preparations, the schedules of the principal people invited and the availability of a suitable place.

December 8 is an important date because it is the Feast of the Immaculate Conception, the name by which the Virgin identified herself to Bernadette, when the girl was charged by the priest to discover how the "beautiful lady" called herself. "Que soy era Immaculada Conceptiou.[1]" Mary, full of grace, the one who had never sinned, the one in whom God prepared a dwelling worthy of his Son! This date served as a ratification of our project. In a way, it seemed as if Mary herself was telling us: "Come in procession, you the littlest and the poorest of my children, you who are the dearest to my heart." Those who God has chosen to reveal his mysteries...

We met at Montmartre, at the house of the Dominicans of the Holy Family. We were a small group of about fifty persons.

---

1. "I am the Immaculate Conception." – Translator note

The presence of two people from England, two Belgians and one Moroccan made our international aspect visible. And we represented very well the diversity of "civil states" that we desired to integrate in the Charter of the future pilgrimage. Twenty parents who had a child with a disability, four directors of institutions or special educators, three of them from religious orders, seven friends, six priests, two of them Orthodox. One of these was Father Virgil Georghiu, this well known political figure from Romania, who suffered a veritable martyrdom during the Second World War and the period following. He was known especially for his novel, *The Twenty-fifth Hour*, in which he defends the sacred character of all human persons, no matter how limited the person might be. The presence of the two Orthodox priests underscored our desire for ecumenical openness, even if the pilgrimage was born in Catholic soil and was to take place in Lourdes.

Bishop Desmazières, bishop of Beauvais and reference bishop for l'Arche, was a delegate of Bishop de La Chanonie, responsible for the "Pastoral for the Maladjusted" in France. In this way, the Church was represented.

He opened this day, giving it direction through a reflection on the Word: "Are you the one who will come, or do we need to wait for another?[1]"; and the reply: "Go and report to John what you see and hear: the blind see, the lame walk, lepers are cleansed, the deaf hear, the dead are raised and the good news is announced to the poor[2]..." In this way, he told us, the weak reveal the presence of Christ. But today Jesus Christ is not sufficiently present in the face of the Church. Where are the sick, the "handicapped", the poor? Our pilgrimage must be an authentic sign of the Church of Christ present in the world. Jean Vanier followed, reminding us of the origins of the pilgrimage: the coming together of many

---

1. Matthew 11: 3
2. Matthew 11: 4

people who carried the same idea, the same desire. These are signs of the presence and of the will of the Holy Spirit. And there was the growing interest of friends from other countries.

Laying the foundations

Jean invited us to reflect and to work together in two groups to lay the groundwork. One group worked on the spiritual basis for the pilgrimage and the other on the general organization.

He asked each participant in the first group to present one point that seemed essential to him/her and that he/she would be ready to develop. Father Hillairet had the task of putting all of these ideas together coherently in a brochure to nourish the reflections of the future pilgrims.

Among the themes that came out in that time of sharing, four major orientations shaped the rest of our work. First of all, it was necessary to think of the very great number of parents and children with disabilities who would not be able to come. They must not feel alone. The spiritual preparation needed to address them also, before as well as during the pilgrimage. It was of equal concern to address the perception that some parents could have, those for whom the presence of a child with disability was a scandal. For some, this impairs their love for God. It was also necessary to think of those without faith. It is a long journey for parents as well as for educators to discover what persons with disabilities bring us, and how God can look at them with a preferential love. Finally, the prayer of the pilgrims needed to be very open to the whole world and to all types of suffering.

The "general organization" group also worked a lot and presented to all the participants its propositions around three essential points: the draft constitution of an association called Faith and Light, with the goal of "organizing pilgrimages for the mentally handicapped". The creation of five international committees respectively charged with the spiritual and liturgical preparation and animation, finances, transportation and lodging, health and security, and finally communication. It was necessary to create "Faith and Light regions" in France (following the country's administrative areas, with a delegate in charge of forming a regional committee) and to establish links with the countries that had already joined us, or that would do so.

We kept a very simple organizational plan. There was a national committee made up of the regional delegates, and an executive committee limited to only five persons.

For the international component we designed the same type of structure, which fell in place in a very pragmatic way. It consisted of an international committee made up of the national delegates elected by each country and an international executive committee.

December 8 resembled a constitutional assembly. A structure was created. Certainly it was still tentative, the names of the entities kept changing. Sometimes we talked about "persons in charge", as well as "correspondents" and "delegates". The number of specialized committees varied according to the reality and the needs. Sometimes these were divided into sub-committees and their names were not fixed either. However, all this was secondary to us.

Our big concern, as it still is today, was to create structures that were flexible and light, at the service of life; structures that would never become confining or rigid but would allow the breath of the Spirit to freely pass through.

We chose a team and designed an organization. Even if, on this day in December 1968, we did not have a precise idea of how the event we were preparing would turn out, we determined three objectives. First of all, we would not make a pilgrimage *for* persons with intellectual disabilities, but *with* them. Secondly, in order that the parents would not find themselves alone once more with their children, we would invite *friends*, especially young people, to accompany them. And finally, the pilgrims would not make individual registrations, but would create small communities (twenty to thirty persons), a type of family, where people would get to know each other and come to love one another. In Lourdes each community would stay together in the same lodging and would participate together in the celebrations.

A name, a place, a date

Three main discussion points animated the first debates. How to name this type of project? Where should it happen? Which date to keep?

In the beginning it was not as simple to determine the type of project as you might imagine. In fact, the question was this: is it a "pilgrimage" or a "meeting"? For most parents it was clear that it should be a pilgrimage. With them, we wanted to answer Mary's request: "May people come here in procession." For them, the grace would be to be able to go with their children with disabilities, who had been excluded from all activities of this type until then.

Others, the priests in particular, objected to the word "pilgrimage", saying it was out of fashion, and pushed for the term "meeting".

After the discussions left each one set in his/her own position, Jean Vanier proposed a formula for a consensus: "international meeting-pilgrimage". By luck, it was welcomed unanimously! That is the formula that appeared on the first posters and in the documents presenting the project. In fact, it proved to be prophetic. It truly was a pilgrimage, and it was truly a meeting.

Next it was necessary to choose a place for the pilgrimage. Some contested the choice of the city of Lourdes, "high place of the merchants of the temple, a locale of superstition, of magic, of the glorification of suffering and of triumphalism". They wanted us to find another place. But which one? Where would we find a place that offered the exceptional qualities of Lourdes: abundant lodging (thirty-two thousand rooms), all close to the areas for the gatherings, hospitals, an international airport, the beauty of the setting, world renowned, a center for international peace, holy ground walked by the Mother of God who chose a little marginalized girl, in many ways similar to the future pilgrims?

It was necessary to accept the evidence: no other place was comparable to this one. Finally, everyone accepted.

As for the date, since May 1969 the international committee had unanimously confirmed the choice of the month of September 1971, a period without any big liturgical feasts, which allowed us to plan a program and a liturgy free from heavy external constraints (it was enough to deal with ours!). The only true difficulty and the real goal was to adapt the pilgrimage, as well as possible, to persons with intellectual disabilities.

But things did not stay this way. When Jean Vanier met Bishop Théas, bishop of Tarbes and Lourdes, in July 1969, the bishop strongly insisted that the pilgrimage take place at Easter 1971. Many were against this change. Some challenged it. These expressions of opposition persisted until the international meeting in March 1970, when it was decided that the date of Easter 1971 was definitive and could no longer be changed[1].

Later, we realized, once more, that Providence was watching over us. Certainly this new date obliged us to speed up the preparations, but it offered the best conditions for welcome, because Faith and Light would be the only pilgrimage present during these days. It also satisfied those who pointed to the

---

1. Despite the difficulty for many chaplains, parish pastors, for whom it was impossible to be away at Easter.

difficulties with the school year. Finally, and above all, the period of Holy Week and Easter seemed highly significant to everyone even in regard to our project. In fact, we often live the suffering of the disability of our children in darkness, and we long for light and for life. Indeed, one year later, we lived these days in profound union with Jesus, sharing his sufferings, his Passion and death, and walking with him towards the Resurrection.

One of the miracles in these years of preparation, which were often very difficult, was the fact that each of our differences, sometimes about fundamental points, were overcome or turned around thanks to a common hope that this project would bring new light and renewed faith for so many persons with disabilities and their families. After the confrontations, sometimes very animated, it was beautiful to see how completely each one was engaged in his/her own particular mission, giving intelligence, heart and time without measure.

CHAPTER 3

An Immense Construction Site (1969-1971)

On the evening of December 8, 1968, we looked out over an immense construction site, because, practically speaking, everything still needed to be done. We were aware of our fragility. It is necessary to remember that we were all volunteers, and each one of us was busy with a profession or studies. Many of us were responsible for a family, and sometimes the added weight that comes with a child with a disability. Many had other social or ecclesial commitments.

Besides that, we did not have the competence or the experience to carry out such a project. Certainly, as much as possible, we asked for help from competent persons or services. Frequently, however, even they admitted having no experience in many areas because this was an unprecedented adventure.

Each one dove into the project in his or her own way, with his or her own motivations and unique personality. Some held onto their underlying apprehension of a burden too heavy to carry or their fear of a big triumphalist demonstration. From these persons came the repeated demand to limit the number of people registered and to fix the number of participants, at least for France. I remember that early in 1970 a delegate from the SCEJI came to ask me to give him an estimated number. We were totally unable to answer him. He did not want to leave without at least a range for the possible number of registrations for the event. Finally, we told him: "it will be between three hundred participants and thirty thousand." It was obviously a joke, but in the end, not far from reality, since the pilgrimage brought together around twelve thousand persons!

For most of us, the awareness of our deficiencies, sometimes with the feeling of being overwhelmed and anguished, was side by side with the exultation of participating in a pioneering mission. Neophytes in this matter, we had a certain naivety that made it possible for us to overcome the obstacles one after the other. That pushed us to be creative, to invent and to adapt based on what was in front of us. I remember the words of Jean Vanier: "Let us not be fainthearted, thinking of a nicely organized little pilgrimage." Many found unsuspected strengths in themselves. In this way, the little team consisting of Pierre Leborgne, Father Hviid, Jean Vanier and myself returned to Lourdes a number of times. We would meet at ten p.m. in Paris, at the train station Gare d'Austerlitz, and we would arrive in Lourdes very early the next morning. We would go to Mass, then appointments and meetings, mixed with a warm lunch at Jean Buscaye's restaurant, and a bath in the icy waters of the pools that reinvigorated and rekindled us. We would go back home in the evening, to arrive the following day to a regular, nonstop, workday - a little harder than usual since we had to make up for the day we had been away.

Here is another anecdote that seems significant to me about what we lived at the time. We were going to Lille with Camille to animate the first big informational meeting. Camille arrived at the train station, Gare du Nord, with a terribly heavy suitcase – without wheels at that time – filled with documents to be distributed. Immediately I wanted to take it from her, because she suffered from serious back problems. She refused and told me simply: "Marie-Hélène, you won't believe it, but since I have been engaged in Faith and Light, it's done. I do not have a bad back anymore!"

We received anecdotes of this type, *fioretti*, throughout this time of preparation, from all the regions, countries and local communities. We felt that we were living something exceptional, something beyond our comprehension.

A word about Father Jorgen Hviid, whose role, although very discreet, was essential to our history. This Danish priest, whom I had met at the Bureau International Catholique de l'Enfance, was a psychologist, spoke five languages fluently, was very close to persons with disabilities and was very engaged in different areas in his country.

During the international meeting in Geneva in 1970, it was absolutely necessary to appoint an international chaplain. We had the idea of asking Father Hviid to take this role, to which the French priests aspired. However, the other countries thought that France already had too much influence on the international council. I called Father Hviid to talk to him about the pilgrimage and I dared to ask him on the spot if he would accept to become the international chaplain.

Yes, he could free himself from other commitments and go to this weekend in Geneva. Yes, if this were God's will, he would commit himself. This is how, for thirteen years, Father Hviid was the spiritual counselor, the priest, the providential man who by his wisdom, faith and total trust established himself at the heart of our small team.

A priority: spiritual preparation

The spiritual animation committee had a central role. It had the responsibility to clarify the broad spiritual and doctrinal orientations of the pilgrimage. It was in charge of the program in general, including the celebrations and the liturgy, as well as the conferences and meetings organized before and during the pilgrimage.

It was an essentially spiritual program that would unfold in the context of the Easter Triduum, the "source and the summit" of all liturgy. All the other committees were more or less dependent on this one. It was the heart and the soul. Therefore it is not surprising that lively discussions sometimes took place during its meetings, and what joy when consensus was reached!

The most important reference for this committee was the Charter whose outlines Jean Vanier had drafted. At each international meeting this draft was on the agenda and discussed again and again until its final adoption in September 1969. After that, it was the final authority. We distributed it everywhere to the bishops, the parishes, the coordinators of different movements, the local groups that started to be formed…

In the introduction to the Charter we were careful to mention the support of the Church through the voice of the bishop responsible for the Pastoral for persons with disabilities, Bishop de La Chanonie. We recalled our desire to see persons with disabilities included in Diocesan pilgrimages. It was written in this way: "If, *once*, it was found helpful to organize an international pilgrimage that focused on them, it is with the goal of being one step toward integration as the general and usual norm."

Already at that time we wanted to bring together families from all Christian traditions, even if this concern was not spelled out explicitly in the Charter. Since the "decisive lunch" that I already mentioned, we had thought about the ecumenical dimension of the pilgrimage. Camille volunteered to enter into contact with other Christian traditions. Unfortunately this was impossible for her. But our desire still remained: we cannot be a disciple of Jesus without answering this call: "That they be one as my Father and

I are one, so that the world might recognize that you have sent me and that you love them as you have loved me.[1]"

We were "born ecumenical", even if some thought it was awkward to invite our Protestant brothers and sisters to Lourdes, a Catholic city, with the prevailing presence of Mary, her messages, the affirmation of her Immaculate Conception, the processions... But what unites us is so much more important than what separates us. In fact, from the first pilgrimage, there were some Orthodox participants. Anglicans and Protestants came from Great Britain and especially from Canada. A group of seventy Anglicans, who were not officially registered, participated in all the events. In our common faith, one point particularly united us: Jesus' words and welcome towards those who are the weakest. "I bless you, Father, Lord of heaven and earth, who have hidden this from the wise and intelligent and have revealed it to the littlest ones[2]" and his urgent demand that we invite to the feast "the poor, the crippled, the lame, the blind[3]". We were in total agreement also because we did not go to Lourdes to ask for healing for persons with intellectual disabilities, but for the healing of our hearts, so that we might fully recognize them in their unique beauty and help them to find their place in the Church and in society.

We did not want to hide our differences, but beyond our differences and with our differences, to create links of friendship and prayer, encouraging each person to deepen in his or her own tradition, and to show the privileged place of those who are weak within that tradition.

---

1. John 17: 22-23
2. Matthew 11: 25
3. Luke 14: 13

Adapted animation and liturgy

The activity of the spiritual animation committee did not finish with the writing of the Charter. It also worked on all the other instruments for animation and preparation. They decided upon the reflection themes, the songs, the pilgrim's booklet, besides the brochures and the posters.

The participants at the international meeting on December 8 determined the reflection themes. It looked like a kaleidoscope, but it was truly the work of all. During the time of preparation for the pilgrimage, these materials helped the animators of the local groups to avoid meetings that would be like a "ghetto", where people only talk about their own personal suffering. They brought nourishment that paved the way for the conversion of spirits and hearts.

Songs also had an essential role in the pilgrimage. We know that persons with disabilities are usually very attuned to music. It seemed obvious to us that we needed to have a "theme song" for the pilgrimage and we asked for help from many composers. Their propositions, although interesting, were too complicated, not accessible to the "littlest ones". Finally, Christiane Gaud, a teacher and specialized catechist, offered her collaboration. She had launched with me the collection of recordings, *Comme un Oiseau*[1], and had composed a wonderful repertoire of songs for children and for those who kept or rediscovered the heart of a child. With Father Georges Plaisatin[2], she wrote the words, while Father David Julien, a great composer of religious songs, created the melody. Their

---

1. *Like a Bird* - Translator note

2. Dominican, member of the *Centre National de Pastorale Liturgique (National Center of Pastoral Liturgy)*, was one of the persons in charge of the liturgy commission. Later he became national chaplain for Faith and Light in France.

song *"Amis, chantons notre joie"*[1] immediately gained unanimous approval. Its words were very simple and theologically profound, easy to learn, with the rhythm of the full Easter "Alleluia" repeated in chorus. We made two 45RPM vinyl records, one in French; one with songs in languages from different countries. These were accompanied by a music booklet with the translations. This music made it possible to create a common soul before the pilgrimage. The songs carried a message that went far beyond the duration of the project and the audience of Faith and Light.

Next we prepared the pilgrim's booklet in the four languages most commonly used by the pilgrims (French, English, Dutch and Spanish). We were aware that it would also be used by persons with disabilities, so we reserved four pages especially for them. As one young lady said, "mine, personal, belong". Each one could write in it (or have someone write in it for him or her) his/her name, address, the lodging in Lourdes, the name of someone he or she loved who could not come to the pilgrimage. As soon as a song started, people would take the booklet out of their pilgrim's pouch, even if they could not read. Many have kept it as a treasure, a souvenir of these bountiful days.

The essential task of the committee was around the liturgy with all its challenges. It was necessary to harmonize as much as possible with the Paschal Liturgy lived in Lourdes, keeping in mind the specific needs of persons with intellectual disabilities.

Liturgy needed to be simple and "bare bones", so that persons with intellectual disabilities might have a true moment of union with God, in his Church, celebrating the death and resurrection of its Savior and a new hope. At the same time, the liturgy had to deeply nourish the parents and friends.

The three grand themes marking each one of the days came very naturally from the Pascal liturgy. Good Friday: a penitential

---

1. *"Friends, let's sing all our Joy"* - Translator note

journey in the Light of God. We, together would all ask forgiveness for our sins and for the sins of the world in union with Jesus' death. Holy Saturday, the day where the disciples were without hope, everything seemed to be finished. Judas committed suicide. The body of Jesus was placed in the tomb. However, there is still the heart of Mary, where all the hope of the world finds refuge. It was a day of waiting and of trusting with her. Finally, the Easter Vigil: the day of the resurrection. Christ is alive. He has triumphed over all suffering and death.

This Easter liturgy can easily be connected with the liturgy of Lourdes. Besides the mystery of suffering and hope, so present in Lourdes, there were other common points in these two liturgies: the liturgy of the fire and light in the Easter Vigil, with the fire and light in the procession of lights and in the candles, omnipresent in Lourdes; the liturgy of water and baptism, with the "miraculous" spring and the pools. We tried to imagine what we called an "adapted liturgy".

When Bishops Donze and Viscaro welcomed Jean Vanier and Father Hviid for the first time, in July 1970, they were very open and interested in the perspective of adjusting the liturgies according to the needs of the project. They also accepted the request for collaboration between Faith and Light and the Sanctuaries. They delegated Father Décha, who was responsible for liturgy in Lourdes, to work with Father Hviid, Father Georges and the members of the committee. Father Décha was familiar with international celebrations. He, as well as the bishop, was very concerned with liturgy marked by the sense of the sacred and of beauty. At the same time, they were willing to study every new gesture, sign or symbol that could help persons with disabilities to fully participate, to help them in this way to awaken or to deepen their interior life.

One of the symbols retained particularly touched the pilgrims: blowing out all the candles after the Celebration of the Passion on

Good Friday, until the end of the Easter Vigil. The city of Lourdes agreed to illuminate the Basilica and the streets, at the very same moment, at the time in the liturgy when all the candles were re-lit, symbol of Jesus' Resurrection, Light of our hearts and of our lives.

During the Easter Vigil, there were slides illustrating the magnificent story of the creation of the world, the light and the night, the heavens and the waters, the plants, the lights in the sky, the animals of the air and in the water, all the beasts on earth, big and small, and then the unimaginable, man and woman created in the image and likeness of God.

Bishop Donze was also favorable to the idea of shortening and simplifying a number of prayers and texts submitted for his approval. These adaptations also needed to be accepted by Bishop Boudon, bishop of Mende, president of the Bishops Liturgical Commission. After that, they would be sent to translators in the different participating countries, and everything then needed the approval of the international commission for the translation of liturgical texts. This considerable work was entrusted to Father Plaisantin who, in the end, bound all the texts together in one "Missal for the priests".

Another major, unprecedented idea also needed the approval of the bishop: the organization, on Holy Saturday, of a great fiesta on the esplanade, "the celebration of meeting and of waiting".

We dreamed of having this fiesta at the heart of the sanctuaries. Simply put, this was impossible to imagine in Lourdes, because the esplanade was reserved for "paraliturgical" celebrations, such as the procession of the Blessed Sacrament or the candlelight processions. However, Bishop Donze and Bishop Viscaro were very sensitive to our desire to organize an event that would be a true celebration, marked at the same time by religious and sacred meaning, and an opportunity to unwind under the eyes of God. Perhaps too frequently we have experienced joy without God and God without joy.

Yet, an authentic celebration opens us to the Holy Spirit, because it is a fruit of the Spirit. In the Gospel, Jesus tells us that the kingdom of heaven is like a wedding feast, a time of joy. We thought that it was indispensable that the pilgrims, with their visible or invisible disabilities, be able to express their joy: sing, dance, rejoice together under the eyes of Jesus and on this land of Mary. Bishop Donze gladly gave us his permission.

The organization of this celebration was laborious and tricky, because many of the persons invited to animate it "fell through our fingers," one after the other. However, we were certain of the participation of John Littleton[1], who was also invited for the Easter Vigil, and of Raymond Fau.[2]

We planned to have a very large stage with a sound system, adjacent to the Rosary Basilica. The countries, the regions and the departments were invited to say if they wanted to have a place in the program with a song, a dance, a banner, a mime, and if possible, dressed in their traditional costumes.

Besides this large, central stage, we also imagined having other venues for more personal meetings. Throughout the paths along the esplanade the countries and regions would set up their stands so others could get to know about their geographical area and the activities they had during the preparation period (posters, photos, paintings...). Finally, tents for free expression would permit persons with disabilities and others to paint, play music, dance, model with clay, etc.: a way to express oneself and to pray in one's own style.

The spiritual dimension of the pilgrimage depended not only on the liturgical committee, but also on all who were carrying the event. We were very aware of the huge gap between our very

1. American singer especially known for his gospel songs. He had extensive experience animating religious celebrations and could sing in several languages.
2. French author, composer and singer. He composed many religious songs.

modest means and the big project to be accomplished. With Camille, when we reached the limit of our strength, we would find comfort saying: "God only asks us for one thing, our five loaves of bread and our two fish. The multiplication of the bread to nourish all the hungry crowd is His business!" Then, we would cling to prayer and as much as possible, to the daily Eucharist.

As a means to mobilize all the pilgrims from all countries, it was suggested to have a meeting point in our hearts each Thursday, around a special prayer. Finally, we chose the Magnificat, Mary's prayer, offering her poverty, her praise and trust in God who raises up the humble and sends the rich away with empty hands[1].

Transportation and lodging

If liturgy was at the heart of the pilgrimage, it was nevertheless necessary that practical questions follow, or even, precede it! Two fundamental questions needed to be settled: the transportation and the lodging of the pilgrims. We wrote down in a notebook all the tasks to be done. This notebook continued to get thicker throughout the time of preparation. Camille Proffit took on the responsibility to get in contact with agencies that might be able to respond to our needs.

The choice was easy: the Touring Club of France. It accepted the originality of our project and its practical consequences for a lesser cost than its competitors. One of our needs was that all the members of the same community be lodged in the same place. A second was what we called an "equalization system", where the price of the pilgrimage was the same for all. A third was that the most comfortable hotels and the ones closer to the Grotto be reserved with priority for the communities that welcomed persons

---

1. Luke 1: 46-55 - Translator note

with greater disabilities or that had come from the most distant countries.

The Touring Club contacted all types of lodgings, religious communities, family pensions, hotels of all categories, beginning with the simplest ones, in order to fix a price that was accessible for all.

The agency accepted that the pilgrims would register by communities from twelve to forty people instead of individually. Their names appeared on a single card, and for each person with disabilities, it indicated his or her two accompaniers: parents or friends.

The motivation, gifts and abilities of their agent, Jean Charrière, were decisive in the choice of the Touring Club. He wanted to participate in all the international meetings to get to know well the spirit that moved us and to be better able to respond to our needs and desires. His ability to adapt, his efficiency, his creativity, his discretion and his professionalism were a key element for the event.

Calling himself agnostic, he did not hesitate to write, several months after the pilgrimage: "For us, the fact that everything took place, in the final analysis, without conflicts and complications, this is a miracle." Having become a partner and a friend, he also participated in the pilgrimage to Rome in 1975 and to Lourdes in 1981.

A challenge: balance the budget

In relation to the financial aspect of the pilgrimage, we had to immediately face criticism from those who were anxious, or who were even shocked that so much money be "thrown away," without a concrete outcome, for persons with intellectual disabilities.

Father Dominique Tommy-Martin, a French priest who lived in Tunisia, serving persons with intellectual disabilities, wrote to us after having news about the project: "The Faith and Light project shocked me. Being with people, day after day, who are not able to satisfy their most basic needs: for food, clothing, shelter, at first I believed that this international meeting was offensive to me. It ran up huge expenses and had an enormous organization, without any tangible result, and without any solution to the tragic problems of people in the third world, and especially persons with disabilities in this third world."

But Father Dominique continued his response: "Now I think that this shock became the shock of a spiritual reality that brings light to the mindset of a world dominated by the search for profit. What disturbed me most deeply, but which represents the whole value of Faith and Light, is the gratuity of the project proposed. More than ever, we need to be liberated, and humanized, by acts without the intention of profit. What can be more gratuitous than a "useless" trip made by the people considered the most "useless" in the world? Finally I find it a stroke of genius and of a higher order than the best works of art, sports records and the conquest of space." In a way he said everything, and he had understood well the meaning of our pilgrimage.

As far as finances were concerned, we had begun a huge construction project; we did not have, at that moment, a single penny. Truly something to be concerned about!

It was necessary to look for financial help. Until that time each one was a volunteer and took care of the little expenses related to their particular responsibility. But it was already necessary to cover the expenses of longer trips, and month after month, the number of these trips increased in an exponential way. We certainly would need contributions to offer scholarships to persons with disabilities from countries in economic difficulty, the ones coming from the third world or from the countries of

Eastern Europe. It became crucial to find resources, but it was difficult to knock at the door of charitable associations when the project was only "on the drawing board" and was still, for many, if not totally crazy, at least imprudent.

Pierre Leborgne presented us to his founder, Bishop Jean Rhodain. This meeting made a deep impression. Bishop Rhodain listened to the presentation of our project in impenetrable silence. After that, he simply said: "I trust your project and I trust you. Bernadette was considered "good for nothing", just as the persons you care about. I will ask the Board of Directors to give you a grant. Besides this, I will personally write to all the delegates to give you all the support that they can afford." This meeting took only about twenty minutes, but was a decisive moment. Some days later we received a check for ten thousand francs, as well as a copy of his circular-letter to all the diocesan delegates in France that finished with a line in his own handwriting: "Here is another occasion to serve the poorest." The support of the *Secours Catholique* opened the doors of the Board of Directors of the OCH and of other associations, because they had so much trust in Bishop Jean Rhodain. If he approved the project, it was because it was valid. Some weeks later, the OCH, even more directly concerned than the *Secours Catholique*, gave a grant of fifteen thousand francs. Others followed.

It was essential that the use of funds was irreproachable. These funds came from associations or friends, from big institutions and also from the widow's "small coins". They were destined for the spiritual journey of the littlest ones. Each "penny" was important.

I remember a critical moment, at the end of 1970, when we had no assurance about the number of participants and therefore about the balance of funds. The three thousand printed copies of the "themes for reflection," destined to nourish the meetings of the local communities, were sold out. The community leaders urgently asked for more. We were then confronted with the need to print another thousand copies, which would cost three thousand francs. "Impossible", said the treasurer, "we are already on the tightrope. You will need to find the money." What to do? The best solution we could come up with was to make a list of ten people, who were convinced about our project or who might be open to be convinced, who could accept to give three hundred francs each, without straining their budgets too much.

Not one of these persons we approached avoided us, and most of them made efforts to take away our feeling of shame for coming to them as beggars. The widow of Marshal Leclerc de Hautecloque added a little note to her check: "Thank you for your trust in asking for my help." Jean Roux de Bézieux, president of the OCH, wrote to us: "with what joy I send you what you need. To know that I am in communion with you in this work increases joy and light in me and nourishes my hope." I mention these examples, but there were many others.

Even the question came up about what to do, in case at the end of the pilgrimage, we would have some money remaining. It was a wise question, because we did not want to stir up any covetousness. The international committee decided that if we had an excess of money it would be given to a center for persons with disabilities in India. The international committee asked the national committees to talk about this hypothesis and the proposal to not keep any surplus.

Two imperatives: health and safety

To bring together a large number of vulnerable persons includes another aspect that necessarily needs to be taken into account: security. It encompasses two fronts: health and safety. The task forces in charge of these questions were called to work closely together. They had a certain number of parameters in common, including the need to prioritize prevention.

Also, since the first international meeting in Lourdes, in December 1969, we had asked Jean-Baptiste Camino for his help. He had founded many establishments in the surrounding area for the ADAPEI. His wife and he were parents of a young lady, Bernadette, who had Down syndrome. He would be "the man on site". Native of the region, he knew all the civil and religious authorities, as well as people engaged with persons with intellectual disabilities. In addition, he accepted to be a regional coordinator for Faith and Light and to be the link with the different entities in Lourdes for us. This was particularly valuable for us in January of 1971, when the climate between us deteriorated.

In Lourdes we discovered another friend, Father Joseph Bordes, a pastor, who started a community in his parish to participate in the pilgrimage. The youth gave him the nickname of "Father Alleluia," a memory that he carried with emotion, because having become the rector of the Sanctuaries, he welcomed the pilgrimage of 1981.

The question of "health", foreseen since the beginning of the preparations, needed the assistance of medical doctors. This collaboration was decisive and multifaceted.

When fear of the pilgrimage's adverse affects on the psyche of young people with disabilities was expressed, the reaction of some physicians was invaluable. This is how Dr. Préaut, psychiatrist, member of the Board of Directors of l'Arche, vice-president of Special Olympics, responded to this objection by sharing fruits from this large sporting event. Five hundred children and youth with disabilities participated in them. He underlined all the benefits. For them, there was an immense joy. For their parents, the comfort of a warm and cheerful environment, the appreciation of their children, a renewed commitment from special educators, etc. "In Lourdes," he later wrote in an article in *Ombres et*

Lumière, "as in the Special Olympics, the feeling of rejection and abandonment can only be transformed into something positive through a call to strive for one's best and through communion."

Professor Jerôme Lejeune, world renowned due to his discovery of the cause of "mongolism," as it was called in 1959, expressed himself in the same vein. In addition, with Dr. Marie-Odile Réthoré, he suggested that we include in the program of the pilgrimage a dialogue between physicians and educators on the theme "The psychological repercussions of rejection or of welcome for the mentally handicapped". After the international team approved the idea, he accepted to moderate this dialogue.

During the press conference organized by Faith and Light in Paris on June 4, 1970, the journalists were particularly impressed by this initiative and by the presentation given by Jerôme Lejeune. They pointedly asked him the question: "Why would physicians participate in Faith and Light?" In his answer, he was careful to underscore how much segregation can break apart one's personality, and how, on the contrary, love can build it up.

According to the Charter, the committee for health was to be concerned with taking all measures "for overseeing medical issues". These would be numerous. Given the needs of a large portion of the pilgrims and the totally new character of this experience, we could not allow ourselves to avoid preparing for the smallest foreseeable risk. There would be plenty of improvisation, given what we could not anticipate.

First of all, it was necessary to study the conditions for admission of persons with disabilities. The pilgrimage Charter presented as a condition that the person with intellectual disability could be integrated in a group without danger to herself or himself, nor to others around him/her.

But how to verify this? At the time of registration, who would determine the possible risks? The parents themselves hesitated, either because this step generated fear in them or, on the contrary, they wanted by all means that their child would go to Lourdes. The committee on health decided to establish a medical team, at the departmental or regional level, including a medical specialist, a psychologist, a special educator and a priest. The parents or the tutors would fill out a form and send it to this team, with a certificate from the current medical doctor. These were the documents that made it possible for the committee to establish a choice "for the solution that seemed the most beneficial for the person, from a psycho-pedagogical perspective." The wisdom and the gentleness of the local teams made it possible to avoid nearly every challenge to their decisions.

The process seemed, *a posteriori*, very hard. Some even found it to be superfluous. Finally, despite its complexity, it worked very well and made possible the participation of four thousand persons with intellectual disabilities from all over the world with the maximum safeguards possible. The only hospitalization that occurred was of a grandmother who broke her leg when she fell on a staircase!

Four medical stations were planned: one during the day in the Esplanade, three operating day and night at the Accueil Notre-Dame, at the Hospital des Sept-Douleurs and at the Cité Saint-Pierre. Working with each medical doctor were members of the Red Cross and of the Civil Defense. Four ambulances were stationed at the Esplanade. After eleven o'clock at night, after the celebrations, the ambulances were at our "headquarters," the Hôtel Lécuyer. Finally there were beds reserved at the hospital in Pau and at the psychiatric hospital in Lannemezen. A veritable state of siege!

On the part of the city of Lourdes, we knew that sufficiently serious security measures were necessary, due to the general lack of knowledge of persons with intellectual disabilities and the fears that this aroused.

A new concern: communication

How can we explain that a plan considered a bit crazy, dreamed up on April 9, 1968 by a handful of nine people with no money, had given birth, three years later to the day, April 9, 1971 to an event bringing together at the Grotto a crowd of seventeen thousand people, including four thousand with an intellectual disability? It was made possible in part by public relations for this event. It was not just a matter of organizing a pilgrimage but we also had to publicize the event, especially for those for whom it was planned.

Certainly, this pilgrimage responded to a deep spiritual thirst of parents and their aspiration that their child be recognized by the Church and by society. But how could we bring together those concerned, often very isolated, and how could we inform the Church of our plan? This was part of the work of the public relations team.

Even before the public relations team was formed, Jean Vanier sent a letter to the bishops in France. At the same time, a letter was sent to diocesan officials responsible for services for children and youth with disabilities, and those involved in "Special Catechesis". We informed them about the project and asked for their support.

To reach parents and also friends and associations, the public relations committee prepared various tools. First, a flyer with a simple and powerful message, as well as a poster directed primarily to parishes, and institutions that welcomed people with disabilities. We hoped that these documents would be illustrated with a logo, which would convey the spirit of the pilgrimage much better than words.

This logo, which is still the logo of Faith and Light today, has a story. First, there was a contest, open especially to persons with intellectual disabilities, to send us possible designs. But the results were disappointing. Then we decided to contact Meb, a painter with Down syndrome, who made a living through his art, and had a place of his own.

I went to see his mother, who acted as his agent, in order to meet him. I then explained to him what we needed and I asked if he accepted to make a design that people would be able to clearly understand. He silently listened to my request without giving any reply. At a time that he himself chose, he asked his mother to read to him the Charter for the pilgrimage, the words of which were beyond his capacity to understand. The theme song for the pilgrimage, "Amis chantons notre joie" served as background music while he worked. We later saw his creation – a boat carrying twelve little persons, with no oars and no sails. In the midst of very threatening clouds there appeared luminous rays of the sun. The sea was boiling out in the deep water, but was much calmer near the boat. Meb, who does not know how to count, seemed to have been inspired when he made his composition. He explained that Jesus slept in the bottom of the boat, but that we should not be afraid because Jesus kept watch.

His painting was accepted unanimously. It became our trademark and the insignia that all pilgrims would carry. One of us suggested a legend, which he said came from a verse in the Bible: "The clouds are opened, Lord, and your light comes upon us." But the reference was never found! We consulted a well-known biblical scholar, Father Feuillet, who confirmed that this text was not in the Bible. But the verse corresponded so well to Meb's drawing that it was adopted.

Meb's story doesn't end here! Régis Malherbe-Navarre, a master-painter, whose workshop is in Lourdes, asked our permission to reproduce Meb's painting in gemmail[1].

---

1. An art form that uses fragments of glass in different colors and thickness, which makes it possible to use the palette's most subtle nuances - Translator note

It is a work of real beauty, which Meb came to sign in the master's workshop before it went on public display for several months. After the pilgrimage, it was decided, with the agreement of Mr. Malherbe, to offer it to the Saint Pius-X basilica to be put in a place of honor to signify the place the littlest ones have in the heart of the Church. It is there until today. This logo was, and continues to be, the best means of communication throughout the world. It unites all the communities in a way that is much livelier and more direct than the Charter. Since then, Meb's painting has been reproduced in all countries in dozens of different artistic media.

Once we had gathered the indispensable information, the dates and the schedule of the pilgrimage, the costs, thirty thousand folders and posters, all of course carrying Meb's boat, were sent to parishes, youth movements, schools, chaplaincies, associations, etc.

Three networks proved to be exceptional channels. The magazine, *Ombres et Lumière,* because its priority was to address families who had a child with disabilities with a Christian perspective. At the time, the magazine gave a certain emphasis to those with intellectual disabilities because they were among the most ignored and marginalized.

The first information about the pilgrimage was published in the magazine in March 1970, then in the following edition there was an article by Camille Proffit with the title: "Why the Faith and Light pilgrimage?" This triggered significant correspondence from readers in the following editions. Finally, there was a special edition about Faith and Light called "It is he who leads us." This came at the right moment, only a few weeks before the pilgrimage.

The second network was through UNAPEI. As an organization, it had an openly non-religious approach, but it accepted news that had a spiritual or religious character. Camille Proffit wrote a circular letter to all the persons in charge of the regional UNAPEI, asking them to publicize the pilgrimage. The magazine *Nos enfants inadaptés* [1] published an article. Camille also wrote directly to leaders in several regions to ask if they would personally take on some responsibility or indicate names of persons who might help us. Many agreed and served as very valuable connections well beyond the pilgrimage.

The media, especially the written press, had an important role. We were surprised because we touched on three themes that are not at all "newsworthy" and around which, many preconceived ideas prevailed. Persons with intellectual disabilities were synonymous with fear. Pilgrimages were considered "archaic and triumphalist" at a time when the only conceivable image of the Church was something very quiet and out of sight. And finally Lourdes, which was perceived as the city of miracles and superstition, city of the "merchants of the temple" making profit from religious objects that had no artistic value! These are just some examples...

Despite all this, they participated in three press conferences, in greater numbers than we expected. It seemed to us that they were attracted by the novelty of the project, its international character, the atypical and media-genic career path of Jean Vanier and by his charismatic personality. They were reassured by the welcome in the Secours Catholique, which offered us a room and a reception at the end of each conference with a cordial ambience. The first, June 4, 1970, was targeted at "certain journalists" likely to understand the depth of our project and able to objectively spread news about it nine months before the event.

In this group we found Geneviève Lainé, from *La Croix* [2], who was an exceptional partner due to her sensitivity, eloquence and faithfulness. She has never let us down over all these years. I found an extract from her first article: "No, this will not be chasing after

---

1. *Our maladjusted children* - Translator note
2. *The Cross* - a Catholic daily newspaper – Translator note

miracles. No, this will not be a patronizing charitable gesture towards these 'poor little ones.' We are all 'poor little ones' in relationship to the Eternal One. It will be a great celebration in the light of God, a meeting without the barriers of national borders, race, social status or IQ, as should, in fact, be all Christian gatherings, children of the same Father. For the Lord, no one is maladjusted." And she was insistent in her invitation: "Whatever and whomever you might be, if you are 'grabbed' by the idea of this gathering that sees itself as 'spiritually humble, poor, friendly, prayerful and harmonious,' if you would like to participate in the party, or to help in any way, write to Faith and Light."

La Vie catholique was equally present through Georges Hourdin, who put aside his personal reservations to give us support. But also *L'Homme nouveau*[1], with Marcel Clément, who was convinced that this was an exceptionally important issue for the Church and for the world, and a dozen other journalists sometimes with very diverse religious sensitivities, but united by those whose weakness calls us forth. They were the first ones to officially put Faith and Light "into orbit."

The television magazine *Le Jour du Seigneur*[2] gave us five minutes to present the event, and we were also allowed to make a financial appeal on the air. In addition, the channel reserved the offerings from the daily televised Mass that day to help the participation of pilgrims in financial difficulty. I particularly remember the special request of two parents whose two sons had intellectual disabilities and lived with them. Their dream was for all four of them to go to Lourdes. This dream was realized.

The regional press was present at the second conference, which had a much larger participation. Its support proved to be

---

1. *The New Man* – a magazine - Translator note

2. *The Day of the Lord* - Translator note

extremely valuable because this made it possible to communicate with families that were not linked to any support services.

Finally, on January 27, 1971, there was an even bigger press conference, "the last chance", for all the pilgrims still hesitating and for all those who had not yet been contacted. Two "headliners" attracted the journalists, Father Jorgen Hviid, international chaplain, who came from Denmark to emphasize the universal dimension of the project with the participation of pilgrims from fifteen countries, and Professor Jérome Lejeune, who renewed his invitation to all medical doctors for a dialogue designed especially for them. "A pilgrimage of this type," Professor Lejeune said, "is a school of hope, and if this school brings forth fruit, this by itself is an enormous miracle that I would very much like to see." In fact, two months later, he saw it along with the three hundred physicians from all over the world, the twelve thousand pilgrims and all the city of Lourdes.

One of the most beneficial aspects of our relationship with the media, which very much wanted to communicate our difficulties, especially for the pilgrims coming from the third-world, was the collection of funds, which was far from insignificant. At the same time, all the publicity initiatives made in France were retransmitted in other countries and this multiplied our impact throughout the world.

All of this made it possible to publicize the pilgrimage, often beyond our expectations. However, besides all of this indispensable organization, person-to-person communication was definitely the most effective way because, in reality, who can better convince a family than another family? Or a friend, than another friend? A priest than another priest? Even today, we must not neglect any means to make the movement known to those who are still isolated and alone, and nothing will be more effective than the "Come and see" addressed personally to all who might join us.

Finally, the public relations committee was in charge of editing all the documents related to the pilgrimage. They needed to do all kinds of "acrobatics" in order to complete this work. We gave ourselves a parameter: "That all be beautiful". Nothing is too beautiful for persons with disabilities, so often despised. In this way, the Charter of the pilgrimage was presented in the format of a booklet, on fine card stock, with the title in golden letters. Beauty signals our respect for the dignity of the littlest ones. I am convinced, as we have so many times experienced, that they are able to perceive the aesthetic dimension of things and are very sensitive to it.

Grassroots: the communities

As it was written in the Charter, this pilgrimage "did not aim to be the coming together of individuals, but a gathering of small, 'human-sized' communities, at the heart of which, persons with intellectual disabilities could be perfectly integrated. The preparation will be done in the context of cordial meetings of sharing and prayer." This provision came as a response to the fear that group thinking would prevail over personal participation, and that suffering multiplied by thousands would be unbearable. It was also necessary to be attentive not to revive the feeling of isolation, which parents with children with disabilities might experience.

The term "community" was not immediately adopted. We would say "base community", "Christian community", "Life community", "Faith Community", or "Base Group[1]". This lack of precision lasted for a long time, but this was not our biggest

1. To simplify the reading of the following pages, we will adopt the term "community", even if it only became official in the Charter of 1982.

priority. However, there was total unanimity that "community" was necessary. It would always come up, like a recurring theme, in all meetings, at all levels. During the international meeting in Lourdes, in December of 1969, we insisted on the following points: "it is necessary that we create living communities, Christian communities with those who will go to Lourdes together. It is necessary that we think about and put into practice all the pedagogy necessary so that people with disabilities may truly benefit from the pilgrimage. So that it may not be just a beautiful trip, but even more, the beginning of a new life in the Church. All your proposals, all your experiences will be the biggest service to all." And on June 8, 1970, Jean Vanier, in a letter to all the members of the international committee, came back to the topic: "In our next meeting in Lourdes, in a month, you will find in the agenda the meetings for the preparation of the local communities. I remind you of our desire to establish these communities of twenty to thirty pilgrims: persons with disabilities, parents, educators, friends... You know the importance that we need to give to the preparation for this big gathering."

The members of the communities were, first of all, persons with disabilities and their families. The presence of friends, and especially of educators, also seemed to be essential. We owe to François Demptos, leader of the "White Scarfs[1]", the very blessed intuition to especially invite young people as friends (from 18 to 35 years old). They would accompany the parents so that they would no longer be alone with their child. The presence of the young person would give the parents a certain freedom to participate in the activities planned for them. The youth, who would register individually, would be integrated into a

---

1. The more experienced members of the Scouting movement who had made the commitment to serve at Lourdes according to the spirituality of their movement. After two, or three internships of fifteen days, they had the right to wear the white scarf.

community, to live a partnership with a family. Some offered their contribution in general services, babysitting, translations, cleaning, help in the hospitals, peeling vegetables... In this case, as much as possible, they would be attached to a community for lodging and celebrations. At this time we had no idea that these young people, who came to "serve", would make the tremendous discovery of relationship with the person with disabilities.

The participation of special educators seemed to us to be basic. Jean Vanier wrote: "Our pilgrimage involves a very strong cooperation between parents and educators. We need educators with experience, competent men and women, and not only youth. If we do not make efforts to bring them into our project, we risk a big split between the world of the parents and the world of the medical-pedagogical institutions and specialized centers."

This concern was even more consequential because we were, as I have already said, in the middle of the upheaval of 1968, that affected, in a special way, professionals in the socio-educational sphere. These professionals, sometimes, considered parents responsible for the difficulties of their children and even found them guilty and took the children away from them. They frequently questioned moral and spiritual values. The pilgrimage could be a unique opportunity for meeting in a different environment and with different responsibilities: establishing a mutual relationship of trust with the parents, around, and with, the children or youth with disabilities.

The number of educators who participated in the pilgrimage surprised us. It is difficult to know their exact number because frequently they were registered as "friends", if they did not participate in the pilgrimage with a pedagogical function, but to simply live a positive, friendly experience with the parents and the young people.

Also, some directors of institutions that welcomed persons with disabilities contacted us. We reflected together on necessary adaptations to welcome their residents, given that the pilgrimage was first of all addressed to families. This pilgrimage was above all an invitation. It was necessary, first of all, to invite persons with disabilities, who were to be the first beneficiaries. They were to be totally free to answer yes or no to our invitation. They needed to be accompanied by at least one person, with priority given to their parents, brothers, sisters or friends, but it was very desirable that the members of the medical-pedagogical team would also join them, and be integrated into the community closest to them. Depending on the numbers, an institution could also form one or several communities open very broadly to people from the outside to accompany the persons with disabilities.

Future pilgrims

We observed some very interesting initiatives. I particularly remember Bec-Hellouin, a Benedictine monastery in Normandy that welcomed about twenty young people with Down syndrome. A partnership was established between them and the youth of the school, Sainte-Marie de Neuilly et de Blois. This was the initiative of a ninth grade teacher, Jeanne-Marie Pardoën, along with the parents of some students. It was an incredible discovery by the students who, until then, had more or less despised these persons called "retarded", and now discovered their heart. And as for the persons with disabilities, from morning to night, they were in awe with everything.

In Alsace[1], half of the residents of a big institution of three hundred persons with disabilities chose to go on pilgrimage with accompaniers, educators and friends from widely varied places. The director, Sr. Gabrielle, wrote: "Even if we did not exactly fit

---

1. A French region, close to Germany and Switzerland – Translator note

the criteria for participation, Faith and Light profoundly marked our institution. We discovered a fraternal and festive dimension that was totally foreign to us. We opened ourselves to the outside world and got in touch with families and young friends." Almost always, these connections remained.

L'Arche was a special case, because it is not an institution, but communities. Its environment does not depend on professional educators, but the assistants are the ones who share life together like family with persons with a disability. In l'Arche they already had the custom of going on pilgrimage with families and friends from outside. The three communities that existed at the time, Trosly, Courbillac en Charante and Daybreak in Toronto decided to participate and organized themselves as communities for the preparation meetings.

In the last image of the film, made by a team of Canadian filmmakers, about this pilgrimage of 1971, a group from l'Arche is interviewed. When Marc thinks that it is time to leave, he separates himself from the group, moves closer to the team of filmmakers, gives a very warm handshake to each one and departs. He turns around once more, radiant, both arms lifted up to the sky, and shouts: "Goodbye! Goodbye! See you soon…" It is a cry of friendship and hope that truly was the cry of all the pilgrims at the time of leaving Lourdes.

We also invented another category of pilgrims: those who could not come! When we fixed the conditions for participation in the pilgrimage, we thought of all those who would be excluded by the medical teams because of some serious difficulty in addition to intellectual disabilities: serious personality disorders, or those whose intelligence was unaffected, but had severe psychiatric disturbance (schizophrenia, paranoia, serious depression…). The context of the pilgrimage, with such an enormous crowd, would not bring them anything good, but just the opposite.

We also had in mind all those who could not participate due to other reasons: fatigue, sickness, family events, professional commitments... They all were in our minds as we developed the "themes for reflection" and as we laid the foundations for the communities. We wanted to encourage them to integrate themselves by participating in all meetings, Masses, and all preparation activities.

The fact of going or not going should not cut us off from each other. We were preparing ourselves to go to Lourdes in our hearts, even if this was not physically possible. Those who would go would bring the prayer intentions of those who stayed, and would place them at the feet of the Virgin Mary upon arrival. The pilgrims who stayed at home would remain in communion with those who went and would accompany them throughout the pilgrimage. They could also help with financial aid, taking care of children or any other service that might be necessary while the others were away for several days.

And then, during the days of the pilgrimage, why would those whom we called "pilgrims at home" not get together for an evening prayer, for a Mass in the parish, or for a pilgrimage to a nearby sanctuary dedicated to the Virgin? And this is what happened. From Peru to Denmark, stretching across Canada or Morocco, invisible strands wove an invisible web throughout the world.

The creation of communities was entrusted to the regional or diocesan coordinator. This person was responsible for appointing a coordinator and a spiritual accompanier for each community.

A community could start with two or three families with a child with disabilities and invite other people who would be happy to participate in this great adventure to Lourdes (parishioners, friends, families, professionals, neighbors, educators...) and whose relationships could continue beyond the pilgrimage.

Another option was to invite a very large audience to an informational session, to make them aware of the difficulties and the richness of people with disabilities. Those who wanted could then be invited to a second meeting to get to know each other better, to create bonds and to register for the pilgrimage, if necessary.

A daunting commitment

The preparation for the 1971 pilgrimage and the first steps of Faith and Light was an exceptional time. Forty years later, quickly looking through the archives, recently, I felt both wonder and dismay. How could anyone make an account of the work of all those who, in a manner so discreet and so hidden, carried the gestation of Faith and Light: coordinators for the countries, regions, departments, communities?

It is impossible to put together a comprehensive picture of all that was done during this period of preparation. What emerges from the reports or from the mail sent to us is infinitesimal compared with what was actually lived at the time.

However, it is possible to demonstrate the magnitude of the heavy and demanding task that these leaders accepted, particularly the regional and departmental coordinators, led by Camille Proffit, national coordinator for France. It is staggering, today, to see its scope. It was necessary to create a regional team with strong people able to invest themselves totally. After that it was necessary, using all possible means, to inform the associations for persons with disabilities, the youth movements, Catholic schools, religious orders... and invite them to join us. Another focus, and the most fundamental, was to create local communities and to assure their accompaniment. That is where the spiritual preparation and animation was to take place.

These tasks would become the responsibility of the diocesan coordinators, who could implement them with relative ease, given their closer proximity to the local and the emerging communities.

Camille counseled, supported, encouraged, visited, supervised… But there was also the seriousness and enthusiasm of the local representatives, who knew how to carry the project in their regions, to the point of making the announcement of the pilgrimage everywhere to the persons directly concerned, but also to those who knew nothing about intellectual disabilities. Young people were particularly moved.

The regional meetings, that happened everywhere, were really amazing. The one in Paris brought together four hundred persons. Six of the eight dioceses were generally represented and we could feel the vibrancy of the coordinators, united beyond any superficial differences of sensitivity and opinion.

The role of the regional and diocesan structures was decisive, because their existence and the quality of their coordinators made it possible, ultimately, for Faith and Light to be born. Without their engagement, our initiative would no doubt have been limited to a "unique pilgrimage", as many did experience, but also to a single pilgrimage, a happy memory, but without any continuity. Today the organization of Faith and Light is a little different but the essential has not changed: the structures that are in place, deliberately light, are at the service of the communities, to accompany them. In their wonderful simplicity, they continue to transform so many hearts, so many lives.

The international dimension, desired since the first steps of Faith and Light, was already present at the decisive lunch of April 9, 1968. We can read in the report of that meeting: "We, Christians, believe in the value of the prayer of persons with disabilities and we know the importance of their place in the Universal Church." And, from the beginning, we had planned the famous international meeting that took place on December 8.

During the summer of 1968, the medical-pedagogical and psychosocial commissions of the International Catholic Bureau for Children (BICE), for which I was the general secretary, organized a conference about persons with intellectual disabilities in La Turbie, close to Nice. Jean Vanier was invited to give a talk and he was given permission to present information about the pilgrimage project. Many participants showed interest and asked to be kept informed, particularly about the date, which was still uncertain. Through this channel many coordinators emerged, including a mother from Portugal and Father Jorgen Hviid, our international chaplain. After December 8, we had six other international meetings, two in 1969, three in 1970 and one in 1971.

In the middle of the preparation we lived a tragedy: the sudden, wrenching death of Gérard Proffit, on June 18, 1970. His wife, Camille, national coordinator for France, performed her mission with incredible energy and efficiency. We were with her, at the office on Mézières Street, for an afternoon of work, when she received the news that Gérard was hospitalized for some tests after a minor heart problem. The couple was to get together for dinner.

The phone rang at the end of the afternoon, during Mass in our little chapel.

Camille received the Eucharist and took the road to Amiens, accompanied by Jean Vanier. Gérard died just before they arrived. Camille, broken, knelt for a long time beside her husband and then prayed the Magnificat. Gérard's death was an immense shock to Camille and to their family, for our team and for all Faith and Light. We were halfway through the preparations for the pilgrimage. How would Camille react? She was a cornerstone in the organization for France, and had a central place on the international flowchart, given that France was the "engine" of the project?

At the funeral, Jean spoke about how Gérard had been a just man, farmer, head of the family, a man of prayer, engaged with Camille in the Équipes Notre-Dame, consecrating half an hour each morning to meet with God. Camille took in these words. In profound communion with Gérard, she continued her task, which she had not chosen but completely accepted. And she did so with exceptional courage, competence and conviction.

Cancel the pilgrimage?

Early in January 1971, three months before the pilgrimage, a major crisis that had been "simmering" for several weeks exploded. It manifested itself in three interconnected areas: lack of registrations, the collapse of the secretariat and alarming rumors. Each problem made the others even worse.

The anxiety centered on the number of participants. The general budget for the pilgrimage had been established with an estimate of eight thousand pilgrims, based on rough approximations from the countries. It was impossible to have precise numbers, with the exception of countries like Canada or England that, a year in advance, had reserved chartered planes and could give notice of one thousand seven hundred and eighty participants. The Touring Club had reserved eight thousand beds, paid the deposit, and had the option of another three thousand beds. It would be a disaster if, in the end, the places reserved were not filled.

By January 1, 1971, the deadline for sending in the final registrations accompanied by the down payment, we had received only seven hundred French registrations of the five thousand expected!

Since the month of December, fear dominated the international administrative secretariat. The assistant director, a key piece in the operation, resigned. The very competent and very motivated priest, who had securely carried the coordination and many other responsibilities, including the Fiesta, closed the door behind him due to differences with another very committed priest on the team. François Demptos, who left the Scouts of France, also had to abandon the project...

Alarming rumors spread. During a meeting of the SCEJI's board of directors, certain members asked Bishop de La Chanonie to ban the pilgrimage. According to them, "the Church should not be involved in such a catastrophe!" The bishop refused to take this action. He thought that too many irreversible commitments had been made, particularly financial ones, and, besides, such a decision did not belong to the SCEJI, which was only an organism of coordination and information.

On another front, Jean-Baptiste Camino informed us that this frightening news was spreading in Lourdes and had begun to alarm different authorities there. Didn't we risk "chaos", as some had predicted, or at least a "monumental financial fiasco"?

It was necessary to act on all these fronts.

The closing of registrations was reset for February 15. Even after that, the Touring Club continued to receive new registrations which arrived until fifteen days before the pilgrimage. And for the workers of the eleventh hour, those who did not decide until the last moment or that arrived without having registered, a welcome stand was organized in Lourdes by the OCH, so that they would also be able to participate in all activities. These came principally from the region nearby and they were able to join a registered community or register together as a community in groups of fifteen or twenty. We know that the total number of pilgrims officially registered through the Touring Club was twelve thousand, not counting the innumerable others who showed up in Lourdes, asking us to "enlarge the tent".

Facing the disorganization of the secretariat, while waiting to find a replacement, all the responsibilities taken before the resignation were shared by other members of the team. I went to Mézières Street every morning for a debriefing. We diligently searched the highways and the byways for the wonderworker who would organize and animate the fiesta. But we had to wait until March 11 before finding a marvelous young couple, Jean-Marc Molinari and his wife, who took up the challenge that grew exponentially day-by-day.

Back in Lourdes, on the advice of Jean-Baptiste Camino, we extended an invitation for a meeting of civil authorities, military officers and religious leaders concerned in any way with the project, to take place on January 29, 1971. We also invited the hotel and merchants unions, the rector of the sanctuaries, the person who coordinated lodging, the president of Hospitality, the Red Cross, the Civil Defense...

We were around thirty persons, including a small international delegation from Faith and Light. Mr. Whigam agreed to come from England to witness to the investment of countries other than France and to the seriousness of the preparation.

At the beginning of the meeting I was struck by the faces: tense, defensive. In his welcome and during all the back and forth, Jean Vanier did everything to speak to the hearts of the men and fathers there (who greatly outnumbered women). He described the situation of persons with intellectual disabilities, their suffering from being so often put away, when their biggest need was to be welcomed, loved, called to share all the gifts of their hearts. When considered in this way, they no longer feel themselves "disabled", but persons. And we can discover them as capable of being "our masters". This is what we want to say with this pilgrimage where they will know the immense joy of being among family and friends, especially the young people. It is a unique opportunity for the parents, to help them to get out of the isolation in which they still too often find themselves.

Questions started to come from all sides, and little by little there was some dialogue. The necessary measures were identified. Trust was established with the desire that each of us would do our best. It was impressive to see the extent of the means that were put at our disposal and the mobilization of all.

Two other similar meetings took place, one on February 24 at the main office of ADAPEI, and the other on April 5, three days before the event, at our headquarters in the Hotel Lécuyer. Together, we reviewed all that was necessary. We wanted this big international gathering to take place in a climate of relaxation and peace, so that the only memory the pilgrims would have would be of profound joy.

From the crisis, we emerged strengthened.

The home stretch

During the last two months, everyone was continually on the go. Everywhere, in the countries, the regions, the local communities, the teams, the international secretariat, etc., everyone was working double shifts. Mr. Charrière slept less and less. Each day brought its share of new problems. Very often prayer took the form of a cry for help: "Lord, come save us. Save us, we are perishing!" Despite the unending setbacks, the documents were finished, new communities were formed in France and elsewhere and financial gifts arrived, at times large and generally unexpected, reminding us that we were not alone. Indeed, we experienced insecurity, doubt and sometimes anguish, an impression of being crushed by the task to be accomplished, and, at the same time, great trust.

Deep within us resided a joyful hope, a sort of fervor that carried us forward. But, to be honest, I must say that we were not really aware of this until after the event.

An incident illustrates well the atmosphere of this time. About three weeks before the pilgrimage, we had a regular meeting of the small Faith and Light team and the person responsible for the liturgy requested to speak. He said that he was delegated by the SCEJI to ask Jean Vanier to sign a paper committing to stop all Faith and Light activity once the pilgrimage ended. Jean's response was clear: "It is impossible for me to make such a promise, since we do not know the future and because I am not the only one involved in this." In spite of the priest's insistence, Jean continued to be unwavering.

From the pilgrims' side, there was so much to think about. What to put in the suitcases? Remember the medications, warm clothing, raincoats, umbrellas, health insurance cards... There was also, for many, the anxiety of taking the train or the plane sometimes for the first time. Among the pilgrims, there was, for example, a seventy-year-old man with intellectual disabilities, who had spent all his life in a psychiatric hospital.

Finally, the moment of departure arrived. First there were the reunions at the train station or at the airport. There was all the hustle and bustle, pleasant for most, frightening for some. Then the moment of the last good-byes to those who came to see us off arrived. From that point on, everything seemed to simply unfold, at least in appearance: the plane took off, the train started rolling, the bus turned onto the road: the pilgrimage had begun. There was noise everywhere. The friendly chatter in the close quarters of the train car was accompanied by pleasant greetings from the conductor, pilgrimage songs and times of prayer. Although we had prepared carefully for any possible medical needs, nothing was needed, and the journey went without incident. In each train was a team with a medical doctor, two nurses and some paramedics. This team had the chart of the hospitals, which had been well informed, and each one knew exactly what to do in case of emergency.

The regional coordinators, for their part, would walk back and forth through the train cars to get to know the people that had been entrusted to them. People shared their picnics. People tried to sleep as best they could. The silence was frequently disturbed by snores, cries from nightmares or by those who woke in the middle of the night... But on our arrival in Lourdes, we were no longer strangers.

Chapter 4

Manifestation of the Holy Spirit
(Easter 1971)

These four days of pilgrimage were, from beginning to end, one single event unified by the presence of grace that manifested itself in what we lived in community and in the deep, hidden places of our hearts. I will summarize it in three words: liberation, consolation and communion.

Josette Audret, on special assignment from *La Croix*, who participated in the pilgrimage with a local community, wrote at the end of this weekend:

"For me, this pilgrimage was nothing grandiose or sensational. The essential is that Jean-Luc who, blind and weak, felt his way forward to meet Jacky in his wheel chair and comforted him, because he was in tears; François, who is said to have an IQ of 40, who hummed all day "Amis, chantons notre joie"; the little unknown girl with Down syndrome who came to hug me; Michel, also blind and with limited intelligence, at the Adoration of the cross, who waved a small wooden cross each time the crowd sang "Amen"; Marie, herself in deep suffering, who said to me as we left the Basilica: "I said to God: see how unhappy they are."

Before D-Day

The beginning of the pilgrimage had been fixed for Good Friday, April 9. But the international team, trusting and ready, arrived Monday at our "headquarters", the Hotel Lécuyer, by the Gave River. The hotel's management, with marvelous understanding, let us use all the operations and meeting rooms that we needed. They were attentive to all our requests.

The last meetings of the different committees started immediately with the authorities in Lourdes: security, liturgy, medical committee... The communication was constant with the secretariat in Paris and with the offices in the different countries. The Hotel Lécuyer was a veritable beehive, where each one would carry out his or her tasks early in the morning, late in the evening or even during the night on behalf of the Touring Club. Meals were taken very quickly, but cordially, and we were as taut as runners before a race.

Wednesday, the evening before most pilgrims were to arrive, we were all very aware of the gravity of the moment. The following day, after three years of mobilizing so many people and resources, would start an adventure without historical precedent, and that would remain a unique event. We were like those on the eve of battle; we all held our breath. Those who believed in God placed everything into God's hands.

Everybody arrives

Beginning Wednesday, we looked for the pilgrims coming from the farthest countries. Some members of the international team were assigned to offer welcome at the airport and others at the train station.

The first chartered plane was a Boeing transporting four hundred and eighty Canadians. In the film of the pilgrimage we see Jean Vanier walking on the landing strip in the direction of the Canadian plane that had just landed. The doors are opened. It is a scene of emotion, joy, and happiness to be welcomed and to welcome the first Faith and Light pilgrims.

Thirty other planes followed. We also waited for nine special trains from France and two from Belgium. Many also arrived by regular trains, buses or by car.

In a matter of minutes, the platform of the train station in Lourdes was swarming with humanity. What would happen? Normally, we know that there are always unexpected occurrences, such as lost baggage, mistakes about hotels, the exasperations of a tired traveller... With Faith and Light, we risked much more. A great number of the pilgrims were fragile: worn by the long journey, plunged into the unknown, without their familiar routines...

However, no incident was reported. All arrived without problems at their places of lodging. I was frequently told by the hotel personnel how much they marveled at the kindness and gentleness of these tired people, and at the contagious mutual help among the pilgrims, among the families, whether they knew each other or not. The anxiety of expectation gave way to a feeling of peace; everything was going well, mysteriously well. This was in contrast with the atmosphere of Lourdes, which seemed to be preparing for war. There was a soldier stationed every fifty meters along the banks of the River Gave, to assure that no child or adult would fall, or throw themselves, into the river. They even had divers ready to intervene if needed. The police guarded the roads leaving the town in case there might be people trying to run away. Some shopkeepers lowered their iron grated security doors because they believed their stores would be ransacked!

The headquarters received those who were not happy, sometimes very unhappy, but these were few. It was cold in

Lourdes, and although we made all necessary arrangements, some hotels where the majority of the Canadians had been booked were not heated. Their coordinators immediately wanted to go back home, fearing for the health of the people with disabilities. Fortunately, the coordinators for the north of France offered to change hotels with them. "For us," they said, "it is less difficult. We do not suffer the time change, nor the change of country, nor the difference between the cold outside and the warmth indoors." This little anecdote gives an idea of the caring atmosphere that prevailed throughout these days.

Since Holy Thursday is the entrance into the Paschal Triduum, although the pilgrimage would not officially begin until the following day, the numerous pilgrims that had already arrived packed the Saint Pius-X Basilica for a celebration accessible to each one, whatever his or her level of intellectual ability. We remembered and relived the institution of the Eucharist and of priesthood, the washing of the feet, and the entrance into the Passion of Jesus with the adoration of his Body given for us. The liturgy was presided over by Bishop Donze and was concelebrated with the priests of Faith and Light.

Meeting at the Grotto

The first action of the pilgrimage took place at the Grotto on Friday morning. We were grouped by country or by region during this moment anticipated so intensely by all the pilgrims, especially persons with disabilities and their parents.

The Grotto is the heart of Lourdes. It is in this place that it all started. Mary chose a small, young girl, the person most depreciated in Lourdes, to repeat the message of Jesus on earth. The Grotto is the place that Bernadette loved so dearly. When she left Lourdes, she confided to those who accompanied her: "The Grotto is my heaven."

Every fifteen minutes, groups of pilgrims would go, one after the other, to take their personal intentions and those of the people who could not come, but were there in their hearts. Everyone, by their songs and their prayers expressed their gratitude, their joy, their intentions and requests for help. Some were more recollected or inward, others more spontaneous, more exuberant. A family expressed the feeling of many: "At the Grotto, it was like we were in a dream, with our son, thousands of kilometers from our little home."

The countries gather for the welcoming

The big gathering on the esplanade was the second moment of this opening day. In the early afternoon twelve thousand pilgrims met, some with their typical regional dress, carrying the name of their country on wooden signs – Germany, England, Belgium, Canada, Denmark, Spain, United States, France, Ireland, Italy, Luxemburg, Morocco, Switzerland, Czechoslovakia, Tunisia. An immense crowd so marked by suffering, hearts very open, came together. It was three in the afternoon, the time when Jesus died to save and to gather into one all his scattered children.

Bishop Donze, who had been so faithful to us since the beginning, spoke after a deep silence. He welcomed the pilgrimage as an act of audacity, which some had believed to be reckless. I had the desire to respond in kind: he also spoke to us in a courageous and audacious way. Out of caution, the other bishops preferred to remain silent. He acknowledged "the organization, laboriously prepared with love and hope during many months", before emphasizing "the exceptional and prophetic character" of this pilgrimage, not like others. "For the first time in history", he said, "thousands of persons with disabilities of all ages were brought together to live, with their parents, friends and educators, in one community of prayer, the last days of Holy Week."

In his turn, Jean Vanier spoke: "Coming to Lourdes from all the corners of France and from fifteen countries in the world, we believe that each one of us can become a messenger of hope. We did not come here to weep, but to seek joy, to live a meeting of peace. It is necessary that together we make rivers of living waters spring forth that make possible the growth of this society of peace, of love and of truth where each one will be loved, respected and will be able to believe."

The crowd was deeply moved. As we interacted with one another more and more, we were no longer a large anonymous group, we were one family whose hearts beat as one. At the end of this message, there was an impressive silence. Then, unending applause. At my side, a young dad exclaimed: "Wonderful, it worked!" At that moment the pilgrimage song planned for the Easter Vigil started spontaneously, filled with alleluias. The word "alleluia" became a password, the only word common to all of us. It substituted for "Good morning", "Sorry", or "Thank you". Like from a hidden spring, a sweet joy started to grow. Alleluias on Good Friday, is this possible?

Celebration of the Passion and meeting of parents

In the afternoon we went in procession to the Saint Pius-X Basilica to re-live the Lord's passion, presided over by Bishop Mamie, of Fribourg. It was a very plain ceremony, in a dark, underground church. To tell the truth, it was not a very adapted liturgy. It took too long and, because of the tiredness of the pilgrims, some found it boring. We could hear groans of "Let's go!" and "Is it over yet?"

Outside it was cold and rainy. The return to the hotel after the celebration was not at all euphoric. In the headquarters the line of people who came to complain kept growing. Fortunately, the meetings with the parents, so well prepared, brought back hope.

Although they were planned later in the process, much attention was given to these meetings. This had been entrusted to Camille Proffit and Father Delpierre. It seemed to us so important that the parents have the possibility to meet together in small groups to share their suffering, their hope and where they found support. They had so little opportunity for this.

However, when the hour arrived, it was very difficult to have these meetings. The pilgrims were exhausted and wanted to go back to their bedrooms. Some hotel owners apologized saying: "We do not have places suited for group meetings." The evening had a bad beginning. However, it turned out wonderfully! With the promise that the meeting would be very short, the parents agreed to come. And then, nobody wanted to leave. In fact, it was the first time that the parents had the opportunity to talk about their suffering in light of their faith, and that in the context of Good Friday. The sharing was simple and profound. Everyone had known Good Fridays in their lives where all seemed lost. For some, the news of the disability of their child seemed to have shattered their lives forever. "And now, said one pilgrim, we remember Jesus' Way of the Cross, in the presence of Mary. Like her, our hearts have been pierced. We become aware that Mary can understand us, and that she walks with us on the road. Jesus has given her to us to be a Mother at our side and to open up a new way for us." The evening program ended with a Magnificat, and the decision to meet again for sharing once more, during the pilgrimage.

This time together was one of the most important for the parents. It was a preview of what could be done later on in the Faith and Light communities. Sharing in small groups, in the middle of each gathering, is a privileged and life-giving moment, where we share our burdens and carry those of others.

Following in the steps of Bernadette

On Holy Saturday morning there was a round table for the parents about faith education, while the pilgrims with disabilities and their friends were invited to become "close to Bernadette," which was the theme for the day. Different activities were suggested: to watch the movie "*It is Enough to Love*", go to the pools, visit the museum or visit the places where Bernadette lived.

Having heard something about her life so simple and so poignant, this last activity, a "mini-pilgrimage," tracing the steps of Bernadette, in the heart of the big pilgrimage, seemed essential to us.

Our brothers and sisters with disabilities often feel a natural attraction to Bernadette. It is like the one they feel toward Little Therese. There is, between these two and persons with disabilities, a certain spiritual similarity, a kinship, a "co-naturality" of hearts.

It is certain that Bernadette did not have an intellectual disability. If she did not know how to read and write at the age of thirteen, it was because of the circumstances of her life. Once she started to go to school, she quickly caught up. When we read the texts of the interrogations she had to go through, we notice her good sense and astonishing capacity for quick responses. In the convent in Nerves, the infirmary was entrusted to her. There she showed herself to be very precise, organized, considerate, and with real authority. On the other hand, as far as society was concerned, Bernadette was very miserable. Her family was humiliated, slandered, despised.

Physically speaking, she was a sickly, asthmatic child. She says about herself: "If the Holy Virgin would have found anyone more wretched than I, it is her that she would have chosen." After the apparitions, it was very difficult for Bernadette to find her place. When accepted by the sisters in Nerves, she entered the Saint-Gildard Community. Later on, so often sick, she would repeat: "As always, I am good for nothing."

Persons with intellectual disabilities find themselves, intrinsically, in a position of weakness. Even if they live in rich families, or are welcomed by institutions and homes having very good standards, even if French law in 2005 grants them all the rights of citizenship and, "in principle," to seek inclusion in society, they know interiorly and by experience that they are different. They know that they are in a condition of inferiority and of dependence. Most of them are aware that they will never be able to live autonomously, start a family, or "succeed" according to society's definition. A young man with Down syndrome, René, who is part of l'Arche, states this with simplicity: "Alone, I am not able!"

If the Virgin chose this "good for nothing", as Bernadette called herself, it is because she was simple-hearted. Bernadette did not seek beauty, power, or efficiency, but truthful relationships, a communion of hearts. Her meetings with Mary were forever engraved in her heart as a deep happiness and the great light of her life.

The simplicity of heart of persons with intellectual disabilities profoundly touches me. They do not let themselves be impressed by fame, or fortune, or status symbols. They are as direct with the bishop as with the cook. I remember a reception honored by the presence of the Prime Minister of the time. Jean-Claude approached him, put his arm around his shoulder and told him: "It is difficult to do your job, Mr. Balladur. Courage, courage, courage." This first contact, open, warm, unguarded, lacking social, religious or political etiquette, generally touches those who come into a home of l'Arche or a Faith and Light community for the first time.

"God loves me as I am."

The round tables, in several languages, about awakening the faith of a child with intellectual disabilities, were addressed especially to parents. Normally they are the first ones to kindle faith in their child, but many of them have doubts about the goodness of God or even about God's existence. If God is all-powerful, isn't God more or less responsible for this tragedy? Many also ask questions about the capacity of their child to have a spiritual and religious life. There was still a trend at the time to believe that these children would go straight to heaven, that they were "little angels". Some parents were very hurt by the attitude of some parishioners colored by pity, fear or indifference. They were wounded by the lack of understanding of priests who had refused the sacraments: Eucharist, Confirmation, sometimes even Baptism for their children, under the pretext that the children could not understand. This shows the range of expectations before this meeting.

In the Rosary Basilica there were more than three thousand French-speaking pilgrims who came to listen to a mother, a catechist and a special educator. These were: Denise Legrix, a young woman without limbs, Canon Bailleux, in charge of special catechesis for the Diocese of Cambrai, and Father Mesny, from the diocese of Lyon. Most had been formed in the school of Father Bissonier.

It is impossible to describe the richness and the density of their words. They all blended together to convey the beauty, the simplicity; the spiritual depth of those whom we call "disabled".

I take this opportunity to speak a little about Father Bissonier, who had a big place in my life, even if we had times of disagreement, particularly in relation to the Faith and Light pilgrimage[1]! In the Church, very discreetly but very deeply, he left his mark on the second half of the twentieth century by his lifework on behalf of persons with disabilities: whether in catechesis, education or the formation of those who worked with them. Father Bissonier, dazzled by the hidden treasures in the heart of the humble, literally "obsessed" by the privileged place that they should have in the heart of the Church, never ceased shouting the Good News from all rooftops, if I may say so. He searched for new methods. He taught. He helped to found and direct specialized organizations. He travelled the world. He was the pioneer of special catechesis.

He was convinced that the child, even the one who does not speak, must be able to discover in his or her own way that God is a father who loves her/him with infinite tenderness, that God sent his Son, who became our brother, our friend and who gives us the infinitely precious gift of his Spirit. This child has the right to be welcomed into the Church by Baptism, to be nourished by the body of Christ and to the help needed to grow in his or her Christian life by the outpouring of the Holy Spirit that is the sacrament of Confirmation. Father Bissonier wrote: "Isn't it a wonderful thing to know that even the littlest child, who might have the greatest handicaps or disabilities imaginable, has a divine vocation? To him, also, God says: 'I have called you from your mother's womb.' Even to little children such as these have I spoken about our God and I never believed I should regret having done so[2]."

---

1. A few years after the pilgrimage, he overcame his fears and became a true support for the movement.

2. *Provoqué à l'espérance*, Mame, 1985, p.165. Read also *Henri Bissonier, pionnier de la catéchèse pour les personnes handicapées*, Éditions Jean Bosco, 2011.

This is what each one expressed in his or her own way. Canon Bailleux reminded us that, "we have the temptation to place ourselves ahead of the person with disabilities, when we are simply with' him or her. The person with disabilities does not exist on one side and we on the other side, we have the same destiny, the destiny of the children of God..." Father Delpierre, in his turn, added that in the loving relationship with God, the one who has an intellectual disability "is not more disabled than we are. It is really the only area where we are certain that this person is less disabled", because certainly there is between him or her and God a secret dialogue that surpasses our ability to understand.

There was also the witness of young François, a boy with an intellectual disability, who had just made his first communion. After the ceremony, his mother had invited some people in for a family gathering. François's godfather whispered to her: "What a beautiful liturgy! What a pity that this poor little one understood nothing." Tears came to his mother's eyes. François, who had understood everything and seen everything, approached his mother and softly told her: "Do not be troubled, Mommy. God loves me as I am!" In these few words he had spoken the essence of the Gospel, that we ourselves have so much difficulty believing and living, and that the theologians will never fully comprehend.

Two important conclusions from all these "round tables": the child with disabilities, no matter the degree of disability, is capable of a life and of a vital relationship with God. Every child must be able to benefit from awakening of faith, and if possible, from religious education, particularly through special catechesis. Each one of us, parents, educators, friends, was concerned that this become a reality. For the first time these findings were expressed clearly, openly and directly to such a large audience.

The celebration of waiting and of resurrection

Up to the last moment, the big celebration of Saturday afternoon, planned for the esplanade, was marked by uncertainty. Four small stages had been set up along the path of the Crowned Virgin, and a bigger one right next to the Rosary Basilica. It was therefore necessary that there be good weather, otherwise we would need a Plan B, laborious and catastrophic, in the underground basilica. It happened that on that day the weather was threatening. Our team and those in charge of the celebration met at noon at the meteorological station in Lourdes. Verdict: "Uncertain weather, threatening rain, mostly in the evening." And the experts concluded: "We cannot guarantee you anything. It is up to you to decide." And we opted for the celebration outdoors.

Starting at two thirty in the afternoon, there was incredible joy in the esplanade. The communities, the regions, the countries arrived singing, many of them in their traditional costumes. The four stages came alive with folk dances, songs with mimes - a variety of activities. Then all attention turned to the big stage from which music and songs of all types literally sprang up. There were also, one after the other, spontaneous speeches mixed with cultural acts prepared well in advance. There was truly a fantastic atmosphere of joy, into which the other pilgrims, not part of Faith and Light, were also spontaneously and warmly invited. A brochure explained who we were and that we formed together, them and us, the beloved people of God. Hundreds of colored helium balloons carried messages of peace and love far up and away.

At the time for fireworks, rain began to fall, transforming all the colors of the rainbow into a thick smoke, with hues of yellow, green and blue, which enveloped and choked us. But nothing could tarnish the joy, neither the smoke nor the heavy rain that had started to fall. There was no panic, either. We simply opened our umbrellas and put on our raincoats and the celebration continued even more beautifully. John Littleton, the African-American singer who came from Louisiana, continued, with his magnificent voice, to sing gospel hymns and alleluias that conquered Lourdes. Children with disabilities, adolescents and youth, singing, would climb the steps to accompany him with drums and dancing, some with an excellent sense of rhythm. The crowd sang and clapped hands. The rain continued to fall, the disabilities had certainly not disappeared, but I believe we lived these words of Saint Athanasius: "The risen Christ, making all suffering bearable, comes to animate a 'perpetual celebration' in the deepest part of each one of us." This is really what we lived thanks to the littlest ones whom we had in mind when we planned this celebration.

The symposium of the medical doctors

The prospect of a dialogue exclusively for physicians, scheduled for Saturday evening, piqued the curiosity of the journalists. All of them mentioned it in their articles. Why a scientific meeting of physicians during a pilgrimage such as this one of Faith and Light, that came together with one third of the persons having intellectual disabilities?

There were a good number of medical doctors, three hundred and fifty, dozens of whom oversaw medical services for the Faith and Light team in Lourdes and were integrated in a community. The theme of the dialogue, as mentioned before, was: "The psychological repercussions of rejection or welcome for a person with an intellectual disability." Professor Lejeune opened the debates clearly announcing the goal: "We are gathered here, a good number of physicians, not so much to discuss medicine as to be helpful. It is important to see how segregation and rejection can dislocate a personality, and how, on the contrary, love can build it up."

In the room, there were also other professionals who served persons with disabilities, who were not physicians, most of them special educators, and we did not feel any barrier. All were united in the same cause.

I was struck both by the quality of the comments, competence supported by experience, and by the very human approach, filled with warmth and respect regarding each person. The assembly was very impressed by the atmosphere of the pilgrimage: the large number of persons with intellectual disabilities, the diversity of their origin, their age, and degree of disability. Most of them expressed joy and the feeling of freedom. We had concretely experienced how the quality of welcome radiates in persons with intellectual disabilities. And, reciprocally, how their happiness shines out on all their surroundings. The whole city of Lourdes was itself transformed!

Professor Bamatter from Geneva made this public statement: "The person with an intellectual disability is often considered by society as dangerous, or beyond all help. The first thing to do if we want to make a difference is to show that this is false. What we see here proves it."

Doctor Lamarche, who had founded an association "The Homes of Living Waters", where persons with psychiatric disorders live together with persons considered "normal", confirmed: "It is important not to have a theory driven too much by questions of rejection or welcome. The person with a disability, himself, senses and knows very well when someone regards him in a negative or a positive way." And Doctor Réthoré went further still: "What is lived in this very remarkable experiment of Doctor Lamarche needs to be lived in the miniature society that each family is, and I think very specially of the important role of brothers and sisters."

And Professor Lejeune concluded: "We do not do great things, but we, physicians, we do a little something each day. However slowly the results might come, we will never give up."

"He is truly risen!"

Holy Saturday concluded with the Easter Vigil. This celebration that marks the summit and the source of the Christian liturgy was equally the source and the summit of the pilgrimage. With the Christians of Lourdes and of the region, we were twenty-three thousand filling the basilica for the Mass celebrated by Bishop Cleary, auxiliary bishop of Birmingham, who accompanied the pilgrims from England. Several symbols, other than those customarily used, adopted on this occasion for the persons with disabilities, touched the assembled participants. For example, the Exultet, which so joyfully proclaims that Jesus is the light of the world, was accompanied by a slow and expressive dance of pilgrims with disabilities and friends around the altar. After the blessing of the baptismal water, which was brought from the miraculous spring, around three hundred priests carried this water to the crowd in small bowls so that each person could touch it, make the sign of the cross and be sprinkled with it as a symbol of purification and of entering new life. During the Our Father, each one said this prayer in his or her own language, and the priests, who made two big circles around the altar, were hand in hand, in this very simple gesture as children of the same family. It is a gesture that united the whole crowd, a gesture that we love so much in Faith and Light and in l'Arche.

I am touched by the memory of this magnificent celebration. Having been detained at the headquarters by an emergency, I arrived later and could not join any of the three communities that had invited me to participate with them: l'Arche, Paris and

Moulins, in which group there were some members of my family. I wandered around in the basilica, deeply moved by so many people marked by suffering but seemingly illuminated from within. In that immense crowd, it was impossible to find any of the three groups that I looked for. Not one empty seat. So I found refuge, sitting on the floor, by one of the pillars. Curiously, I was not unhappy in that relative solitude, and I was surprised by the tears that overflowed, filling me with peace and joy.

At the end of the ceremony, Bishop Cleary, who had presided, read a long message signed by Pope Paul VI, addressed to the pilgrims of Faith and Light. For us, it represented a truly incredible encouragement. Half of his words were addressed directly to the persons with disabilities, who were particularly touched by this passage:

"Be assured: you have your place in society. In the midst of people, often intoxicated by productivity and efficacy, you are there, with your simplicity and your joy, your eyes in search of a freely given love, with your marvelous capacity to understand the signs of this love and to respond to them with delicacy. And in the Church, which is above all a House of prayer, you have an even more fitting role: to understand the secrets of God that are hidden from the wise and the skillful[1]. To ask God, also, for all that is needed: by your parents, your friends, priests, the missions, all the Church, the peoples who do not have bread or peace or love. We know that Christ listens to you in a privileged way, that our Mother, the Virgin Mary, presents your prayers to him, as she did in Cana.[2]"

Then Paul VI assured the parents that he was near to them in their suffering. At the same time, he encouraged them to take it on and to move beyond it:

---

1. Luke 10: 21
2. John 2: 3-5

"Yes, look at your child with tenderness, as God himself looks at him. And may your trials, with the grace of God, unite you to the mystery of Christ, spur on your search for a human advancement, no matter how small, strengthen your solidarity within your home, and open you to all the other parents of children with disabilities, whom you understand much better than anyone else."

Finally, the pope addressed an urgent appeal to all society, friends, neighbors, physicians, psychologists, educators, teachers, social workers:

"We hope that your witness shakes the indifference of a society that in its materialism does not always know how to respect life, that willfully closes its eyes to what is not comfort, power, efficiency. May the people responsible for the economy and those holding power, not forget to integrate in their plans the excluded poor in their own country as well as those in the third-world! For us, this is the test of this true humanism that we want so much to prevail. And may all pastors of the Church know how to welcome these little ones, as Jesus did, with a preferential care! May this pilgrimage leave behind, for all, a trail of faith and of light."

Going out from the Easter Vigil, each one, with his or her lighted candle, discovered the illumination of the basilica and of the whole city. We hugged each other with alleluias, in the manner of the Orthodox who, in never-ending jubilation, continually repeat to one another: "Christ is risen! Yes, he is truly risen!"

In this milieu, Hubert Allier, a young friend from Grenoble, had a wonderful inspiration. With the members of his community, he took the lead dancing, all hand-in-hand, and singing the pilgrimage song. Spontaneously an immense farandole[1] was formed that went all over the esplanade. Continuously, the crowd

---

1. An open-chain communal dance popular in Provence, France – Translator note

repeated the seventeen verses of this song. The last verse is: "Jesus opens the way for us, to new life, to a more beautiful world. We can live his message, Jesus gives us a new heart."

And the celebration spontaneously flowed through the streets of Lourdes, where groups sang and danced, hand-in-hand, until very late at night.

"Alleluia!"

For Easter day, the Masses were planned in several languages, especially in English and Spanish. The French-speaking pilgrims met at Saint Pius X Basilica for the international Mass prepared by the Faith and Light liturgy team and the Sanctuaries team. There were also many other pilgrims coming from the area and a few from everywhere at the Mass. This signified the inclusion of the "least" within the Church, Jesus' Body, where each one has a place.

The Solemn Mass was presided over by Bishop Jean Rodhain, founder of the *Secours Catholique*, whose support was so decisive for the birth of Faith and Light. At Lourdes, he was at home. He had created a permanent place of welcome beside the Grotto and on the mountain nearby, the *Cité Saint-Pierre¹*. This facility welcomes pilgrims who have great economic difficulties, sick persons, persons with disabilities, the homeless, families with many children, who would be excluded from this holy city if not for the inventive and boundless love of Bishop Rodhain. It was in this place that all the pilgrims coming from distant countries or in very difficult financial situations were welcomed in the 1971 pilgrimage and in the others that followed.

---

1. St. Peter's City – Translator note

Bishop Rodhain celebrated Mass with simplicity and seriousness, visibly happy to be surrounded by the weakest among the weak. He recalled in his homily that "the preferences of the Lord are not the preferences of the world: 'Until this day (Easter), the apostles did not know', and we also did not know." Then he finished with this prayer: "Teach us, O Lord, around your consecrated bread, around our shared bread, teach us how much you love us, each one, in your way that is so secret, so considerate, so direct, that surpasses all justice and has the name, Charity." At the end of the Masses, the message of the Holy Father was distributed in the three official languages. For those who did not speak any of these languages, translators went to work and all received copies of the text before going back to their countries. Each one also received a holy card with the image and dedication by the Holy Father.

"Forward!"

Would we participate in the procession of the Blessed Sacrament or the candlelight procession? This was the question of the day. The leader of the liturgical team initially said no to both. He considered these to be old-fashioned rituals. Besides, the candlelight procession risked being mixed up with the Easter Vigil and greatly confusing the persons with intellectual disabilities.

However, both of these manifestations of faith fit very well in the program. Didn't the Virgin Mary herself tell Bernadette: "Go, tell the priests to let the people come here in procession"? And we, pilgrims, weren't we a little like the crowd in Jesus' time that followed him or pressed around him to hear his words? Just like them, we had a thirst to be healed of our maladies and we longed to be liberated from all that tormented our spirits and our hearts.

Those who had already been to Lourdes were very attached to the processions, these strong times of prayer, at the same time communal and personal. Those who came for the first time had heard others speak of their simplicity and beauty.

This Easter Sunday, after the large universal prayer in the esplanade, the pilgrims we regrouped at the Grotto where the procession with the Blessed Sacrament would start.

Before the procession began, there was an incident that spoke for itself. At the scheduled time there was no priest in sight, no raised platform or monstrance. The pilgrims were surprised and began to become restless. In one group, a man was visibly impatient. Finally, exasperated by this unexplained delay, he exploded: "But, well, what is going on? This is unacceptable!" And he repeated without pause: "What is going on…?" His anger grew. Just then we heard the tranquil voice of a young person with disabilities, about twenty years old: "Sir, what is going on, it is that today Jesus is risen and now we wait for him to arrive at any moment!" Immediately, the storm calmed. The very simple and fervent faith of this young man reminded us of the essential: Easter is Jesus alive, Jesus Risen, Jesus among us, with us.

A few moments later the procession began and thousands of people followed Jesus present in the Blessed Sacrament accompanying him with their songs and their prayers of trust and of petition, taken from the Gospel: "Lord, come help me!", "Lord, make me see!", "Lord, make me hear!", "Lord, heal my child!", "Lord, say only the word and my child will be healed!", "Have pity on me, my child is very sick!", "I believe that you can do anything!", "May this chalice be taken away from me, but your will be done, not mine!", "I place my life in your hands!".

Night came, and it was time for the procession of lights, which also starts at the Grotto. The esplanade was illuminated by this immense procession that repeated "Ave Maria" of the song to the Virgin Mary, known throughout the world, with verses that tell the story of the apparition. We also sang: "Give us your Son!" the light of the world, with whom darkness is no longer dark.

That Easter Sunday evening a mother confided to me: "I have lived so many Good Fridays in despair. Today, Easter Sunday, for the first time since the accident when our little boy became profoundly disabled, a little light appeared in the darkness."

A great moment: the evening for the young people

It was absolutely necessary that there be a time where all the young people from the fifteen countries could meet, share and express how they were affected by what they had lived so intensely during these very exceptional days.

The meeting of the youth, animated by Jean Vanier and Raymond Fau was planned for Easter Sunday, at ten o'clock in the evening, after the candlelight procession. They had already lived three intense days followed by very short nights. Between three and five thousand young people arrived in the underground basilica, a noisy horde, exuberant, overly excited, wanting nothing more than to give loud expression to their feelings.

Jean Vanier, who is very tall, dominated the situation. He made a sign to Raymond Fau, the singer, to begin. Raymond picked up a guitar and played a song composed especially for that evening: "How much time is still necessary, how many years, how many days, how many nights, how many springs and dawns so that this world may live out of love?"

Jean, peaceful, indicated with a gesture that it was time to sit on the floor. Little by little, the tumult diminished. Just a brief time after the disorganized invasion, there was silence. Jeanne-Marie, amused, whispered to me: "We have seen Daniel facing three thousand lions..." In a few words Jean drew forth the meaning of that evening. He told how, from his position in the Navy, which he loved, he went to study philosophy, theology, then to sharing his life with persons with intellectual disabilities: "They have mysteriously transformed me."

Those young people who desired were invited to give witness to their encounter with a person with a disability, whether it was for the first time in Lourdes, or as brother or sister, special educator, assistant in l'Arche... Some students in the last year of high school shared about their "twinning" with persons with profound disabilities whom they had the opportunity to meet for several months before Lourdes: at Lourdes, "it is very different, we are lodging with them at the hospital, we sleep in the same room. We are touched by their simplicity. They find everything beautiful. They are always kind. They gently expose our way of being, of appearing, of seeing the world...". One young man witnessed: "I am fed up with this society of consumerism, of money, of promotion. I believe that Jean-Jacques, who has not stopped following me one second for three days, is in the process of taking me out of my depression." In the same way, another confided his desire to leave business school to enter l'Arche. He needed support to move on...

An Irish Jesuit, Father David Harold Barry, wrote to us about this evening: "Is fraternity impossible? These accompanying volunteers, students, in the full vigor of their twenty years, of their bodies, of their success, the future open to them, could have been moved by a condescending charity, bending over those who are miserable. If there was equality, and consequently fraternity, between these young people so different in possession of earthly riches, if there was friendship without condescension, it was beyond this earth. Not beyond after life or death, but an already present beyond, an immensity opened up in the depth of humankind."

Mass of send-off by countries and time of goodbyes

The last official morning of the pilgrimage was short, dense, intense. First, there were the Masses of sending-off organized by the countries. These had the feel of being sent on mission and of a new communion. For the French pilgrims, Mass took place in the underground basilica, presided over by Bishop Donze, and the homily was given by Father Plaisantin. "When back home, it is necessary to look for others, especially for those who are still alone, search for everyone to share our pains and our joys. We have what we need for this: God loves us and Jesus is alive." The countries with a small number of pilgrims had the privilege of celebrating Mass at the Grotto.

It was beautiful that day to see the French-speaking and the Flemish-speaking Belgians joining together around their common flag for the Mass celebrated by Bishop Cammaert. It was the same for the French and English-speaking Canadians, who met together in the joy of only one Eucharist. During these three days with persons with disabilities, all sorts of barriers came down.

It had been planned that during the morning each community would be very free to meet together in friendship and thanksgiving.

For a last good-bye, many found themselves at the Grotto, where we had so intensely discovered the tenderness of Mary, her desire that Lourdes, her city, become our city, for all of us, but especially for all those who are the most dear to her heart.

In Lourdes, during these four days, we lived, in a way, the transfiguration at Mount Tabor. We saw the glory of God, the presence of Jesus in the celebrations and in the hearts of our brothers and sisters with disabilities and their parents. And then each one took the road. At the train station, or at the airports, we saw luminous faces, radiant, relaxed. We had the desire to say, like Peter: "We are so well here, we would like to stay. If we pitch three tents…"

This desire was expressed, by a young boy with disabilities, François, in the airplane at the moment of departure for Canada. He exclaimed: "And now, all of us will stay in Lourdes!" There was no nostalgia in his voice, but the desire that this unimaginable climate that we had lived, we would find there where we were going. We all had the responsibility to recreate it in our homes, our schools, our institutions, our workshops... We were all messengers of peace and of joy, all artisans of these communities where we fashion covenant with one another, carrying each other's burdens, marveling at the gifts of each one.

In the airplanes, in the trains, the journey back home was very different from the trip to come.

"In the overnight train," tells a pilgrim, "we were six members from our community. When we came, without saying so, we all had fear of staying beside Frédéric, very disabled and agitated. When we returned, each one asked to sit next to him. Frédéric had certainly felt our rejection. Then, in Lourdes he received waves of attention and of friendship from all. These were present in our compartment. Frédéric was reassured, peaceful. We felt that, with us, he lived moments of true happiness, of communion."

I would also like to mention an arrival at the train station of Austerlitz, in Paris:

"We left the train laughing, singing, 'Amis chantons notre joie', along the very long platform. It was the same environment in the streets, or in the cafés, the restaurants that were invaded, and then in the taxis, the buses, metro, as long as some pilgrims were still together. We wanted to tell everybody: 'Rejoice with us, God loves us!'"

However, after Mount Tabor and the Transfiguration, many will again find themselves abruptly back down on the plains. Life will resume with solitude, fights, tiredness... A dad told us: "In the metro, with my daughter, I understood we were no longer in Lourdes, with the other passengers' looks of pity, or pretending not to see us." This is why so many wanted to continue! They did not know, but this continuing had already been inspired that very morning.

Faith and Light with the "authorities"

On that Easter Monday we had invited all the "officials" from Lourdes and from the region, and all who had made it possible for this pilgrimage to take place without incident, in an atmosphere that no one had dared to expect. In the name of the international team and of all the pilgrims, Jean Vanier expressed our deep gratitude. Each person had carried out his/her responsibility as a servant and a friend, not out of duty.

We were touched by what they had seen, heard, lived and wanted to share: "Never could we have believed that contacts with persons with 'disabilities' could be simple and truthful." A hotel owner witnessed: "They were happy with everything. A young man with disabilities was enchanted with the flowered wallpaper in his bedroom – and it was old! Another appreciated the good soup. When they left, we all hugged each other." A military man, who spent his time escorting young persons with disabilities, affirmed: "I never believed that so much happiness was possible for them. What a lesson for us, army recruits, who are well, but we easily slide into discontentment, criticism, and are so quick to denounce what doesn't go well!" A journalist whispered: "I think that one day we will be proud to say: 'That pilgrimage, I was there...'"

During the meeting, the witness became more and more personal. The Superior of a convent that had welcomed several groups told me how her community was touched by the pilgrims' kindness, their patience with each other: "For us, this was a true reflection, perhaps more powerful than a retreat." A police colonel approached me, opened his wallet and took out a small broken daisy: "You see this, it was one of your little ones who gave it to me, and I keep it so I never forget what I have seen."

And, in echo to the cry of the pilgrims that same morning, unanimously they said: "Come back next year."

"May Faith and Light continue!"

Before leaving, we organized a farewell party with the coordinators from communities, dioceses, regions, countries and the international committee. It was impossible for us to let them leave without having at least a few minutes to tell them thanks and goodbye - a final "goodbye" - since the pilgrimage charter clearly stated that there would be only one international Faith and Light pilgrimage.

There were just a hundred of us, a small handful compared to the twelve thousand participants. We felt deeply united. Each of us realized how completely the event had been protected and blessed. We had asked for the miracle of hearts, and there had been many. After giving thanks to God, Jean Vanier expressed our appreciation to all those who were there and who had been the architects of these four days, often at the cost of great sacrifice.

They had just finished these thanks when a delegate rose before the assembly and stated, "I have something important to say on behalf of all of us here, all the pilgrims. We cannot accept that it's all over. We are linked to each other. We want Faith and Light to continue." A round of applause confirmed that this was indeed the cry of all. Jean responded: "Be faithful to the Holy Spirit. Continue meeting together in communities of prayer, friendship, and mutual support. Organize celebrations, pilgrimages. In some months, we will meet again and see how things stand."

Then the Magnificat, the song of Mary, sprang forth, celebrating divine love for children, the humble, the hungry. The Lord has done wondrous things for us!

The Faith and Light pilgrimage was over, but the Faith and Light movement was born. Several days later, Jean made this birth official through a letter directed to all of the leaders and to the cooperating associations.

After all, there was the revelation of the participants' great joy, in the simplicity of what they had lived and shared during these four days, and the almost unanimous expression of their expectation that this event not be the end. The following months would show us that this would not be done without difficulty.

CHAPTER 5

The Season of the First Fruits
A unanimous press

The press was unanimous in their astonishment and their praise. Here are some reactions:

Georges Hourdin wrote in *Le Monde*[1]:

"This world pilgrimage (it is good to call things by their name) was considered by the wise to be a crazy adventure. Why bring together men and women wounded in their intelligence and, sometimes, in their motor ability, with the risk of provoking serious accidents, unhappiness and a sort of chaos? It happens that the reasonable people were wrong... During three days, from daybreak into the dead of night, the song of the pilgrimage was raised towards the sky of Lourdes in an immense alleluia repeated indefinitely."

In the west of France, Father Chevré, in charge of children and youth with disabilities in the diocese of Nantes, marveled:

"Have you ever seen a bishop dancing in a circle with children and young people? Have you heard completely spontaneous acclamations and applause during liturgies? Have you known a whole city inundated by songs of Alleluia? Well, all that, and so

---

1. *The World* – a daily newspaper – Translator note

much more, we witnessed in Lourdes. And also actors, almost in spite of us…"

In the newspaper *La Croix*, Maurice Abdad insisted on the ecumenical dimension:

"What a beautiful demonstration of faith, but also what touching solidarity, said an Anglican priest, underscoring the participation of Anglican communities…"

Marcel Clément, in the *L'Homme Nouveau,* was full of enthusiasm:

"It was necessary to see the spontaneous dances, which expressed the joy of the ghetto finally being broken, it was necessary to have lived these days where these children (and these adults) dared to search for the smiles of the people passing by, because they were certain that they would find them; finally it was necessary to have experienced the quiet but ever present charity of these suffering and brave families to discover, from within, that we had participated in an extraordinary event."

The newspaper *Le Journal de la Grotte*[1] dedicated its front page to an immense photo with the caption: "The celebration of joy". We also could quote articles in the regional Catholic press, as relayed by its correspondents or even by the pilgrims themselves, who became reporters upon their return home.

Lourdes has changed!

The first astonishing thing that was reported to us immediately after the pilgrimage is the impression that it left on Lourdes. I remember the witness of a chaplain who, in a sentence, summarized this climate in the *Le Journal de la Grotte*: "A wall has fallen, one not made by rejection, but by ignorance."

---

1. *The Journal of the Grotto* – a local newspaper - Translator note

A woman religious from Lourdes wrote to us about what she was able to see: "Before, we saw very few persons with intellectual disabilities in Lourdes. There were so many in the summer following the Faith and Light pilgrimage, that sometimes there seemed to be more children with intellectual disabilities in Lourdes than children without disabilities. None of the families I met had come at Easter, but they all were there because of Faith and Light and talked about the pilgrimage with genuine emotion. It is refreshing to see the ease of contact with these parents, and their simplicity. They stop in the street, and ask the pedestrians: Where can I park the car? How do we go to the Grotto? They present their children. Before, you would rarely meet these families, and they did not dare talk to anyone... and nobody dared to make the first move. We saw small groups of Faith and Light joined with bigger pilgrimages: groups of persons with intellectual disabilities surrounded by many accompaniers, lively songs, musical instruments, helium balloons... Sometimes families who came alone would join these groups. Their joy radiates"

A permanent place for persons with disabilities

In this period that followed the 1971 pilgrimage I had an idea that never left my head: to have a permanent welcome center for persons with disabilities, it did not matter what type of disability, and for their families, who would come to Lourdes "alone" or as participants in a pilgrimage. I wanted them to feel welcome in the holy city in a special way, with the look of trust that Mary had bestowed on Bernadette.

This could not be the mission of Faith and Light, which had the call to be close to persons with intellectual disabilities and their parents. But wouldn't it be within the mission of the OCH, broadly open to all persons with a disability, their family, their environment? The OCH had helped Faith and Light to be born. Faith and Light could, in its turn, call the OCH to grow a new branch.

In this place of welcoming, we wanted each one to find listening, compassion, counsel, support, with a little light of hope to continue the journey. The rector of the Sanctuaries, Father de Roton, was not opposed to this idea and gave us free rein to go forward.

First of all we needed a place. This is not easy in Lourdes! We even thought of further excavating the rock where the *Secours Catholique* has its welcome center! At just the right moment, the L'Action Catholique Générale Féminine[1] needed to downsize, and left us a miniscule office. Madeleine Dupui, born in Lourdes and member of the Fraternité chrétienne des personnes maladies et handicapées[2], took charge of this initiative. In the first year, it had eighty visits. Eight years later, when Madeleine retired, we had about two thousand per year.

Martine Guénard followed, and stayed there for thirty years. Thanks to volunteers, today we welcome more than twelve thousand pilgrims and many groups annually. One of the big concerns continues to be that each one leaves with at least one address, that he or she be encouraged not to remain alone, to join a group, and where there is nothing, to start something. Martine tells how a medical doctor, an Italian mother of a small child with intellectual disabilities, fell apart when she arrived at the Welcome Center. She was beyond her limits and had a tremendous need to talk about this. The priest at the center counseled her to join Faith and Light in her region, but he noticed, as he consulted the directory, that there was no community in her region. Then he

---

1. Women's General Catholic Action – Translator note
2. Christian fraternity of persons sick and with disabilities – Translator note

told her: "Start something." The following year she came back to Lourdes with her family and a community. The next year, three communities arrived with her. "This is extraordinary, says Martine, how from listening to one mother, the inspiration of the Holy Spirit and the grace of Lourdes, the life of one family has completely changed, and also the lives of hundreds of others."

In 2005, Bishop Jacques Perrier wanted to express in a more striking way the preferential option of Lourdes for the poorest ones, as John-Paul II had frequently encouraged. Bishop Perrier decided to create, within the several services offered at the sanctuaries, a service for persons with disabilities and their families. He entrusted the responsibility for this service to the OCH, at a place that symbolizes welcome, by one of the entrances to the sanctuary, Gate Saint-Michel. This center is at the service of all persons with disabilities.

The inclusion of persons with disabilities in the diocesan and national pilgrimages was not immediate, nor massive. But progressively things started to become simpler. It became easier to welcome individuals with disabilities. The welcome of a whole Faith and Light community that was included with other pilgrims seemed the best way to mutually "tame" each other. Depending on the tiredness and specific needs of its members, the community would meet for a vigil, a liturgical celebration, a sharing among parents, while the children would be with their friends. All was done with flexibility and gentleness.

We experienced great joy when we heard that in a diocesan pilgrimage the presence of a Faith and Light community was very appreciated and people asked them to come back again. I remember the witness of a diocesan leader: "We were surprised to discover the climate – contagious – of simplicity, truth and joy that the persons with disabilities transmitted, and with them, all the group. They let us live the Gospels more fully."

The movement is launched

As to the movement, it was necessary to follow up on the cry of the pilgrims in Lourdes on Easter Monday: "We want Faith and Light to continue!"

Immediately after the pilgrimage, Jean Vanier wrote a letter to all the leaders, and to the principal movements that were interested. He made the birth of the movement official: "This meeting, without doubt, was protected and blessed by a special grace of the Holy Spirit. It was truly a manifestation of the Spirit. It would be unthinkable, on our part, not to be aware of the importance of what happened and it would be a serious lack of fidelity by all of us not to see the consequences for the future. It is up to us, now, in our countries, in our regions, in our dioceses, to reflect on our responsibilities."

Then Jean warned us to guard against two cowardly dangers. One was to say: "It was very good, but this is enough", and the other, to attach the local communities to an already existing organization, both risked suffocating the movement of the Spirit.

Now, Jean Vanier reminded us, Faith and Light was not created by a structure and it was not the fruit of a hierarchical decision. It was the fruit of an outpouring of grace carried by a certain number of persons, who, at the same time, wanted to be free and intended to act in the Church, linked to existing structures. The essential, now, is to continue the efforts in the communities: to strengthen the bonds of prayer, of friendship, of mutual support, to make the meetings a time to renew hope and, for some, to discover the sign of the Father's love. And finally, to reflect, with the accompanying young friends, on the creation of a new type of community, organized around the littlest ones, which the world so badly needs.

Jean then suggested several possible ways for the groups to engage themselves: to collaborate in diocesan pilgrimages for the full inclusion of persons with disabilities and their parents; to create special catechesis linked to the existing structures; round tables, meetings of friendship between young persons with and without disabilities. Besides, there could be Easter celebrations, and the organization of Faith and Light fiestas in cathedrals all over the world.

Jean finished like this: "The future of Faith and Light is in the hands of each one of us. May the Holy Spirit give us his light, his strength, his creative breath, his wisdom." This letter was considered to be like a roadmap for the leaders of Faith and Light.

First international meeting

In the months following the pilgrimage, we kept the commitment of Jean and of the international team by organizing a meeting in Paris for September 25-26, 1971; it was necessary to make an evaluation of the pilgrimage and to look at the future. The meeting was marked above all by thanksgiving, joy and full determination to continue the movement.

We worked on very concrete questions: the financial report and the film made during the pilgrimage. Pierre Leborgne, our treasurer, informed us that there was a surplus of a hundred and twenty thousand francs. Since the beginning of our meetings, we had planned that, in case of a surplus, we would donate it to a third-world country. After sharing ideas, the assembly decided to help India, which had fundamental needs. Part of the donation was given to Mother Theresa for her centers that welcome children with disabilities, another part would contribute to the creation of a center for persons with intellectual disabilities that had been entrusted to an Indian bishop with the collaboration of Caritas-India.

The film about Faith and Light, a forty-minute documentary, came out in the beginning of 1972 in French and English with several interviews in each of these languages. Several countries made versions with subtitles and it had a big impact everywhere. In France, for example, it was presented on the TV program *Le Jour du Seigneur.*

Faith and Light teams presented the film everywhere in France and they were usually surprised and happy to see the rooms fill up. After seeing the movie, the public was touched: "We did not expect this…" Personally, I had the opportunity to present the film to very diverse audiences. No matter who they were – parish, schools, colleges, and the very large room *La Salle de la Mutualité*, with a thousand and five hundred seats – when the film ended, the reaction was the same: an impressive silence. We observed that very frequently after having seen the movie, a desire was awakened, a certainty grew: each one of us can always do something. Perhaps simply being more attentive to the neighboring family that we had pretended not to see, or to whom we had not dared to talk. Hearts change one by one.

It is impressive to see that this film still touches hearts and changes the way people see.

We observed this again when it was shown in Lourdes at Easter 2011, during a gathering of fifteen hundred persons from France, Canada, Peru, etc., on the exact date of the birthday of Faith and Light, forty years before.

On the international scene

The big question during the international meeting at the time was this: "Do we want to keep some link among ourselves? If so,

---

1. *The Hall of Mutuality* – a large events center in Paris – Translator note

what would this look like?" Each country was invited to give their opinion. There was unanimous agreement to keep connected through one annual gathering and a letter every three months. The team gave a mandate to Pierre Leborgne, Jean Vanier and myself to oversee the publication of the letters, with the content coming from the different countries. An international meeting was scheduled for the following year in Luxemburg.

Jean Vanier introduced the report by reminding us that the Faith and Light pilgrimage was truly an experience of "God passing among us." The pilgrimage, which started so poorly, was already having a social and spiritual impact around the world. As all the feedback attested, Faith and Light was very original. There was its dimension of celebration and of joy. There was its giving access to parents and to persons with disabilities who could feel that they were part of the human and Christian family. There was the collaboration of the young people. And there was the way the communities prepared for this event and continued to gather, to support one another, to pray and to rejoice together. It was important now to be faithful to this impulse and to respond to the graces received. There was a strong unity expressed in the reports coming from the different countries, which confirmed Jean Vanier's words, with the exception of France, which had a different opinion.

In Belgium, they emphasized the meetings of parents, giving them a strength and courage that they could have never imagined before. Parents of children living in institutions or in families who, until then, felt like strangers during visits or gatherings, now met as "members of the same family".

In Canada and in the United States, they told us: "Faith and Light resonates in the souls as a sign, dense and very charged with love, of a new manifestation of hope. Truthfully and humbly, we can say that, since our return, this is a new era." The Canadian national team wrote a personal letter to each one and kept in touch with the leaders to support any initiative. It had visited several communities, with the goal of encouraging the creation of local groups, establishing links between them and organizing a national meeting, based on the needs expressed by those they met. A Canadian cathedral decided to host a Eucharistic liturgy each month, designed to assure the full participation of persons with intellectual disabilities and hoped that other parishes would take similar initiatives.

In Denmark, Anne Storm, a young medical student who had been present at the meeting on December 8, 1969, witnessed:

"We knew that there were around five hundred Catholics with intellectual disabilities. How to find them? We began by telephoning all the pastors of parishes in the whole country. Almost no one knew these persons with disabilities, which revealed how great was the need to put something in place for them and their parents. In August 1970, we sent an initial invitation to all parishes, convents and to all the people who had contacted us to come together for communal prayer at the church, followed by a friendly meeting. There were only eighteen persons and only two with intellectual disabilities. Each month, we re-sent the invitations. The number of persons increased each time. Finally, we were about fifty. The pilgrimage has stirred us. Everybody talks about it non-stop. There is a true openness toward the parents, persons with intellectual disabilities, friends and the young people. We decided to organize monthly gatherings where we all meet, and specific meetings for the parents, particularly to help them with religious education. We feel so united after having shared the great Christian feast of Easter. Bishop Rodhain, president of Caritas International, said to Bishop Ballin (Denmark): "The days of Easter 1971 were at the service of the poor. It was Charity (Caritas) in its pure state!"

In Spain, the groups continued to meet and each one remembered the feelings and emotions lived in Lourdes. It was decided to continue the gatherings and to always invite more families and friends. The principal project was to celebrate Easter 1972 together at a national Marian shrine. They did not yet know the place, or the particulars, but they all desired to continue to be aligned with Faith and Light.

In Luxemburg the delegation that went to Lourdes was made up exclusively of children from a big institution, Saint-Joseph de Betzdor, accompanied by some parents, their assistants, a medical doctor and a chaplain. They were all surprised and even amazed by the children's behavior. The physician insisted on what he called "our Lourdes miracle": among the fifty children that he accompanied, he had anticipated that certain ones would have great difficulties. Well, all the medications they brought were unnecessary. The doctor did not open his medical bag, not even once. According to him, this was due to the fact that each child had an accompanier. "We were able to observe, above all, the importance of an environment that creates an atmosphere of calm and avoids, in this way, the harsh effects of medication. The children lived extraordinary things and went from one wonder to the next. Even the long liturgies did not tire them because everything was such a novelty and so beautiful for them: to be mixed in with this crowd of warm pilgrims, to see their work displayed on a large panel during the celebration; they were so proud..." The person representing Luxemburg added: "For the children, this was the first big event of their lives. We made a scrapbook with countless photos and clippings from newspapers and magazines. They do not get tired of looking at them. Six months after the pilgrimage, the house still resonates with the Easter song. The little souvenirs they brought back – statutes, rosaries, images – they never abandon them. Their memories of Lourdes are still in their drawings and in the stories that they tell..." The delegate from Luxemburg was part of what he called "a happy follow-up in our country: the awareness on the part of the public of the children with disabilities in our institution; their welcome in a boarding-school constitutes for many families an embarrassment, if not a shame. The artistic gala, in the presence of the Grand-Duchess of Luxemburg, the many articles in the press, all this has contributed to tell the larger public that the child with disabilities is as fully a member of the Church, as anyone. We have really felt, since that moment, that something has changed". And he added: "Next year we have already planned a national pilgrimage, during the annual solemn ceremonies, after Easter, in honor of Our Lady of Luxemburg. Finally, we agree to participate again in an international pilgrimage!"

In Switzerland the pilgrimage was considered a success that filled "everybody and each one" with enthusiasm. The warmest testimonies came from parents who had never dared to go to a church with their child with disabilities and who now found themselves truly at home. For them, it was a veritable resurrection. Their unanimous desire: "May everything continue…"

And the French exception?

After this full overview, filled with hope and expectation, the French team was the last called upon to speak. They gave a very positive written report of the follow-ups in the French departments, then surprised us by giving the participants a note, jointly written with the SCEJI,[1] where it announced its decision to disappear. It planned to organize a last meeting with the Faith and Light correspondents in France to make an evaluation, invite viewpoints and to discuss and ratify the proposal of the national team. The correspondents could continue the activities if they so desired. They would be given the name and the address of a

---

1. The Catholic office of children and youth with disabilities – Translator note

person, as a contact, responsible for sending on to the dioceses and to various organizations the requests that came to them. Each local community would discover its own way.

Curiously, the national team's plan to resign did not create any significant waves in our assembly. How can we explain why the international council did not react more to this strange news? We can easily explain this apparent indifference for two reasons. On the one hand, we had thought of a very simple, light structure, leaving great autonomy to the countries. The International Association was not even constituted as a not-for-profit organization. The scope of decisions of the international team was therefore limited. On the other hand, we thought that if the national team would disappear, another one could easily be assembled, nominated by the diocesan correspondents who seemed to be full of energy. Being a little naïve, we were not aware of all that was going on in the national team, under the influence of the SCEJI.

Gérard and Camille Proffit with their children
They inspired the first pilgrimage

On their engagement day

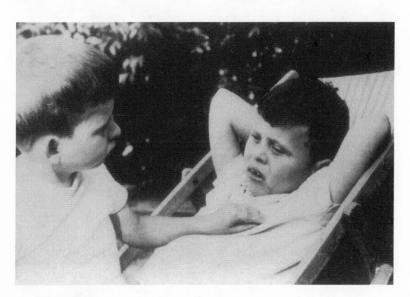

Thaddée and Loïc

Lourdes 1971
The fiesta: a big HALLELUJAH !

"She looked at me as a person."

The pilgrimage is over; a movement is given to us

Jean Vanier and
Marie-Hélène Mathieu

Emblem of Faith and Light
(Meb's painting)

Together: sharing, friendship, prayer, fiesta...

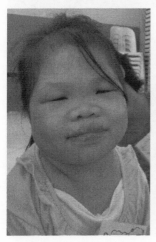

Rome, October 1975
"You have a great mission to spread Faith and Light throughout the world." Paul VI.

Rome, March 1984
"May the Holy Spirit enlighten and strengthen all the members of Faith and Light" Jean-Paul II.

Amongst so many servants...

Mariangela Bertolini, Betty Renaud, Bella Feliciano, Marie-Vincente Puiseux,
Teresa de Bertodano, Marianne Abrahamsson, Marie-Hélène Mathieu, Father David Wilson,
Roland Tamraz, Jean Evariste, Marcin Przeciswewski, Jean Vanier.

Ghislain du Chéné

Artkin Muwishi

Roy Moussalli

Corinne Chatain

Fr Joseph Larsen

Viviane le Polain

Maria-Cecilia and Tim Buckley

François and Marie-Noëlle Bal

Maureen O'Reilly

Lourdes, 2nd February 2011

For the 40th anniversary of Faith and Light, 40 pilgrimages all over the world

"I came to bring fire to the earth,
and how I wish it were already kindled."

CHAPTER 6

The Crisis
(1972)

The months that followed the 1971 pilgrimage were difficult for Faith and Light in France. They have an important place in this book given the prominent role this country has in the life of Faith and Light. Those who were the origin of these difficulties certainly had good faith. For them, it was better that the new wellsprings of life brought by Faith and Light would nourish the official organizations rather than create a new "shoot" in the Church. This position was understood, but the means that were used, sometimes against the will of the members, and by questionable methods, were not at all acceptable.

In fact, on the day following the international meeting of September 1971, without further delay, Father Georges, the national chaplain, decided to bring together the national team to persuade its members that it was time to inform the diocesan leaders of the dissolving of the team and to announce the new mission of Faith and Light: to become "yeast in the dough" in the existing structures. They would call a national meeting to do this.

The planned disappearance of Faith and Light!

The invitation to this meeting, belatedly sent to the French leaders, did not mention the outcome that Father Georges had determined. It was written like this: "After having had a break since Easter, it seems important to us to make an evaluation together in the spirit of friendship and mutual support that unites us. It is good and helpful that each diocese brings its own experiences, inquiries and projects to share with all."

Jean Vanier and I were invited simply to be participants. Immediately before the date of the meeting, fixed for November 28, a member of the national team told me, confidentially, the real goal of the meeting: the disappearance of Faith and Light. I was therefore informed, but my feet and hands were tied.

The evening before the fateful day, three young Faith and Light community leaders, whose human and spiritual qualities, as well as their commitment to the movement, we had already observed, asked to have an appointment with me. Among them was Hubert Allier, this young man of twenty-two whom we noticed in Lourdes, who had begun the incredible farandole after the Easter Vigil. They told me what was bothering them. The person in charge of special catechesis in their diocese asked them if they would agree to give their personal testimony to the marvels of the pilgrimage and to the new call from the Holy Spirit today. This "call," they were instructed, is to be committed to the service of persons with intellectual disabilities in catechesis or in associations for leisure activities, to bring the spirit of what had been lived in Lourdes, but abandoning the name "Faith and Light", since it had become useless. This leader had asked them to keep it secret, to preserve the effect of surprise. They were worried.

This confidence put me in a very difficult position. Should I tell them the truth about the role that they were being asked to play, since the true objective to which they would be contributing had been concealed from them? Moreover, if I had knowledge of the meeting's objective, wasn't it to make the best possible use of it? I decided then to share with them what I knew. They were very relieved. But what could they do? There was very little room to act. Suddenly, Hubert's face lit up: "I think I have found what to do!" The invitation from the diocesan leader for him to participate in the meeting came indirectly. The other two had received a direct invitation. In this way, he had not made any commitment and he felt free to act according to his own conscience.

That meeting of November 1971 was the meeting of all the misunderstandings about Faith and Light. It was the first national meeting after the pilgrimage. There were around sixty leaders representing thirty-five dioceses, happy to come together again at the youth club at Saint-Joseph-and-Saint-Louis parish, in the heart of Belleville. Several persons from "outside" Faith and Light had also been invited. Among them there were the leaders of the Action Catholique de l'Enfance[1], Guides de France[2], as well as Father Duben, chaplain for centers of young people with disabilities, and Jean Roux de Bézieux, president of the OCH. We were welcomed by Father Orset, the parish pastor and regional chaplain for Ile-de-France. He represented Father Delanoé, in charge of pilgrimages for the diocese of Paris.

The delegates waited impatiently to be able to share their experiences and be nourished by them, in order to return home with new enthusiasm. It is important to say that after six months, many continued to work as they had in the previous three years of preparation. The message of Jean Vanier, in answer to the cry of the leaders: "We want Faith and Light to continue" was sufficiently explicit for them to go on in trust. The greetings

---

1. Catholic Action of the Child – a not-for-profit dedicated to protecting the rights of children and struggling against child abuse – Translator note

2. A Catholic scouting organization – Translator note

were warm. People incessantly hugged one another, recalled the wonders of Lourdes and shared about the present.

Then the meeting began, led by Father Georges. He made an introduction, followed by the presentation of the results of a poll taken in about seventy-one dioceses, of which thirty-one answered. He invited the participants to be aware of the different documents in their packet and announced that Bishop de La Chanonie, president of the SCEJI[1], and his general secretary, would join them in the afternoon. It was the first time that these two would be present at a meeting of Faith and Light. This seemed to show the interest that the Church had for our new movement. If the participants had had time to read the documents they received in the morning, they would have understood better the meaning of the coming of these important officials.

We met again in the afternoon after Mass in the parish and lunch. Some were surprised to see the head table occupied by the bishop, the general delegate of the SCEJI and the national chaplain for Faith and Light. Isn't this strange for a meeting of Faith and Light leaders? Why was Camille Proffit, national coordinator, not sitting at the table? Faith and Light had been created by a team of lay people; it was a movement of lay people; why were none of them present to lead the meeting? But well, it does not matter; the most important thing is to move forward.

Father Georges invited Marcelle B. to read a joint declaration written by the SCEJI and the national team. This reading caused a true electric shock, because it announced, thinly disguised, the disappearance of Faith and Light. Marcelle B. added that it was the parents' obligation to be engaged in the UNAPEI,[2] "a big

1. Catholic Secretariat for Children and Youth with Disabilities – Translator note
2. National Union of Associations of Parents of Children with Disabilities – Translator note

organization of exceptional efficacy and dynamism at the service of our children." The people were baffled. Many were already part of this association, but asked themselves why mention it during this meeting. To be a member of the UNAPEI and of Faith and Light was to belong to very different and complementary associations.

"Faith and Light must live!"

Then came Hubert's turn to speak. Following the instructions that he had received, he had been given the task to make a stirring appeal to the youth so that they would engage themselves in "Christian gatherings", leisure activities and the different already existing ways of accompanying persons with disabilities. He was a born speaker. He expressed himself with conviction and strength. In his diocese, he said, he participated in "Christian meetings" intended for adults with intellectual disabilities. Each quarter they brought together a hundred and fifty adults with some young people. It was a very fruitful initiative begun by special catechesis. Hubert said he was "very invested and very faithful". But in Faith and Light he had discovered something else, a new way of seeing persons with disabilities and living with them. Faith and Light had a very specific vocation, he insisted, to gather persons with an intellectual disability of all ages, with their families, young people and educators. The fruits, during and after the pilgrimage, were exceptional and this was just the beginning. For nothing in the world should this be a fire in straw, quickly extinguished by falling back on the old ways. "This is why," he concluded, "Faith and Light must live! Faith and Light will live!"

These words were welcomed by a torrent of applause. These were the words many had waited for. Hubert's freedom made it possible to have a very open debate about all the questions or objections that might be expressed. On the other hand, this made things much more difficult for those who had prepared the meeting and how it would unfold. Indeed, how to create a favorable climate toward the common declaration, received in the folders, but that no one had had time to read? Let us remember that it announced a final meeting of the diocesan leaders to make an evaluation and to ratify the one proposition of the national team: to dissolve Faith and Light.

Questions came from all corners. Everyone was trying to understand. "Why did the agenda, so simple, hide the real goal of the meeting? We could never anticipate what was going to be proposed. Therefore we had no opportunity for discussion with our teams." "These texts seem to have been "ripening" for a long time. How can you ask us to approve them in fifteen minutes, since we just became aware of them?" "So what you mean is that the diocesan teams must dissolve themselves, as the national team did?"

These confusing discussions took nearly three hours. I had the impression that we had just stepped on an anthill. The diocesan leaders understood more and more clearly why they had been summoned. Among the decisive statements, here is the one from Father Orset, who had been asked to represent Father Delanoé, in charge of diocesan pilgrimages. Both had read the "common declaration" and had studied it until late at night. Father Delanoé had entrusted to Father Orset the following message: "In our world today and in our Church today, no decision can be taken without the base, that means, the communities of families with a child with disabilities. In conscience, I cannot ratify this declaration, which goes too far. It can only be a beginning of a discussion." Father Orset also emphasized another point: Faith and Light was the work of lay people. "I myself," he said, "was contacted by the leader of Ile-de-France and a group of laypersons. I gave myself totally, but I worked as a priest under the direction of laity. Today there is this desire to make this movement, the work of lay people, subordinate to the SCEJI; it is impossible to ratify this."

For M. Couillaux, father of a child with disabilities and diocesan leader in Rouen, to let the dioceses continue to act without the support of a national organization, without statutes, was like creating "groups without bones, with only a clergyman, often disinterested, sometimes hostile, for support." And he added: "At least, this is what I have lived in 'my corner', during the preparation for and after the pilgrimage."

Pierre Leborgne, our national and international treasurer pointed out an inconsistency: the secretary of the SCEJI had made it clear that it had a role of coordination and not of animation. This supposes that there are movements and associations to coordinate, but now the matter at hand was to suppress them. He asked the question directly to Bishop de La Chanonie: "Why does the national team dissolve itself?" Answer: "Because its goal was to organize only one pilgrimage. But it is not forbidden that it continue with other goals."

Marcelle-Renée, mother of a daughter with disabilities and diocesan leader in Clermont-Ferrand spoke up: "We are witnessing something strange. What is an association? It is something democratic. Who must take the decision? It should be the members, in any case not those who, in the course of three years, have given us no support!"

Father Georges gave assurance that the national team had only acted faithfully to the spirit of Faith and Light, adding this: "The name disappears but the spirit continues."

We arrived at an impasse. The discussion became worse and we looked for a way out. Some asked for a vote on the text, but this was avoided. Camille Proffit then proposed to follow up on one of the items of the "common declaration": "to give the leaders the name and address of a person who would act as a liaison". Finally Father Georges accepted, on the condition that this person acts only as a "mailbox". When the liaison receives a request, he or she would immediately send it to the SCEJI if it would be best able to respond.

Marcelle-Renée recommended that we not leave without first appointing this person: "I accepted a responsibility in my department from people who trusted me. To go back without a link, I would have the impression that I betray them."

Realizing that there was no other way to get out of this impasse, Father Georges accepted the suggestion: "For now, I propose we vote on the name of Camille Proffit, temporarily, as the liaison." Applause. Camille had proven herself, and much more than this, through her considerable work during the preparation of the pilgrimage, and she was well regarded by all.

Bishop de La Chanonie, without any doubt badly informed of the situation, suddenly discovered the complex reality. It was expressed by the parents who had suffered much. They had discovered a treasure and did not want it taken away. He concluded the meeting, then, with a more reassuring statement: "I have said, and I repeat, the SCEJI is not an organism of animation but of coordination, of information and relationship between the Church and the world of persons with disabilities. Consequently, I can only accept this fact: an organization that was Faith and Light and which has accomplished its goals tells me: "Bishop, we inform you that, having accomplished our goal, we no longer exist as such." I acknowledge this, but I also acknowledge, and with much joy, that this which has been born continues adapting itself under other forms, at the service of persons with intellectual disabilities, their families and their friends. I ask that all of this be coordinated by the SCEJI, pastoral center for all persons with disabilities in France, in the name of the Church. Therefore, we do not ask you to disappear..."

The diocesan leaders were a bit more reassured. However, one still asked Bishop de La Chanonie: "Bishop, does the Church give us permission, yes or no, to continue Faith and Light in our region?"

"Yes, my answer is clear: you can."

It was clear and pleasing!

The incident of the files

The next morning, having just arrived at my office, I received a phone call from Camille Proffit: "I am almost certain that the SCEJI wants to seize the files of Faith and Light. They are in the office next to yours. This represents a treasure because it is our link with all the communities of the international movement. As liaison, I have the obligation to watch over them. These files do not belong to the national team that no longer exists, certainly not to the SCEJI, nor to special catechesis. I entrust it to you, then, as vice-president of the Faith and Light international association. Put them in a safe place. But do it quickly!"

What to do? The Faith and Light file cabinet was not a disc. At that time, the files were made on card stock and organized in wooden boxes. That means a lot of weight and volume. Luckily, my office had a very large closet with shelves from top to bottom, providentially nearly empty; and it could be locked by a key. The move was just from one office to the next. The two young secretaries who worked in the offices strongly believed in Faith and Light and helped me with complete trust. We used a big stepladder and we organized everything.

We had barely finished the last box when the bell rang. While one of the secretaries went to open the door, I quickly locked the closet with the key. Someone knocked at my office: it was Father Georges. Without any greeting, we had the following conversation:

"The general secretary of the SCEJI asked me to come and take the Faith and Light files."

"I am sorry, but Camille, as the liaison, called me this morning and asked me to please put them in a safe place. That is what I immediately did."

"Where are they?"

"Camille asked me to keep their whereabouts secret."

"This does not make sense! I want to talk with her immediately."

"I will call her right now."

Then I explained to Camille the "conversation" that we had just had, and passed the telephone to Father Georges. He gave a suspicious look at the tall stepladder, clearly out of place in the middle of my office, but he did not dare interrogate me. Completely beside himself, he picked up the phone. I left but could hear shouts for quite some time.

Camille had just made a radical choice: until that day, she had not wanted to poison the relationship with Father Georges. They had teamed up to coordinate Faith and Light in France, he as the chaplain, she as the national coordinator. She had witnessed the enormous amount of work that he had taken on. But she became aware that he sought to impose another project, one that belonged to the SCEJI. By keeping close to him, she had hoped to maintain a certain influence and avoid the dilution of Faith and Light within structures that were unsuitable to welcome it. But during these last weeks Father Georges' attitude made this collaboration more and more difficult. The previous evening she had made her decision.

Father Georges' attempt to retrieve the files was not much talked about, but it increased the atmosphere of anxiety. It was sure that on November 28 we had escaped the immediate, outright dissolution of Faith and Light. It was also certain that the concluding statements were more reassuring. However, they were just words. They did not correspond to the decisions that had been prepared in writing and they left big questions about the future.

Faith and Light activities, on the level of the diocese could continue, but on condition that they be coordinated by the SCEJI. Well, the SCEJI did not have a totally positive image among those who had participated in the pilgrimage to Lourdes. In some cases it had manifested a benevolent neutrality and had sometimes given its collaboration, but in many other cases, it had hurt leaders and future pilgrims by a kind of disdain and even malice.

Pierre Leborgne tried to conciliate between the differing points of view. His role as treasurer and his title as vice-president of the *Secours Catholique* gave him some authority. His levelheadedness and his desire for unity motivated him. He tried to use all his strengths so that the SCEJI accomplish its own proper mission and nothing more. He sent a "man to man" letter to Father Georges, in which he clearly analyzed the errors of the SCEJI and suggested actions that could calm the tense climate and, little by little, restore the trust of the Faith and Light diocesan leaders.

One of the passages of his letter shows well the spirit of the French team: "If, on November 28, the SCEJI had declared: 'We recognize that we made a mistake. We were very afraid about your pilgrimage, which was a risky gamble. We, as a service of the Church, were not able to commit to such a daring enterprise. But today we thank you because you were definitely successful, and in reality you have helped to advance the pastoral service to persons with intellectual disabilities and their inclusion in the Church.' If this passage had been read out loud, there would have been thunderous applause to greet these words. Then, the SCEJI diocesan leaders would have welcomed people representing Faith and Light on their teams, and they would have shown, by attitudes and deeds, the reassuring statements that had been verbally given.

Then you would be certain that the game was won." And I would like to add that we all would have won together.

Was it too late? Unfortunately, at the time, the blockages proved to be too great and, because of this, it was necessary to wait for another door to open.

Rising up from our roots

The very evening of the famous meeting, several leaders gathered. They had received the news of the dissolving of the national team like a whiplash and they insisted that Father Georges reconsider the decision made, but he declared that it was "irrevocable". That meant that sooner or later Faith and Light would disappear, and this they could not accept. They wanted to continue. But how? The liaison had the trust of all, but her role, as "mailbox," did not leave much to hope for. With whom was it possible to reflect? The national team? It had just disappeared. How to help Faith and Light to maintain its originality and continue to develop?

In the days that followed, new contacts were established. Finally, twelve leaders met, persuaded that the solution that best matched the desires of the majority, was to have a meeting of the departmental and regional leaders who wanted the movement to continue to live. Christmas was coming and the first date possible was January 8. They decided, then, to send an invitation dated on December 8. It was a gesture to manifest their trust in the protection of the Virgin Mary, the Immaculate of Lourdes. For three years, day after day, she had taken care of the movement with much tenderness. More than ever, during this time of great crisis, it was necessary to trust her and ask her help to find ways of peace.

The "letter of the twelve," an invitation to this meeting, indicated their goals: to choose a national team to maintain connections and to coordinate, corresponding to the reality and needs of Faith and Light, to be attentive not to duplicate the work of other already existing movements and to totally accept coordination within the framework of the SCEJI.

At the same time, another letter was written to the former members of the national team that had organized the pilgrimage. The twelve clearly explained their decision: to make it possible for all department leaders who desired to continue Faith and Light according to its proper vocation. Their message was firm, calm, gentle. It ended with this: "Dear friends, Our gratitude to you who organized the Faith and Light pilgrimage is written forever in our hearts. We hope that the team that will take up the torch now will do so with as much courage and faith as you have put into your work. Because our ultimate goal is the same, we would like to reaffirm here that it is in the unity of Christ that we remain with you."

There were numerous reactions after these events. Pierre Leborgne continued to play a role of reconciler. He kept in touch with Bishop de La Chanonie, who gently asked him to participate in the January meeting, counting on Pierre to act as mediator.

Six weeks later, on January 8, 1972, the "team of twelve" welcomed those who had answered their invitation at the Parish in Bellville, hosted once more by Father Orset, with all his warmth and friendship. After many exchanges of letters, alternating cold and hot, the atmosphere was hopeful.

There were forty-nine participants representing twenty-three departments; four excused themselves, and ten others sent news. Camille Proffit was present as national liaison. Jean Vanier, Pierre Leborgne and I were invited as members of the international team.

Pierre Leborgne, more or less mandated by Bishop de La Chanonie, introduced the day. He began by stressing that we were gathered to see clearly, in serenity and in peace, under the eyes of the Lord. Then he proposed that Camille Proffit lead the meeting. Unanimous accord. Camille invited Jean Vanier to speak. He recalled the signs which so clearly manifested that Faith and Light was willed by God: the uncertainties through which we had passed during the preparation, our psychological and material poverty, the fear of a financial catastrophe, then the multitude of graces received and shared in Lourdes, the immense joy of persons with disabilities, the relief of so many parents. And the unanimous cry of the pilgrims: "We want Faith and Light to continue."

And Jean Vanier went further, saying that it was up to us to continue the movement started in the spirit of the Gospel, and that this would involve struggles and suffering. We needed to fix our eyes, not on the difficulties and barriers, but on these young people, on these men and women with disabilities who wait expectantly, like dry land, for places where they might feel loved, valued and respected.

Camille presented a synthesis of the responses sent by the diocesan leaders concerning their wishes. Four main points emerged: the desire to continue to break open isolation through the local community; the desire to assure services that favor integration of persons with disabilities and their families in the human and Christian communities; the concern to bring human and spiritual nourishment and a renewal of faith to all; finally, the great desire to keep in communion with the diocesan Church and existing movements.

We then proceeded to nominate a national team to support Camille, made up of a couple from eastern France, Paul and Mimi Leblanc, who had a son with disabilities, Hubert Allier and Pierre Leborgne. Camille insisted that this council would not be a national structure that would give directives "from the top", but that we rely greatly on fraternal support from department to department and the sharing of information that this team would be responsible to pass on. "Our work," concluded Camille, "very often, exceeds our capabilities but we have experienced deeply that we can count on one another, and that in our weakness, God is there as our strength."

This meeting closed with a Mass. In the homily, Father Orset called to mind the specific mission of Faith and Light: the meeting of persons with and without disabilities, where the goal is mutual transformation. Faith and Light is a movement created and led by lay people, able to move mountains because they do not rely on themselves, but on Jesus and the Holy Spirit. This is done in close and irreplaceable collaboration with the priest, who offers them the sacraments and who gives the bread of the Word and the bread of the Body of Christ.

Father Orset mentioned that some had questioned the name, Faith and Light: "This name, it is not an identifying placard on a train car, or a sign to carry in procession. It recalls the trust received in Lourdes, as one mother during the meeting of parents said: "When I am discouraged in my heart, just to say the name Faith and Light gives me a little bit of hope". We all know that a spirit without a name is nothing but pure abstraction. When we remove the name of someone, we cross it off the list of free, living persons. May this name be for you a sign of unity, a reminder of a vision, an openness to all persons with disabilities and those around them no matter their age, the degree of their disability, their religious affiliation or lack of affiliation... May it include all who cannot be touched by catechetical instruction. May it be a star lighting up the Easter sky... May it be a full-throated "cry of life" addressed to all who demand the death of persons with disabilities before their birth..."

With these words of hope, we left energized and united, ready to move forward. The first months of 1972 were marked by big celebrations, meetings and pilgrimages, a few throughout the dioceses. We could think that the conflicts were behind us. They were not.

The boat still tossing

La Documentation Catholique[1], in its issue of February 20, 1972, published a common declaration from the SCEJI and the national team of Faith and Light.

The sub-title announced "the dissolution of Faith and Light, which relies on the Church with its diverse specialized services, to maintain the new hope raised by the Easter pilgrimage". The letter was signed by Bishop de La Chanonie, even if he was not the author. This could stir up trouble and awaken opposition. A certain number of events justified these fears.

In this same month of February, the Faith and Light team in Paris had sent an invitation to all their pilgrims and their friends for a day of friendship. The regional leader from the SCEJI reacted immediately with a statement including four points:

1. Since the Faith and Light national team has been dissolved, Faith and Light disappeared.
2. A Faith and Light event will only aggravate the pastoral difficulties experienced by the bishops of the surrounding dioceses both with those who are self-employed and with the working class.
3. If the term, "Faith and Light," does not appear, and it is replaced by "those formerly of Lourdes", whatever a leader does will not be criticized.
4. No initiative can be taken without first being referred to the head of the SCEJI!

This at least had the quality of being clear! But the pronouncements of the SCEJI echoed everywhere. For example,

---

1. *The Catholic Record* – a Catholic magazine published twice a month – Translator note

the Faith and Light communities in Rhone had prepared a large three-day pilgrimage to La Salette. The priests from the sanctuaries had agreed to give lodging to all five hundred pilgrims. But, just before departure, the leaders received a call from the rector saying: "We have read the article in *La Documentation Catholique* and it is impossible for us to receive a movement that no longer exists." The press spread the rumors. It was necessary to appeal to the bishop to save a pilgrimage that in the end, according to the participants, was deeply blessed.

Despite this resistance, we continued to go forward, trying to prevent these differences from degenerating into a hardening of positions and into confrontation. We moved on in hope.

There were signs of cooperation here and there. For example, a leader of the SCEJI asked Faith and Light to help with the birth of a community to support isolated parents. Friends and parents became engaged in special catechesis. Bridges never stopped being built from one side to the other.

Today, the movements at the service of persons with disabilities, with all their differences and complementarity, find themselves united around a common mission.

In the beginning of the year 1973, the international association of Faith and Light was officially created, with three principle goals: to form communities of friendship and prayer with persons with intellectual disabilities, their families, educators and friends; to work for integration in the Church and in society; to foster the human and spiritual life of persons with intellectual disabilities and to help them to grow in all their abilities.

CHAPTER 7

All Roads Lead to Rome!
(1973-1975)

Just when we were hoping to simply live Faith and Light in the day-to-day, suddenly, in 1973, the question arose about our participation in the Holy Year[1] that Paul VI had solemnly announced for 1975.

Many coordinators asked us: Will the communities be encouraged to be integrated into the diocesan or national pilgrimages, or will there be an international Faith and Light pilgrimage to Rome that year?

In France, Bishop Jean-Charles Thomas was approached for his opinion. He was head of the office for pastoral services for persons with disabilities, someone with whom we had woven links of trust. His answer was very nuanced: "Being designated by the bishops of France to oversee the pastoral services for children and youth with disabilities, I have always tried, for a year and a half, to keep my proper place. It is not up to me to make the final decisions for each movement, group or organization with which this pastoral ministry deals. Each one must find its

1. A Holy Year – we can also say a Jubilee Year – is announced by the Pope every twenty-five years. It is a year of graces, centered on a return to God, who calls us to new life on all levels: personal, familial and social. The focus is on a conversion of hearts. – Translator note

own autonomy." However, he was happy to share the fruit of his reflections. His preference was that members of Faith and Light be included in the diocesan pilgrimages, instead of having a separate event. But he indicated that, nevertheless, he would understand a different decision, if it were carefully thought out.

A time of hesitations

During the French national meeting that took place in September 1973, with fifty-eight participants and six guests representing Belgium, Great Britain, and Italy, we studied the two hypotheses, finally eliminating the possibility of an international Faith and Light pilgrimage. The preparation for such an event would require all our energies. Wouldn't it be better if we dedicated ourselves to the creation and accompaniment of new communities? Wouldn't it be more valuable to promote the integration of persons with disabilities in the Church by the participation of the communities in the diocesan pilgrimages? The high cost of an international pilgrimage would require a large amount of funds that could be used for more concrete works: classes, institutions, day centers...

The national team decided then to get in contact with the national pilgrimage director, to study with him how the Faith and Light communities could participate in the diocesan pilgrimages and to ask him to facilitate contacts with the local diocesan directors.

However, this first inclination did not last long. At the international meeting in January 1974, when the French team reported this decision, thinking that it would be immediately endorsed, vigorous opposition arose. Two Italian delegates, Sister Ida Maria, canon of Saint Augustine, very engaged in catechesis of persons with disabilities, and Father Renzo del Fante, chaplain of an institution that welcomed persons with disabilities did not agree. The Sister asked to speak: "You, French, you could go to Lourdes with seven thousand pilgrims and this has given you great momentum. Now you have Faith and Light communities, even if their level of activity varies from region to region. You have a structure that allows Faith and Light to spread. We, Italians, we have nothing. We were a tiny handful that went to Lourdes. We were too small. We were incapable of transmitting the flame, but we are sure, if you come to Italy, the flame will spread, and it will go everywhere throughout our country and beyond." Father Renzo supported her: "If Faith and Light crosses the Alps as Napoleon did, it will be the spark that ignites a great fire in all Italy and beyond our borders!"

It was necessary to open a dialogue. Hubert Allier, recently elected national coordinator, recounted the reasons why France had given its preference to the diocesan pilgrimages.

We looked at the question from the spiritual angle. If the Pope had made an appeal to all Christians to gather together in Rome, wouldn't the invitation be even more urgent for persons with disabilities and their families? In the simplicity of their heart, the weakest go directly to the essential: Rome, it is the person of the Pope. Father Thomas Philippe simply affirmed: "Their heart, frequently less cluttered than ours, is more ready to grasp, by an intuition of love, the mystery of the papacy." All were also touched that Paul VI had set reconciliation as the theme for this Holy Year. The parents with children with disabilities particularly felt the need for this undertaking.

First of all, they needed to be reconciled with reality. Many were at odds with reality since it no longer coincided with what they had justifiably planned. They had dreamed of a perfect child, full of life and of capabilities, and there the child is, fragile, limited in intelligence and perhaps in body. However, this is a unique person whose very destiny depends on how we see him or her. Could we hear the cry of their heart: "Stop dreaming about me, love me as I am"?

And then, they needed to be reconciled with themselves, which was at least as difficult. We so easily condemn ourselves and imagine that our trials are the consequences of our faults. We are so put off by our handicaps, our failures, our pride, our pretenses.

Finally, to be reconciled with God: "If your heart condemns you, God is bigger than your heart."[1] To let oneself be invaded by this infinite "mercy" of God, *miseris cor dare*[2], and to recognize the heart of God that gives itself to those who are in misery. To trust in God, not *in spite of* our misery, but *because* of it, because our misery is what draws the superabundance of God's tenderness to us.

Rome could help us to be reconciled with our children as they are, as they can become. With ourselves as we are, poor "pardoned" sinners, with our life that is like Jesus' life, marked by death and resurrection.

Here we go!

We faced two alternatives: to join the diocesan pilgrimages or to choose the difficult path of organizing a new Faith and Light pilgrimage. The repeated appeal from our Italian brothers and sisters and their deep motivation touched us tremendously. We were very clear about the mountain of difficulties and worries that we would face again, yet we felt that it was important to respond to this request from Italy. We took a break and time for prayer. Only then, did we proceed to vote. Unanimously, the assembly

---

1. 1 John 3: 19-20

2. The Latin word for mercy is misericordia (a heart that responds to suffering with mercy) – Translator note

decided in favor of an international Faith and Light pilgrimage to Rome. However, countries, regions and departments were free to be integrated in a diocesan pilgrimage.

Another important point on the agenda: better representation in the international council. In fact, France, which had more communities than all the other countries combined, occupied a dominant place. The international council was concerned with the unique place of each country, and unanimously approved that, from now on, each national delegation could be represented by ten persons: parents, friends (of whom two or three would be young people), one or two priests, no matter the number of its communities.

At this time when we were taking such an important decision, I asked to meet with Marthe Robin once again. She told me: "Certainly, it is very important to go on pilgrimage to Rome, to reaffirm your gratitude to the Holy Father and your fidelity to the Church. But wouldn't it be important to think about returning to Lourdes for the tenth anniversary of Faith and Light? You have received such an extraordinary gift! The Virgin Mary will be filled with joy that her children come back to give thanks." When the moment came, we did not forget this advice of Marthe and we were faithful to a pilgrimage to Lourdes every ten years until and including 2001.

The challenges of Rome

Even if we had the experience of the Lourdes pilgrimage, going to Rome brought us face-to-face with new challenges.

The practical questions were very different. In Lourdes the whole town was mobilized to welcome persons with disabilities, but in Rome we would encounter challenges everywhere: steep hills, cobblestones, stairs, even in the houses of welcome and lodging in boarding houses, the puzzle of moving through the city, not to mention the Italian language, unknown to the majority of the pilgrims.

Another difficulty, and not at all the least, was the fact that Faith and Light did not yet exist in Italy. It was therefore necessary to create a local team in charge of the organization.

Moreover, it was not certain that we could easily have access to the authorities in the Holy See, whose support seemed to us to be indispensable. Our pilgrimage could not happen unless the Holy Father encouraged it and the Vatican authorities facilitated it. That is why we immediately decided that our next international meeting would be in Rome, April 1-2, 1974, so that we could meet with the authorities, giving priority to Bishop Mazza, president of the commission for the Holy Year.

Mariangela

Our first initiative in Rome was to designate a coordinator for Faith and Light in Italy, who would be at the same time in charge of the organization of the pilgrimage. In February 1974, Sister Ida Maria organized a lunch with Jean Vanier and myself so that we could meet her team of volunteers and some other friends. That day, it was necessary, whatever it took, to name a national coordinator. By chance I was at the table next to a certain Mariangela, invited by the Sister as an "extra" person. This young woman had a small daughter, Maria Francesca, nicknamed Chicca, with a very profound disability. Chicca did not talk, did not walk, did not eat independently, did not communicate. For many years, Mariangela could not accept nor love this little girl. Sometimes, with shame, she asked: "Is this really a child?" It was in Lourdes that she experienced this "little big miracle", as her husband said, the miracle of discovering the hidden beauty of her daughter. As soon as the dinner was over, captivated by this person, I asked Sister Ida Maria why she had never mentioned Mariangela's name as a possibility for coordination. "She would be extraordinary," Sister told me, "but this is totally impossible. She is already overwhelmed by her responsibilities. She is the mother of two other children, including a four month old baby." Jean, who had joined us, asked: "Do you give me permission to talk with her?

"Yes, she will be touched to have a personal moment with you, but do not have any hope."

After a long conversation with Jean, Mariangela concluded with a big laugh: "Jean was able to sweep away all my arguments. I give up. So, maybe I will try! I know this is totally crazy, but I recognize that God has given me, day by day, drop by drop, the grace that I needed and Faith and Light has become a light in my life and of all my family."

From that day on, Mariangela, supported by her husband and Sister Ida Maria, by her team and many others, took on two responsibilities: to develop Faith and Light in Italy and to lead the team organizing the pilgrimage. Very soon there were four groups in Rome. They met once each month, in a spirit of joy and friendship. Each one accepted some responsibility for the pilgrimage. At the same time, Mariangela worked for the creation of other communities, in Vercelli, Milan, Cuneo, Parma and Abario. Later, she would begin to launch Faith and Light in many countries of Southern Europe, as Sister Ida Maria and Father Renzo had predicted.

What became of Chicca, Mariangela's daughter, the littlest one in Faith and Light? Four years later, in 1978, Italy organized a pilgrimage to Assisi. Chicca participated, just before having surgery for a cancer. Then, she slipped away from us and went to Heaven. She gave her silent good-bye to a thousand pilgrims, in her way, as if whispering in their ears: "Good-bye, I have given my message. What I wanted to tell you, I have said. Now I need to do something else." What she has confided to us, with all her love, is that children like herself, mysteriously, have a prophetic message for the world today. We have experienced this, and we believe. They have something very powerful to tell us. In their presence, we cannot even think about the future, because we are given a glimpse of eternity. In this, they help us to be converted to the message of the Beatitudes that Jesus left with us.

Green light from the Vatican

After having taken care of the question of a working partner in Italy, it was necessary, in collaboration with her, to concentrate on the international meeting of April 1974 in Rome, and on contacts with the Vatican.

The welcome by Bishop Mazza was very favorable. In agreement with him, we fixed the dates, October 31-November 2, 1975, due to the All Saints holiday[1], but especially because of the twenty-fifth anniversary of the proclamation of Mary's Assumption. With his advice, we reserved nine thousand rooms through the *Peregrinatio Romana*[2]. Bishop Mazza agreed to send on the file of the pilgrimage project to the Holy Father through Cardinal Villot.

The response was slow in coming. At the end of July, a letter from Bishop Mazza finally arrived: "I am sorry to announce that the Vatican Secretary of State thinks that it is inappropriate to hold this pilgrimage at the same time as the Feast of All Saints

---

1. In several European countries, All Saints Day, November 1 is a national holiday – Translator note

2. A service established by the Vatican to assist pilgrims to Rome – Translator note

and All Souls Day, especially because of liturgical considerations. So, it is necessary that you contact *Peregrinatio Romana* in order to choose another date." This answer, that arrived more than three months after our request, and above all the prospect of changing the date worried us deeply. To us, it seemed impossible to reserve nine thousand places for another time. We decided to go immediately to Rome to fix a definite date.

At the *Peregrinatio Romana*, the person who received us, flipping through the agenda for the Holy Year, began by indicating that there was no other date in 1975. Faced with Jean Vanier's exasperation, he discovered an impossible little niche, between Sunday October 26 in the afternoon and Wednesday October 29 in the morning. We reserved it, even if it did not correspond to any holiday and led us to revise our projections about the number of pilgrims.

We still needed the Pope's consent. Bishop Mazza was unreachable. With Jean Vanier traveling to Canada in August, I was in charge of contacting Bishop Séjourné from the office of the Secretary of State. Very bored with all this, he informed me that he had no authority to intervene in this matter, but he gave me a preview of some reservations of the Roman authorities: Was Faith and Light well aware that Rome presented difficulties far different from Lourdes? Yes, we were clear and "accepted this". He indicated to me that Bishop Mazza would be the better person to talk to, but because of the Synod of bishops it would not be possible to see him until three weeks later.

When Jean Vanier came back to France, the situation was very embarrassing. We had various documents, especially the pilgrimage Charter, ready and waiting to take to the printer. All documents needed to be translated and printed in four or five languages. Jean decided to write to Cardinal Benelli, the Secretary of State, making plain to him the reality of the situation. We were going to have another international meeting in Rome, October

28-29, 1974. We were ready to go forward with the undertaking that represented this pilgrimage in as much as it corresponded to the desire of the Holy Father when he announced the Holy Year inviting all Christians to go to Rome. We thought that it was within the Pope's heart's desire that the weakest ones might come to him. We had carefully weighed all the difficulties, but to continue, we absolutely needed to find support in Rome, but this could only be by calling to mind the Holy Father wishes. The pursuit, or not, of our pilgrimage project depended on the response from Cardinal Benelli. He set an appointment with Jean Vanier on the date requested. Their meeting let us see that many things seemed to have been unfrozen, that we could move forward with the dates for October, and that he would pass on to the Holy Father all our desires, giving us support. In fact, all this was freed up only after Pierre Goursat, founder of the Emmanuel Community[1], placed a file of our pilgrimage project directly into the hands of the Pope.

For nine months, uncertainty had hovered over this response. This was added to the uneasiness that at the time shook more or less the whole world, given the serious political, social, economic and financial difficulties. Italy was particularly impacted. Would we need to limit the number of pilgrims? Or even cancel the pilgrimage?

Without an explicit answer, we decided to move on in the semi-darkness (or better, in the semi-light), but this did not diminish our enthusiasm. In fact, since the consensus of January 30, 1974, the executive team and the international council, the national, regional and local teams were working with energy and enthusiasm.

---

1. An international Catholic lay community whose members commit to live their faith in their daily lives and to meet together regularly – Translator note

We made use of all our experience from Lourdes: the partnerships that we had made, in particular with Jean Charrière and Touring Club for the infrastructure (registrations, travel, lodging…); the method by which the registrations would be made by community and by triads, each person with disabilities being accompanied by at least one relative and one friend; the same principles of organization for security and finances; the planning for a big celebration in one of the gardens of Rome. Another support was also secured in Father David Julien, who had participated in the organization of big regional gatherings in France. He accepted to be in charge of the spiritual and liturgical animation of the pilgrimage. Then we also welcomed another recruit, as if falling from heaven: Anne-Françoise Marès. She arrived at Christmas 1974, after we had been searching in vain for a general secretary for several months. She had traveled around the world and had completed an internship in handicrafts. Her motivations for the role were multiple: to discover persons with disabilities, whom she did not know; to travel to the beautiful city of Rome; to network with people from other countries; and then, she was certain that a job for six to eight months was a perfect fit for her. In reality, her commitment lasted much longer! Thirty-five years later she was still a member of a Faith and Light community and had been appointed by the diocese of Paris to be in charge of the Service of Special Catechesis for children with disabilities for the region. A direct link between these two entities.

In the course of the preparations for the 1975 pilgrimage the progress of the movement after 1971 was made clear, particularly in the unity of the international council and in the other structures. More and more we recognized ourselves as brothers and sisters. This did not prevent differences in our points of view or disagreements, because we were very diverse in our cultures, traditions, personalities… But we loved each other as we were, called to the same mission that was radically beyond us. Little by little, we passed from collaboration to communion. What could have separated us was dissipated by the desire to search for the will of God and by us forgiving one another as many times as was necessary.

In many communities, there were also the deepening of bonds and the discovery of a mission that did not belong to us. We knew that the groups would joyfully throw themselves into the adventure. And unburdened of the material dimension, the preparation could give a much more prominent place to the religious and spiritual aspects. We noticed this, for instance, while we prepared the charter for the pilgrimage to Rome.

The Charter and the spiritual preparation

This Charter was similar to the one for Lourdes. However, it issued a special call to young friends, whose "interest" we had discovered, equally good for them and for Faith and Light. "In our time, many young people are discouraged. They have great difficulty to take up, in faith, their social, political and other commitments. This pilgrimage could be an opportunity for them to live with their wounded brothers and sisters, to discover in them the mystery of the living Jesus and to commit to them. Besides, in this period of confusion and crisis, through this spiritual journey on the soil where Saint Peter and Saint Paul and so many other martyrs gave their lives, where very early Christian communities were formed, they might discover an answer to the anonymity of our society and to the disorder of our times." Thirty-five years later, with completely different profiles and by very different routes, many young people today find, as those before, new meaning for their lives in a Faith and Light community. Others, without knowing, thirst for this same type of spring and wait for us to invite them.

The Charter insisted equally on the deepening of the life of the communities and on the importance of the inclusion of persons with disabilities in the Church (parishes, groups and movements).

Finally, the pilgrimage was not to be an end in itself. Upon return, we were to witness to the Good News that Jesus came to announce to the poor.

During the preparation period, three spiritual activities were proposed to the communities to create a spiritual bond between all the countries and between all the members, both those who would travel to Rome and those who would live the pilgrimage "in spirit".

The first recommendation that we made to the communities was to invite them to choose a saint to accompany them along their way. Having initially hoped that the pilgrimage would take place around All Saints Day, it seemed logical to take as a preparation theme "to walk in the footsteps of the saints". In general, the saint was chosen by all the members of the community. Together, they found out about the saint's life: most often, this was not a very extraordinary person. Just like us, the saint had a job, an occupation. He or she was not without faults, difficulties, disabilities... The saint had also known sadness and joy... He or she simply said "yes" to Jesus and tried to live as He did, in tenderness and humility. "Place yourselves in my school, become gentle and humble of heart." This saint became the friend of the whole community and of each one of its members. We asked his or her help to also become a "disciple," a "friend" of Jesus.

Each community was invited to make a banner, bearing the name of its patron saint and the name of its country or city. The persons with disabilities welcomed this idea with enthusiasm, and the other persons, sometimes reluctantly, eventually let themselves be convinced. The banner was a spiritual symbol and also a gathering point for the groups more or less spread out along the platforms in the train station, or at the airport, or at the celebrations in Rome or during visits to the city. In this way the banners helped many pilgrims to not get lost and made it easier to find those who strayed. The persons with disabilities, paired with two other persons, proudly carried this sign of belonging to the same international family. In Rome, it was so beautiful to see saints from all countries, from all times, and from such different circumstances side by side!

The second spiritual pillar in preparation of this pilgrimage was a call to reconciliation. In this activity, it was proposed that each community reflect on what Jesus asked of them during this Holy Year. *Ombres et Lumière*, in one of it's issues, dedicated a section to help us to enter, more deeply and concretely, on this path of pardon. The persons with disabilities showed themselves to be our masters, frequently simpler and more truthful to recognize their errors and to "make peace". After some misbehavior, they know very well how to make Mommy's and Daddy's smile return. "Sorry" is a word that does not hurt their mouth. To confess, once they have understood the joy of this act, brings peace. They have difficulty tolerating disagreements or conflicts. Even when these are hidden, they sense the atmosphere. They interpret a door that slams; they understand a hostile look. We can say that, with all their being, fragile persons cry out for harmony, this good soil that allows them to grow.

The community gatherings centered on reconciliation with God, with others, with ourselves and with our life and gave an opportunity to create a "parchment", on which each person could express himself or herself.

By these drawings, all expressed what they lived in their community. Here are some beautiful disclosures from these parchments:

"I could not accept my child with disabilities. To see him grow and develop, with the help of my Faith and Light community,

I could discover, little by little all the affection that he brought us. Little by little I accept God's plan and I become reconciled with him."

"My parents, my brothers and sisters refused to welcome my son with disabilities. They always invited me without him. Deeply hurt by this attitude, I decided to not see them again and we were all unhappy. When our son made his first communion, I invited all the family to the party and all has been mended."

"Jesus, forgive me when I sulk, help me."

"There was a wall between my husband and me. We were not in agreement on a decision to be made about our daughter with disabilities. During a Faith and Light Mass, I asked God to change my heart, because I could not receive Communion in this state of resentment and of revolt. Little by little, I felt my aggressiveness diminish and be transformed into a surge of pardon and affection toward my husband. I went to him and I hugged him like there was nothing between us. Since then, we were able to renew dialogue and make the decision to get counseling with a person whom we trust greatly. Throughout this Holy Year I have tried to disarm confrontations… and I feel God's graces deeply."

"I found Bertrand disagreeable. When I saw him, I always had the desire to pass him by on the other side of the sidewalk. I have overcome my repugnance. I have conversed with him. The ice is broken. Now, it is much better…"

And then, this simple sentence: "Dear Pope, thank you for having invited all of us to Rome with Faith and Light!"

The parchments, gathered together in a "Golden Book", were meant to be given to the Pope at the meeting that we would have with him. This speaks to the love that was placed in their creation…

The third spiritual sign that we imagined was intended to emphasize the familial dimension of the community. Our international family was born in Lourdes around the person with disabilities whom Jesus had entrusted to us. In Rome we would celebrate our first reunion at the heart of the universal Church, of which we are members since our baptism.

But we would be six thousand pilgrims, very different in our cultures, our languages and the social milieu from which we come. How might we concretely manifest that we were united to each other through very deep bonds? How might we say to each one: "You are my brother, you are my sister, I love you." If this would, practically-speaking, be impossible, we could at least manifest this desire by a sign. So we decided that all of us would address a message to a member of Faith and Light, as yet unknown to us, to share our friendship with him or her, to express our joy that he or she exists. It could be a word, a drawing; a little letter that we would personally deliver during the celebration.

The preparation in the countries

In the countries, people leapt into action with great fervor, each one according to his or her charism and call. I remember the witness of the coordinator for Canada, which illustrates the way that things could happen.

In Canada it was Betty Renaud who took the helm. A very short lady, very simple, filled with faith and love, nothing could stop her. She had met Jean Vanier at the house, Saint-Benoît, where everyday they serve a meal for the poor in town. She was on retreat. She recounts:

"He asked me if I would like to organize the Faith and Light pilgrimage to Rome for Canada. But I did not know anything whatsoever about organization. I had difficulty balancing my own little family budget, imagine! I shared my objections with him, but he only smiled: "If God wants, it will be done, even if what you say is true." With this viewpoint, I accepted. It was pure madness... And we were many who believed in this folly and met to pray in order to try to understand the meaning of this gathering in the year of reconciliation. It would be necessary to prepare our participation in the celebration having the perspective that each creature has infinite value and the right to live, at least once in life, something that fulfills him or her. We were happy to give our contribution.

It was a totally different matter when I understood that someone needed to make arrangements to reserve a charter flight. In panic, I realized that this 'someone' was myself! We proceeded very cautiously. There was nothing else to do but to go forward with the help of the Lord. When the manager of the travel agency asked how many people would participate in the pilgrimage, I asked him the question:

'How many people are necessary to fill up an airplane?'

'Three hundred and seventy-eight.'

'Then, there will be three hundred and seventy-eight!'

Only God knew who these three hundred and seventy-eight persons would be, because, at the time, I did not know one. The manager greeted me with a little skeptical smile and I went back home torn between fear and hope. Soon all started to get organized: people offered to be leaders in different parts of Canada; days of reflection were set up; we received donations. But I cannot deny, organizing an international pilgrimage was very difficult. So many letters, trips, phone calls, meetings and sometimes tears were necessary!

The moment to make the first payment of eleven thousand dollars arrived. I was on edge when I went to see the treasurer to tell him that I needed to sign the contract the following day and asked him how much we had in the bank. Serge added up the checks and told me: "We have eleven thousand dollars." We looked at each other in silence and I believe we had the same thought at the same time: 'O, people of little faith!' Two other times, the same pattern repeated itself. What an experience!"

Preparations were also in full swing in Great Britain. Eighteen dioceses would be present at the pilgrimage. Seven hundred and twenty-eight pilgrims were divided onto five planes departing from Manchester, Luton and London. The smallest community had six persons; the largest one had sixty. The small preparation groups were busy and planned some celebrations, diocese by diocese, before their departure, so that those who were not able to go could also come together in community.

Many communities were formed in several cantons in Switzerland. Each month a member of each community would meet in Lausanne, or Geneva, for a meeting of the national team. Emphasis was placed on spiritual preparation. We gave priority for young people to accompany their brothers and sisters with disabilities. We wanted so much that Faith and Light be a true encounter of friendship and of fidelity.

In Germany, a group of pilgrims, members of a big institution in Bavaria, had gone to Lourdes. The number of persons had increased, but although very small, the group accepted the Rome project with enthusiasm. People dove into the special issue[1] on preparation, people saved money... The spring wind, despite all our tiredness and difficulties, helped us to wait attentively for the wonders of the Holy Spirit.

"Hope" was our keyword. There was the hope of the parents of persons with disabilities who seemed astonished that others wanted to share and journey with their children. And there was also the hope of persons with disabilities, young people or adults, who had never imagined that one day they would find themselves with the Pope and brothers and sisters from all over the world. Strengthened by all these hopes, we marched together towards the Eternal City.

---

1. Of *Ombres et Lumière* magazine – Translator note

CHAPTER 8

Rome: Pilgrimage of Reconciliation
(1975)

This pilgrimage was called "the pilgrimage of reconciliation", referring to the theme of the Holy Year. It could also have been called "the pilgrimage of the confirmation of Faith and Light". In truth, if Lourdes saw our birth and our baptism, Rome was like a confirmation by the Church. The Pope, it is true, gave many signs to encourage us, and to send us on mission.

First of all, it was necessary to arrive in the Holy City. For those who took the special trains, with stops in each village to pick up other pilgrims, the trip was very, very long. Forty-eight hours, for those who started in Paris, while we stayed in Rome for only two and a half days. However, like a young person with disabilities who loves math, if we count the days and the nights of the trip as part of the pilgrimage, we lived five very full, rich days together.

I was touched, once again, to observe how the time spent traveling is important in a pilgrimage and may be marked by a truly human and spiritual dimension. "At the time of departure," said the leader of a Belgian community, "we were afraid that we would become totally lost. But it was not like this at all. First of all, the trip made it possible for us to get to know one another. We were eight families with children or young people, a priest, a nurse and four friends. From the moment we boarded the train, I felt that we were from the same world, where there were no barriers. We no longer feared that our children would be scrutinized; they could live fully, be themselves without constraints, and we, their parents, did not need to fear that they would draw negative attention."

I also remember the remarks of this priest:

"When night fell, a group asked me to lead them in prayer. Why not? We had chosen a text that was meaningful for the moment. In a poorly heated train car, with very little light, we read Chapter 17 of Acts, the passage where St. Paul was traveling by boat in the midst of a storm, going to Rome, just as we were. Then, we meditated on the words of encouragement and confidence that St Paul addressed to his travel companions: 'Courage, my friends, I trust God.' The discomfort became a source of joy: 'We are doing just like St. Paul!' and when there was no longer any light, a young blind pilgrim added: "This is faith without light!" I could see how much this prayer, repeated group by group, helped us to form a people journeying towards light."

A friend also told us: "After leaving Amiens, we transformed a train compartment into an 'adoration chapel', at the end of the train, and we had adoration all night long."

The arrivals in Rome spanned twenty-four hours, day and night, obliging the Italian welcoming teams to be highly ingenious and to be available literally around the clock.

Meeting at Saint Peter's Square

The big day arrived, with the Mass at St. Peter's and the meeting with the Pope. Early in the afternoon, the banners of a hundred and twenty-five communities converged on St. Peter's, forming a semi-circle at the end of the square. We were an enormous crowd of men, women and children, many with disabilities, sometimes just arriving from the train station or from the airport, tired and a bit dazed, but marveling at the spectacle. We came from Argentina, Belgium, Canada, Denmark, France, Germany, Great Britain, Ireland, Italy, Spain, Switzerland and the United States.

We were at the heart of the Church. In the name of this Church, Cardinal Poletti, Vicar for Rome, welcomed us with great affection. He took a little boy with profound disabilities and a sweet smile into his arms, and placed him in the arms of Jean Vanier. Jean addressed the crowd that had become a family since Easter Monday of 1971:

"The great moment has arrived. After weeks, months and years of preparation and prayer, here we are assembled in the heart of Christianity, very close to the Pope. We carry with us all those who could not come and their suffering, and we open our hearts to receive the grace that Jesus will give us. Then, we will go back home with hearts burning to deepen our communities and to help make our society a place where all people, whatever their disabilities, whatever their difficulties, may believe in Jesus' love and in human dignity."

With exultation, we entered the Basilica where the tomb of St. Peter is located, to whom our Pope, Paul VI, was successor. For the first time in history, this Basilica was invaded by pilgrims, many of whom, because of their physical appearance, their behavior or their apparent uselessness, were generally shut away far from society.

The opening Mass celebrated by Cardinal Poletti was filled with fervor and joy. The songs sung by the famous African-American singer, Willie Mae Wright, ascended towards heaven with all the purity of her voice, and were repeated by the crowd. She had come to know Faith and Light in Cleveland, Ohio very well and particularly their chaplain, Father Jim O'Donnell.

The one hundred and twenty-five banners of saints were carried by the community coordinators and a member with disabilities from each community and they circled the choir. In this way, all these "friends of God" who during their lives had followed in Jesus' footsteps were honored this evening and during all the pilgrimage.

In the Basilica, some people, filled with emotion, asked themselves what solutions could be provided for so much suffering. Painful questions, filled with mystery whose response here was the joy and the trust of the alleluias, the joy of being welcomed by the Holy Father, and also the joy of welcoming him as Jesus had been welcomed in the midst of the crowds of blind, lame, sick, poor people, to whom he tirelessly announced the Good News of the Kingdom.

"You are loved by God... just as you are"

Just before the entrance of the Pope, all the lights were turned on. There was an arch, which recalled the sun, drawn by Meb, bursting victoriously from behind the clouds to illuminate the boat of the big Faith and Light family. But the true light emanated from the radiant faces and eyes. Parents were no less moved than their children. No one was intimidated by the *sedia*, this elevated chair upon which, at the time, the Pope was carried. This sign was not a triumphalist gesture, but on the contrary, one of delicacy so that even the littlest ones could see him.

When the time came to read his official speech, the Pope, visibly touched by so much suffering, trust and filial affection, gave the pages that he had written, or that someone had written for him, to his secretary. And he spoke from his heart. Each one felt that the Pope's words were addressed to him or her, personally.

"In such moments, as I pass among you, I would like to help each one of you to understand: you are loved by God, just as you are. He lives in your heart. Thank Him. Trust in Him. See: He gives you your place among all the other Christians in His Church. With them, you are called to form one family where we love one another as brothers and sisters."

Then, in the name of all of us, Jean Vanier, Father Hviid, Hubert Allier and I had the privilege of a moment of personal contact with the Holy Father. Jean handed him the "Golden Book", containing all the parchments, a tangible sign of the acts of reconciliation and pardoning that he had asked from all Christians in this Holy Year. The Pope opened the book and, filled with emotion, he paused over some pages.

When my turn came, Pope Paul VI turned his very penetrating gaze towards me. He took my hand in his and said, "You have an important mission, to see that Faith and Light spreads throughout the entire world." These words were addressed to all those who were there, physically or spiritually. I had been assigned to give him the symbol of Faith and Light. As required by protocol, to keep the Pope from being overloaded with gifts, a bodyguard rushed to relieve him of the symbol. But the Pope placed it back into my hands and motioned to me to pin it onto the short, white cape that covered his shoulders. Applause and "alleluias" burst forth! If it was important to him to wear this emblem of our family next to his heart, wasn't this his way of expressing that he too was a member. As if he were telling us, "Continue with what you are doing with the littlest. It's good. I am with you."

A few seconds later, we witnessed another gesture of trust. A religious sister placed into his arms Youri, a little child with very profound disabilities, who shared a sustained look of wonder with the Pope. At this moment, a voice announced over the loudspeaker: "It is all of us who are presented to the Holy Father and whom he takes in his arms!"

Then for about an hour, people with disabilities accompanied by their relative or a friend went, one by one, to spend an unforgettable moment with the Pope. A child with autism started to continuously clap his hands, in a joy that seemed to come from very far away. A young friend pushed another youth in a wheelchair, and both, with tenderness and respect, kissed the Holy Father's hand. A mother, smiling through her tears, presented a little girl who was not able to move, except the response of her beautiful smile. Songs continued in Italian, French, English, and in the other languages of the pilgrims. Despite our tiredness, we lost track of time.

Back in his *sedia*, the Pope slowly passed among us. We felt that he wanted to respond to all those who reached out their hands towards him, that simply wanted to touch him or who called him: "Pope, Pope, come toward us." He answered by giving blessings. He grasped hands. He caressed a deformed face that suddenly illuminated. He rested his hand on the head of parents who had so much need of consolation. There was a moment of emotion and of grace when he bent from the *sedia* to hold Chicca, the littlest one in our assembly, a miniscule member of the Body of Christ, broken and raised up. For Mariangela and Paulo, in a flash, all tears dried, the veil torn, with certitude in their heart: God loved Chicca with an infinite tenderness, and, with this same love, all the Chiccas, hidden in the Basilica or scattered throughout the whole world.

"The miracle of faith and of love"

This exceptional moment with Paul VI impacted hearts, and not only those in Faith and Light. Some days later, the *Osservatore*

Romano, the daily Vatican newspaper, dedicated two full pages to Faith and Light, under the title: "In the heart of God." The journalist, Virgilio Levi, stressed three types of reaction before our arrival: "Hostile, focused on suffering, or rooted in the Gospel." A radical brochure had denounced "the multinational exploitation of persons with disabilities"! Others, recognizing the serious character of the movement, placed the emphasis on the suffering that so many persons with disabilities and their families had to bear. "In reality," began Virgilio Levi, "against all logical expectation, the members of Faith and Light gave witness through their happiness. The miracle of faith and of love that makes it possible that joy be present even in the midst of difficulties and of suffering."

And the journalist continued: "If the recent audience with the Holy Father was one of the most beautiful, one of the most moving in the Holy Year, it was especially because of this spirit of joy that the groups demonstrated in unison with their alleluias."

Leaving the Basilica, then in the square, the pilgrims did not go their separate ways. We continued to be in wonder together.

The affection of the Holy Father was manifested again the following day, during the Vigil of Light, in Saint Peter's Square. It was the third day of the pilgrimage, the evening before our departure. At night, the six thousand pilgrims reassembled, each group around its own banner.

To be reconciled with God, with others, with self, it was first of all necessary to recognize our weakness, our faults, and sweep them from our hearts. The voice of Father David Julien was heard over the crowd: "Who rips apart the darkness, who sends away the night? The sun! Who is the sun of our lives? Who is the sun of our hearts? Jesus."

On the steps of the Basilica, twelve priests in white albs, carrying torches, brought forth an enormous book of the Gospel and placed it in the center of the square. "This is the book of

God's love that, after two thousand years, shows the way to his children. It is the way that we have chosen. We are faithful and we are filled with joy." Then these priests, with their torches, descended towards the crowd and passed on the light. Each person's candle was lit. Very quickly the whole square was filled with six thousand little lights and "Alleluia, Alleluia" came from everywhere. The priests then read together this passage of the Gospel in five languages: "Love one another as I have loved you. By this love, they will recognize that you are my disciples[1]." At this moment, each one placed his or her right hand on the shoulder of the person in front, making a human chain that went all the way to the Gospel book. "It is the Word of God that gives us light and makes of us light for the world." Red paper lanterns rose up, in rhythm with the chants, towards the sky and towards the window of the Holy Father. Wheelchairs were lifted up, one after the other, so that each one could enjoy the sight…

With hearts overflowing, the crowd waited for the Pope to come to the window. Suddenly, he appeared. He had placed the symbol of Faith and Light on his short, white cape, a sign of tenderness towards his children that the world so often despises. Then, opening his arms these were his words of affection and blessing: "Dear friends, we are very close to you in this vigil of prayer, even in the night of suffering. May the light of God shine always in your hearts and may Almighty God bless you in the name of the Father and the Son and the Holy Spirit. Amen."

This blessing of the Holy Father, a light in the night, remained engraved in the hearts of many, a living image to guard like viaticum[2].

---

1. John 13: 34-35

2. Literally: provisions for the journey. This term is used in the Catholic Church to refer to Eucharist given to a dying person to help them on their way toward God. – Translator note

The celebration and the visit to Rome

No Faith and Light gathering is truly well lived without a celebration. It happened in the Flaminio stadium.

It was not an exact replica of the celebration in Lourdes. We immediately recognized the charisma of the Italians, their talent to generate an atmosphere of communal joy, with their creativity and life energy. About a hundred young friends had participated in organizing the celebration and filled it with their gifts.

In addition, the French team had gained experience through big celebrations in Belgium, and those in France: Lisieux, La Salette, Bressuire, Cognac… They often brought together big crowds, sometimes up to three thousand people. We had discovered the importance of sharing a meal (or at least a bite to eat) together. Around a table, around nourishment for the body, we would meet each other, heart and soul, in joy and sharing. In Rome, the meal was supplied by a specialized company, but this did not stop us from offering the neighbors a piece of pizza or to receive from them part of their dessert.

A priest reported:

"They danced and sang all day long, in never ending joy. Everyone celebrated, without any barriers, under the astonished eyes of the Roman *carabinieri*[1] who were sent there to protect people who had no need of protection. They alone could not dance, poor ones! They did not have permission. Suddenly, they seemed to me to be old, very old, and we were suddenly very young, with a youthful radiance."

A mother marveled at the capacity of her son to enjoy everything and to wonder at it all:

---

1. The national military police of Italy – Translator note

"Because he was surrounded by attention and affection, everything seemed beautiful to him, everything was grand, all was pleasant. Isn't this what our children mostly ask of us? And it was I who suffered the most because of the disabilities of my heart... During the celebration, they disappeared. How many times I looked up at the sky! And the warmth of the sun penetrated me. How good it was!"

Sister Maura, who came from England, accompanied a little girl, Helen, and her mother. Helen was eleven years old, but looked like she was four. She could not walk, nor talk. Since the death of her father and her grandfather, eighteen months before, she had refused to eat and they had gone back to giving her a bottle. Sister Maura suggested to the mother that she participate in the pilgrimage with Helen. She hoped this would help the mother, because it seemed that Helen would not benefit from it much. Sister Maura writes:

"I took Helen with me to the celebration, dancing with her wheelchair to the musical tunes, holding her hands and clapping them in rhythm with the songs... Helen remained in her wheelchair, indifferent to everything and everyone. After two hours, I stopped. I contemplated the marvelous spectacle around me. Suddenly, Helen started to get agitated in her seat and looked at me with a truly splendid smile. Words cannot describe my joy at seeing this child, with such profound disabilities, come back to life. My only regret was that her mother was not there at that moment with us. Anyway, I did not need to worry, because, from that moment on, Helen found life again. She started to make gestures and to try to clap her hands, to communicate in a hundred ways.

I believe that the love of six thousand people, all gathered in the Lord's name, succeeded in penetrating her being and giving joy back to her. So many happy people, so many nationalities mixing with one another! Before the death of her father, she had loved music. It was as if she had realized at the 'fiesta' that after all, life was worth living. And then, the weather was so beautiful, so sunny."

The musical animation for the celebration was simple, the accompaniment provided by an orchestra of young people with guitars, trumpets, flutes and cymbals. Tirelessly, we repeated by heart the pilgrimage song composed by Father David Julien: "When we are together, how beautiful it is! God comes to change our hearts, how beautiful it is! When we are together, how good it is! Joy fills our hearts, how good it is! And if our smile would carry your Name, and if our courage would proclaim your joy, then, around the world, reconciliation would be your message, You, God of pardoning."

This song was alternated with "Amis Chantons Notre Joie", which remains forever the song of our gatherings, recalling the miraculous birth of Faith and Light. There was also the refrain "Hand in the Hand" repeated a thousand times, immediately inviting us to place our hand in the hand of the person next to us, no matter who the person is, and to form so many circles that sometimes we would come together in an immense farandole.

What is the secret of these celebrations of Faith and Light, so spontaneous, so joyful? It seems to me that there is no other reason but the presence of persons with intellectual disabilities. The "fiesta" addresses a profound need in their hearts. They are very naturally in harmony with communal festivities because they live in the present moment. They are not burdened with worries about performance or proficiency. They don't have the desire to dominate or to pretend to be someone else. Their poor, simple presence is a call to each one to give their best.

In this way, celebration brings down barriers. When we sing and dance together, we find ourselves in all simplicity to be brothers and sisters. We forget our disabilities, our difficulties, our pride. Something changes in us, and we move from indifference to sharing and to communion.

To conclude this pilgrimage, we had planned a one-day visit to Rome and the surrounding area. A true logistical challenge! It would be necessary to gather one hundred and fifty buses at St Peter's Square and six thousand pilgrims coming from all corners of Rome and its environs. It was also necessary to plan the itinerary in such a way that the visits to the different sites would flow harmoniously and to find a competent guide for each bus capable of adapting the presentation of places to persons with intellectual disabilities. Eventually, it would also be necessary to add translators.

Father Michel Charpentier, chaplain of the Italian organizational team, was finishing his theological studies in Rome. He was an extraordinarily key person in preparing this impossible mission. He was both a lover of Rome and a catechist in two centers for children with intellectual disabilities. He knew how to find places that could help us to be better pilgrims in our everyday journey.

He wrote a sort of poem, accessible to almost all pilgrims that gave life again to the stones:

For you, I visited Rome, the sun was warm, the sky was blue.
I went to the Coliseum. I imagined the big festivals of the Roman
    Empire, the chariot races, the wrestlers...
I imagined Paul, Saint Paul who arrived in Rome. Paul, tired by
the journey,
    but full of courage, his heart full of joy, filled with the Gospel.
I imagined Saint Peter who arrived in Rome, he too, to bring the Good
    News.
God loves Jesus and Jesus is alive.
God loves all people and all people can live.

But many did not listen to them.
It is annoying to have someone saying that you need to love one
    another;
    who says that the Savior is not the emperor.
Then, I imagined the Christians who were captured, tied up, put
    in prison, martyred.
I saw the catacombs where the martyrs were buried.
For you, I visited Rome and I send you the fraternal greetings that Saint
    Peter sent to the Christians of the world:
    "May you be filled with love and peace." (1Peter 1: 2)

Despite the inevitable disorder, despite the tiredness, there was much joy at the end of this day. And all were amazed: "We have never seen this before"; "How beautiful it is". Many were eager to find postcards or to buy little tourist guides to show to those who were not there, to help them recount all that was indescribable, especially when we have very few words at our command.

"Go everywhere"

The final morning, this pilgrimage ended in the Basilica of Saint Paul-Outside-the-Walls with a thanksgiving Mass highlighted by the ceremony of sending off on mission. Not in the least sad, but with a great desire to pass on all the graces with which we had been filled. Once more the pilgrims were struck by the celebration, at the same time simple, joyful, fervent and in deep communion. We have never heard a shorter homily than the one Bishop Brewer, from Shrewsbury (England), gave: "Open our eyes. Open our arms. Open our hearts." This cry, accompanied by gestures, was repeated by all the pilgrims as an urgent plea: "Yes, Jesus, come to change our hearts of stone into hearts of flesh so that we might announce the Good News to the poor and so that the poor might lead us along the way of the Beatitudes that they know so intimately, much better than we."

On leaving Mass, each pilgrim received a holy card on which was written, in the Pope's handwriting: "We have recognized God's love for us and we have believed." In the final moment before we separated we danced one last exuberant good-bye farandole around Saint Paul-Outside-the-Walls. Many of us would never meet again, but our hearts would be forever united by the mission that had been entrusted to us.

The coordinators of communities, regions and countries had the privilege of a last word from Jean: "Yes, as in Lourdes, there has been the manifestation of God's protection. In the heart of each one of us there is a cry of thanksgiving for the wonders to which we have been witnesses."

When leaving Rome, I had in mind all that we had lived, that Virgilio Levi summarized so well in his article in the *Osservatore Romano*[1] about these three days:

It seemed like things from another epoch; it might not even seem real. But those who have seen and heard all these things cannot doubt its authenticity. They happened in a world run amok and in which joy cannot be attained by other means. Faith and Light is not a movement that imposes itself by the number of its members: a handful of men or women, boys or girls, people in perfect health and others, more or less seriously limited in their intellectual and physical capacities. However, it makes one think of the bit of yeast that a woman mixes with the flour, or of the mustard seed that becomes a tree where the birds build their nest. It is the continuation of the Gospel; it is a work of God and God uses it to repeat to those who want to listen: "You are all in my heart."

---

1. The Roman Observer – a Catholic daily newspaper with extensive coverage of the Vatican - Translator note

CHAPTER 9

Within the Community: The Joy of Meeting

Barely two months after the pilgrimage to Rome, there was an international meeting in Versailles, from January 10-11, 1976. Wrapped again by the Holy Spirit with new strength, we were no longer the same. We had been deeply impacted by this plunge to the roots of the Church, as part of the Holy Year itself. We gave thanks for the protection that God, once more, had shown us.

Tensions and opposition were always present. They were part of our history and part of the times themselves. These continued over the course of many years, diminishing here and there, remaining stronger in other areas. But we were accustomed to this and at peace, certain that time and the desire of our hearts would do their work.

In 1975 we also had to take into account the social and political context, and especially the law on abortion, which had just passed[1]. This law decriminalized the elimination of the infant in its mother's womb, up to the day before birth, if the child was discovered to have a disability. Facing this frightening discrimination, we felt it our duty to witness to the beauty of all human life and the need to support parents confronted with the great trial of their child's handicap.

---

1. In France – Translator note

At the heart of Faith and Light, the community

From then on, communities really started to exist. Their members were more engaged, the gatherings more regular, new groups were born. However, while emerging from our adolescence, we still lived a time of trial and error. Some communities disappeared. Others continued to be fragile: they had an insufficient number of members, or, on the contrary, too many to allow true community life, where each one can be attentive to the other. This was the case in Belgium, Canada and France, where communities sometimes had a hundred or more members, when the ideal number is between twenty and thirty. In other cases, certain groups consisted only of parents with their children; in those cases we could feel how much friends, with their dynamism and creativity, were missed. In other groups, the young people, in equal numbers with persons with disabilities, met without any family members, and their activities were more similar to a leisure club than a meeting where we share around and with the most fragile. This might be a valuable initiative, but was it Faith and Light? *A fortiori*, if there were no persons with intellectual disabilities, the community lost its reason to exist.

In some cases, the spiritual and religious dimension of the communities was also questioned.

At those times it was necessary to remember our roots: Faith and Light was born out of a pilgrimage, in response to the spiritual thirst of parents and their children with disabilities. We could not wipe out this spiritual aspect, inseparable from the very existence of the movement. This does not mean closing the door. In the initial Faith and Light pilgrimage to Lourdes, there were people who were not practicing their faith and there were non-believers. They were welcome in Faith and Light communities. Deeply rooted in the Gospels, the communities are largely open to those who love its spirit, its ambience and its desire to weave bonds of friendship with persons who are fragile.

It was also necessary to specify the scope of the possible initiatives that a community could take in the name of Faith and Light. In the "mission letter" of 1971, which we mentioned before, Jean Vanier had encouraged creativity and the launching of very diverse activities. It was normal that some took this literally and that gave rise to all sorts of projects. For example: a little school in Peru, prayer groups in the United States; in France, the creation of a house to welcome parents and their children during vacations... But it was soon clear that such projects were beyond the limited resources of our small Faith and Light teams.

That is how we discovered what we should not do, because it was not our vocation: the creation or administration of establishments, homes, schools, workshops, vacation homes...

The mistakes, the failures, the needs, the fragilities of certain communities, as well as the positive initiatives and their fruits all helped us to discover and to deepen what constituted the essential of a Faith and Light community. We came to see its marvelous secret, its power to make pearls burst forth, such as the question from Anne, a young lady with disabilities: "Mommy, do you remember how we lived before we had Faith and Light?" Or the affirmation of Denis: "Before Faith and Light, I only wanted to die." And also from Flora: "Why did I come to Faith and Light? Because of the emptiness of my dried up heart. Why did I stay? Because of Carlos, who asked me: 'So, when are you coming back?'"

What we were discovering, we needed to put clearly on paper. For this, we began the work of writing a Charter to specifically state what the movement was: its inspiration, its vocation, its members, its activities. And we needed a Constitution to define its organization and its structures. The Constitution was like the skeleton of the movement; the Charter was its heart and soul, one inseparable from the other.

Instead of presenting these two documents, I would like to tell how they are concretely applied in a community, making frequent reference to the community to which I belong, the community Notre-Dame du Magnificat[1]. It is not perfect, but it is unique, as each of the one thousand and six hundred other communities in the world is, and it is a reflection of what we live in Faith and Light.

Above all else, the meeting

In contrast with l'Arche, where people live together in the same home, the Faith and Light community is a community that meets regularly. The essential is not "to do things". The director of the charitable association in Rome had reason when he exclaimed: "You do nothing: no schools, no workshops, no leisure activities, not even catechetical activities![2]" In the hundreds of years before us, many religious orders were created to serve needy persons and this was absolutely indispensable. In Faith and Light, we are called simply to weave bonds of friendship and of communion between one another. We have sealed a covenant between persons with disabilities, parents, brothers, sisters, friends, and chaplains.

If persons with disabilities are the heart of the movement, their *parents* occupy a place nearly as essential. So different from one another by culture, their place in society, their reactions in relation to their child with disabilities…, however they have a very profound bond in common, the experience in their own flesh of one of the most poignant sufferings there is, the disability of their child. The tears of a French mother are the same as those of a Russian or Peruvian mother; it is the same for the hearts of the

1. Each community chooses its own name.

2. See the prologue – Translator note

fathers. The little hope that Faith and Light awakens in them is frequently very similar. As a mother from Honduras said: "My life is the same, yet everything has changed. My son is loved. For me, it is no longer a black hole, but a tunnel. At least one Sunday a month, the sun shines for us."

Our meetings, at least monthly, are indispensable times during which the community is formed, nourished and grows in love.

The booklet of the "Guidelines" helps us. Prepared by a different international team each year, it proposes an annual theme, usually centered in the Gospels, such as "The Life in Nazareth", "The Friends of Jesus"...This theme is divided into twelve sections, one for each month, each of which suggests: mimes, questions for sharing groups, ideas for organizing an artist's workshop[1], games, a prayer... Each country and each community adapts the suggestions to its own culture and needs. The Guidelines is a very strong link that unites all the communities all over the world in the same reflection and spirituality. Many communities meet on Saturday or Sunday, which facilitates participation in the parish's Sunday Mass. Others, like ours, meet on a weekday evening, because it is the only possibility for the majority of its members. Time is more limited, the rhythm is very rapid, but we are together, and this is most important.

The meeting consists of three parts that are not rigid: the time of welcome and sharing, the time of prayer, and the time of a meal and celebration. And the meeting is extended by a fourth time, the time of fidelity. These parts are inspired by the life of the first Christian communities, forming, as Saint Luke says, only one heart and only one soul: "The members devoted themselves to the teaching of the apostles, to fraternal communion, to the breaking of the bread and the prayers. They broke the bread with

---

1. An activity that helps less verbal members to express themselves, share and participate through art. – Translator note

joy and simplicity of heart. They praised God. They helped one another and were attentive to the needs of each one[1]."

Welcoming one another

Welcoming plays an important role. For myself, when I arrive in the community at the end of the afternoon, I am tired and tense, and the smile and the notice of each one casts all the weight of the day far away. Thanks to Emmanuel, Isabelle, Patrick, and so many others whose charism is welcoming, we are introduced into another world. Everyone gives a little attention to the others, the chairs are arranged in a circle, a little further away the tables are set up for the meal. We feel that we are expected.

The song, started by Alain, the community coordinator, or a dance marks the "official" beginning of the meeting. We take our place in the circle, always ready to be enlarged by someone's late arrival. The community is a family where all know each other's first name. This is not so easy when we are about thirty persons. A little game helps us to remember them all and brings joy to the person who is named and recognized.

Then we proceed to the "weather report.[2]" We give news of those who are absent. Each person can express whatever, big or small, they have experienced recently: Blaise lost his dog, Delphine might move, François and Mireille, a young couple of friends are pregnant, Sylvain is sad and angry because a "guy" in the CAT[3] called him "mongoloid". Alain announces important things of the life of Faith and Light in France or in other countries.

---

1. Acts of the Apostles 2: 42-47

2. An opportunity for each one to tell what is new in their life or to say something about how he or she is. – Translator note

3. Centre d'aide par le travail (Sheltered workshop).

A word to share

In general, after this time of welcoming, it is time to listen to the Word of God. Today, Alain leads this part. He has read and reflected on the text suggested in the Guidelines and he presents its essence in very simple words. Tonight it is the parable of the Good Samaritan. Father Franco, the Parish Pastor and our chaplain, makes comments about the story, asks questions and we also ask him questions. We are not shy. Then we create a mime of the text. This is not theatre and we are not actors; we only want to relive the Gospel, this true story. We assign the roles being very attentive that no one is left out. Blaise, who has a disability, is the traveler. A father, Louis, is the Good Samaritan, accompanied by Arnaud, as the donkey! It is also necessary to choose a priest, a Levite, the bandits, the hotel owner and all his staff. No need for complicated costumes. It is enough to have one prop, a scarf, a walking stick, a hood, a white apron, a traveling sack, a backpack...

We run through a brief rehearsal then, the moment has arrived, we remind ourselves once more that we are not going to "act a part," but to "live" a word of Jesus that he asks us to take as an example. Celine is chosen to read the words from the Bible. Paying attention to what is unfolding in the scene, she gently prompts those who might have made a mistake. There is often the unexpected, and laughter, but it does not matter, the heart is touched. We will remember what happened and the word of Jesus: "You also do the same thing that this Good Samaritan did."

The small groups

What impact can this Gospel passage have in our lives? The small sharing groups of five to seven members are more or less spontaneously determined, if possible having one person from the coordinating team[1]. In a small group, each one can express himself or herself more freely, according to his or her heart's desire. Sometimes there is an inspired word, as this exchange one day when we asked Vincent:

"What can we say to Jesus?"

"Jesus."

"Yes, but then what?"

"Jesus, Jesus, Jesus!"

This is simply the cry of his heart, because "it is in the mouths of children, the little ones, that you have prepared perfect praise[2]."

Today, three questions were proposed to us: In this Gospel story, what has touched me the most? Have I ever met a Good Samaritan? Can I be a Good Samaritan?

The first question helps us to be certain that the core message was understood by all and perhaps gives an opportunity to repeat it in even simpler words. Regarding the Good Samaritan, each one remembers a person who has come to help in a difficult moment; then according to our abilities or inspiration, we write this name on a little card, we make the name with modeling dough or we mime the name and give thanks for the person. The call to be a Good Samaritan encourages us to step out of our egoism to care for someone else. "It is not easy", said Jocelyne, "but afterwards we are happier." By sharing, we become more aware of each one's difficulties, the circumstances of their life, their pains, their joys... The simplicity and truthfulness of the weakest ones invite

---

1. The coordinating team is a group of four to eight persons, with at least one parent, one friend, the chaplain (priest or pastoral minister) and as much as possible a person with an intellectual disability. The team meets between the community gatherings to plan the animation of the monthly meeting and other activities for the year. It watches over the unity of the community and the unique place of each member.

2. Psalm 8: 2

all of us to strip away our façade. That evening, Dominique and his sister Nathalie were in the same group. Dominique speaks very little, but he was immediately able to recognize the Good Samaritan in his life, his sister Nathalie. He got up and went to hug her. Bernard, a father, in his turn recognizes: "For me, when I come back home from work in the evening, I only want one thing, to sit in front of the TV and to close myself in my own bubble."

In communities of families with small children, parents often prefer to meet in the same small sharing group every month, sometimes with some friends and the chaplain. For some, daily life is so heavy, so overwhelming, that the theme proposed may seem very removed from their worries. We take time to share about their real concerns. To talk is healing. To listen to the other members of the group helps them to get out of themselves. A mom mentions the unexpected smile of her child. A father was touched by the kindness of the gas station attendant who noticed his little daughter with disabilities in the car. In this cordial environment, a wife can hear what her husband says – something that he had never spoken about before. A mother with two children with disabilities, shares about how deeply she suffers when she considers that she will never be a grandmother. This type of sharing does not call for a response, but a reverent silence that understands. A word from the chaplain awakens a little hope so that we can continue to make our way through the whole month, keeping us united.

Community prayer

The "prayer corner" is prepared with care. An icon or a statue of Mary, candles, flowers, Simeon's flute, a meditative chant, invite us to turn towards God. Jesus has assured us that when two or three gather in his name, he will be in our midst. This is even truer when the whole community enters silence to pray. With very simple words, as children talking to their Father, we say the four basic words of everyday: "I love you", "thanks", "pardon", "please". Tonight we particularly say thank you to God for the Good Samaritan that He placed one day along our way. In procession, each one places the name of their Good Samaritan in a basket at the base of the prayer corner and proclaims this name out loud while the community acknowledges it with a refrain of thanksgiving.

Many communities also choose to dedicate some time to the "prayer of the poor person", that Father Joseph, our international chaplain[1], introduced all over the world. It is the prayer of those who are not able to think well, but are able to love. It is also the prayer of those who want to get rid of all that clutters their life, and become very little before God. Therefore, with hands open on the knees, eyes closed, we simply "be with God". From time to time we speak a word of love: "I love you", "You are in my heart", "I am here for you". A peace, a silence descends over the group, interrupted by the surprise of Beatrice: "I do not know how to pray, we say nothing, and I am not bored!" It is true. We discover that God is there and that His joy is to abide in the hiddenness of our heart. In this way, community prayer can teach us personal prayer.

Everyone to the table!

In our community, we have a meal at the end of the meeting: the food is taken from our bags, the plates set on a beautiful table. Whatever it is, it is a moment of relaxation and unity. In the Gospels, Jesus' love and friendship are manifested very frequently

---

1. Fr. Joseph Larsen was International Chaplain 1994-2006 – Translator note

during a meal. He accomplished his first miracle at the wedding feast in Cana. He accepted the invitation of the Pharisees. He loved gathering for a meal at his friends' home in Bethany. There is also that extraordinary "picnic" of the multiplication of the bread and fish, enjoyed on the green spring grass. And there is the very moving last supper with his disciples where he gives himself as nourishment in the Eucharist.

For our meals, Jesus indicates whom to invite: "When you give a feast, invite the poor, the crippled, the lame, the blind; and you will be happy[1]." No doubt, it is because they are there, that there is so much happiness at our Faith and Light meals.

All over the world we quickly discovered how important it is for community life to share the same food, no matter how frugal it might be: potatoes in Poland, crackers and bananas in Rwanda, *pasta* in Italy, oranges in the Dominican Republic, a cup of tea with rye bread in Russia, fries and sausages in France… The blessing whets the appetite. One blessing is particularly appreciated, because we sing it with gestures and it finishes by holding the hands of those beside us, and lifting our hands very high, towards heaven. The text is very simple: "Our five loaves of bread and our two fish, Lord, we offer to you. Multiply them for the hunger of mankind, and together may we sing your name."

Dessert is the much-anticipated moment when we celebrate birthdays[2]. For a brief moment during the year, each one becomes the center of attention. After he or she has blown out the candles on the cake, we celebrate, we sing, we give thanks for his or her presence. Different communities have different traditions, but birthdays are always a special time.

---

1. Luke 14:13

2. Since the meetings are usually monthly, we celebrate together the birthdays of all the members who were born in that month.

Finally, the time comes to say good-bye. Joy might be mixed with a kind of sadness if not for the hope of the fourth time, the time of fidelity.

The time of fidelity

In fact, the community meeting represents only a few hours per month, too few for some. How to maintain the "light" during all the time that passes between two monthly meetings?

First of all, before leaving each other, we frequently exchange a sort of "viaticum," a sign to accompany us during the whole month. I particularly remember the year with the theme: "Ten Words of God for Happiness." Didier's mother had made what we called little "sacks of happiness." Each person had one. At the end of each meeting, we would slip the "treasure" that we had just made or that was offered to us into the sack: a figure for the Nativity Scene, a candle for our prayer corner, a small cross made during the artist's workshop[1], a paper that was drawn by lots before summer vacation with the name of one person in the community, to invite us to journey with that person, in our heart, while we take a break from our monthly gatherings.

Creative expressions of friendship also keep the flame burning. They show us that we are not alone: a phone call, an email, a postcard, a little meal, a movie together, a helping hand, babysitting a child, etc.

Some communities suggest a more explicit connection between meetings and form small groups of five or six persons who carefully maintain spiritual contact among themselves.

---

1. The artist's workshop, which is implemented in the small sharing groups, is particularly appreciated by those who cannot speak.

There is also the Guidelines booklet, which is given to the members of the community to help keep them connected between meetings. Persons with disabilities are happy to page through them, to remember what was lived during the previous meeting and to find one very concrete idea for each day of the month.

A call to grow

Faith and Light communities call us to grow. Persons with disabilities help all of us, with or without disabilities, to move from egocentrism to the gift of self, from the feeling of guilt to the recognition of our limits, our weaknesses, our vulnerability. They help us to discover, by experiencing it, that we all have need of one another. Then our hearts are transformed, divisions disappear, ghettos are thrown open.

It was like this for Victor. When he came to the community for the first time with his mother, he was obsessed with his picnic bag. It took the combined efforts of his mother and two young friends to keep him from devouring everything before the time of the meal. Whenever his mother brought up Faith and Light, "picnic" inevitably came to his mind. He stayed in this stage for a while, until the day when his mother said "Faith and Light" and he uttered the word "friend". And on another occasion, amazingly enough for his mother when, talking to him about the community, she heard him answer: "Jesus."

Picnic, friend, Jesus… What a journey!

I would like to talk about Martial. When he arrived in the community, he had intellectual disabilities and psychiatric difficulties with a paranoid tendency. He was taciturn and wanted to be alone. In the circle, he ostensibly pushed his chair backwards, manifesting his desire to remain outside the group. He usually refused any food. Sometimes he asked to speak, railing against the wickedness of humanity, while always claiming his faith in God. Imperceptibly he became calmer. He agreed to sit at a corner of the table and snack. During a gathering just before Christmas, everyone was happily describing how he or she would celebrate the holiday. At that moment, Martial declared with sadness: "You will all be with family, I will be all alone in my room." So, Émile, a young friend, said to him: "If you want, I invite you for Christmas." Suddenly his aggression and isolation were broken. Little by little, he became closer to several persons. Now, when he asks to speak, it is often to wonder and be astonished that Faith and Light exists. Recently, he made a plea that one day the president of the Republic recognize his merits and those of Faith and Light, "which should exist everywhere in the world". Martial has not been healed from all his wounds and without doubt he will never be in this life, but he now has a little light in his life. He speaks of Faith and Light to whomever is willing to listen.

It happens that we have had some negative experiences and we need to be aware of our limitations in welcoming persons with very serious psychiatric problems.

This is how it was with Diwan, ten years old, who had very disturbed, violent behavior. It was necessary, though it was deeply painful, to make the decision to remove him from the community the day that he attacked a terrified little girl with Down syndrome in an unexpected and brutal way. We took care to suggest other resources to his parents.

Walls of division fall

In "normal life" there are few chances to be side by side and become friends when we belong to very different social milieus. This was the case for Simone and Yvonne who lived in nearly opposite realities and whose hearts were expanded.

Simone lived in Paris, enclosed in a minuscule apartment of two "rooms" with her son Philippe, blind, with epilepsy and a profound intellectual disability. In the evenings she worked in the concert hall, Pleyel. Yvonne, mother of five children, regularly went to concerts with her daughter Constance, who had Down syndrome and who appreciated music very much.

Their meeting took place in the gathering space of the concert hall. Simone dared to talk to Yvonne about Philippe, who was much more severely disabled than her daughter. Simone shared with her about her husband's abandonment, the daily struggles, Philippe's outings in a baby carriage until she got a wheelchair. She also spoke of the words of pity or the gestures of rejection. Just that day, when leaving the train station in a terrible downpour, waiting in the priority line for taxis, a woman cut in front of Simone to take her place, hurling these words at her: "Your 'defective' means nothing to me!" Or when a member of her family asked her why she sacrificed herself for "a piece of trash"! And she added: "I have the opportunity not to revolt, but to feel sorry for them. They were not bad people, and if I did not have Philippe, how would I look at children like these?"

Yvonne, the leader of Faith and Light for Ille-de-France, was shaken. She proposed to Simone to participate with Philippe in the first pilgrimage to Lourdes. This was the first great happiness of her life. For the first time, it was not pity that people had towards her son, but love. Friends who loved him and who let themselves be loved by him, and who helped even in the most unpleasant tasks. Thirty years later, the pilgrimage song still made Philippe smile.

The young friends who frequently came to visit in their tiny apartment found it to be an oasis. Simone, who became a community coordinator, could say: "Thanks to Yvonne and to Faith and Light, Philippe and I were spoiled for life."

The importance of the fathers

Some words about fathers. The birth of a child with disabilities is for them a suffering as deep as their wife's, but it is expressed in a different way. Their shame frequently prevents them from talking about it. Physically less close to the little one, they may have the temptation to become distant or even to flee from their home. Others have a tendency of demanding too much from their child. It is necessary, at all costs, that the child makes progress, learns, "makes it". And then there are those who have understood the profound call of their child, his or her vital need for an atmosphere of peace that is born from the unity of the parents, from their mutual love, something as important as daily milk and bread. The child thirsts for the affection of his or her father, of his encouragement, of his trust. When they accept to open the doors to Faith and Light, it frequently indicates a new step in the fathers' lives. It was a radical one for Francesco[1] and, in a completely different way, a total revelation for Antoine.

Antoine, a CEO, refused to come to the community in spite of the insistence of his wife and, even more so, of Bénédicte, their daughter with disabilities. He was very happy to take them by car and to pass by to pick them up at the end of the meeting: "Do not ask me again." But it happened that one day – it was the meeting before Christmas – a re-living of the Nativity was planned. Very naturally, the "boss" lent a hand to get the materials out of the car and into the place of the celebration. A group of young friends, in charge of preparing the Christmas mime, unaware of his lofty position, asked him:

"We do not have anyone to be the donkey in the Nativity Scene. Would you like to be the donkey?"

---

1. See Prologue

"No, I have never done this, and I would not know how to do it."

"It is very easy. Just get down on all fours; we will place a brown cloth over your back and all you have to do it to walk beside Mary and Joseph."

Bénédicte then exclaimed: "Yes, Daddy, it will be so good!" He let himself be swayed. As he tells it: "This was a great moment in my life when I found myself on all fours, with Bénédicte as a jubilant lamb trotting by my side." This first meeting with Faith and Light was the first of countless others. Since that day, having become simply "Antoine", he finds pleasure in helping other fathers whose difficulties he understands so well.

Long live the friends!

Without friends, especially young people, Faith and Light would not have been born and spread throughout the world as it did. Equally true, thanks to Faith and Light many youth who searched for a better world found meaning for their lives. Many who were attracted by the Gospel but rejected the Church have discovered that these are united. They experienced the words of Frédéric Ozanam[1]: "Become a friend of the poor, become the friend of one poor person. There you will find Jesus."

Young people today are very different from those of 1980. In western countries (with the exception of countries of the Middle East, Africa, South America, etc.) it is very difficult to reach them. Much more than before, they are afraid of commitments. However, they remain the hope of the world, of the Church, of Faith and Light. And they are out there because we have found

---

1. A nineteenth century French scholar and activist who co-founded the St. Vincent de Paul Society – Translator note

many. When they are present, when we trust them, when we give them some responsibility, they are "geniuses" in tact and dynamism. Many young people can say like Yvan: "Faith and Light has made all the difference in my dead-end life. I do not understand how the simplicity of the heart of the persons with disabilities, their friendship, has touched my heart so deeply." Never stop calling young people.

We also discovered how precious is the friendship of families who do not have children with disabilities. This is a reciprocal gift, source of balance and serenity, source of openness to differences and of the natural awakening of the heart toward persons who suffer.

Pierre and Blandine were engaged. The whole community was invited to the wedding. You can imagine everyone's great joy at this ceremony! At the Mass, after the mutual declaration of consent, we saw Isabelle advancing down the main aisle carrying the rings, filled with emotion and pride to have been entrusted with this responsibility by Pierre and Blandine. The assembly was touched and surprised. Later, the young couple explained that they came to Faith and Light to be useful, to do good. The situation was reversed. "Isabelle, with her luminous look and her smile that expresses: "I am so happy to be with you", made us discover an unexpected friendship. Through her, we heard Jesus tell us: "I do not call you servants, but friends." Today, in Lyon, Blandine and Pierre – parents of Paul, four years old, and Madeleine, two years old – are leaders of a Faith and Light community of families with young children, and are laying the foundation for a second group.

Personally, as a friend, Véronique has helped me very much, by her intuition and sensitivity to the pain of others, by her desire of reliving it and by her faith. I was about to leave for India and Australia and I felt overwhelmed by these two missions. But in the community, I talked about this trip joyfully. Véronique perceived my anguish: "Marie-Hélène, don't worry. I offer your trip up for you. You will not be alone. I offer you the angels and the saints and the Holy Virgin, you will see..." Her words re-awoke my trust, and during that whole long and arduous journey I did not feel alone!

And brothers and sisters?

To have a brother or a sister with a disability is never a neutral experience, and it is rarely easy. That is why it seemed essential to us from the beginning that brothers and sisters of a person with disabilities find, if they so desire, a special place in the community. A place that makes it possible for them to discover that others can love their brother or sister as he or she is, but also a place to express what they have to say (including when they've reached their limit!). One example among many others is that of Henri and Nadège.

Henri recounts that for a long time he had the least possible amount of contact with Nadège, his sister with disabilities, because he couldn't stand her presence. He remembers:

"One day, Mom, over-tired, asked me to pick Nadège up at a Faith and Light summer camp. I grudgingly complied, while promising myself that this would be done as quickly as possible. When I arrived, I found about fifteen young people, half of them with disabilities. Everybody welcomed me in a spirit of joy: 'Will you stay for supper?' How could I refuse? 'Will you stay overnight?' I stayed. I was very amazed by Nadège's joy and by how the friends looked at her. She was no longer a person with disabilities; she was Nadège. When she climbed into the car, she was no longer a beaten dog but a happy young lady, she was my sister. And I became a friend; I even became a community coordinator!"

Something I hadn't learned in the seminary

In our community, one of our chaplains, Father Jacques, when he was about to leave for another parish, confided to us how much the community and meeting with people with disabilities had clarified his priesthood. "In the seminary, they taught me that it is necessary to love, serve, give oneself and this is what I was trying to do everyday. In Faith and Light, I learned something equally as important and perhaps more difficult. I have learned to let myself be loved and to receive. Nowhere else have I been hugged, and received attention, care and affection. I never heard people talking so simply about Jesus as someone so close to us."

And then, there are the members we no longer can see, those who are in heaven. Their names are no longer written in the roster of members, but they are so close.

I see again the faces of so many of our community who have already left us: the first, Marie-Odile, who had a mild disability and was a big sister to many. Recently, it was Annie, Marie-Claire's mother; Dominique, Nathalie's brother; Louis, Bruno's dad. Moments of deep sorrow, sometimes anguish, but also of unity and communion around those who are more directly and painfully touched by their parting. With the aging of many communities, we are more and more often confronted by this mysterious trial.

Alice, that young woman who was the first to awaken my heart to the suffering of persons with disabilities, had a very simple faith in the communion of saints, this "intimate, constant, joyful, refreshing union of those who are gone and those who remain[1]". To console Josette at the death of her father, Alice wrote to her: "You see, I find that our dead are always with us. We do not see them, but they see us." She called out to her parents in

---

1. Paul VI.

difficult moments, like when she was crossing the street: "Daddy, Mommy, give me your hand."

While the world has difficulty bearing the idea of death, I think that our brothers and sisters with disabilities have a special vocation to help us to live it, with their very simple faith and their certitude of the mysterious presence of those who remain so close and whom we love to name and call upon. When, in our turn, we enter Life forever, they will be the ones welcoming us. Spontaneously, I think of Chicca, Sophie, Thadée, Philippe, Véronique, Clémence, Emmanuel[1] and so many others, whom we will discover in the light of God. We will finally understand the hidden meaning of their lives and see all the fruit that their lives have born.

A treasure to hand on

We would like so much to share the "treasures" that we have found in the community with those around us. How to do this?

It happens very naturally without us thinking much about it. In our community, we invite many people to simply come… to see: "Come and you will see". Persons with disabilities invite residents from their homes or co-workers. One young couple brings another. Now they are several, two couples with their little ones. Some people will just pass through, but they carry with them a picture of what Faith and Light is. Others stay. In this way, the community grows.

When we get to about forty members at a meeting, interpersonal relationships become more difficult. It becomes necessary to look toward the future with the Faith and Light

---

1. Gilles Delaunet, *Emmanuel, mystère d'amour (Emmanuel, Mystery of Love)* Éditions Traditions monastiques, 2001.

leader who accompanies the community. In our history, we have been led to give birth to a new community, to designate a team of community members who feel called to support its beginnings, and to send reinforcements to a community that has become too weak or too small. If we do not give life to others, we risk drying up...

But to leave one's community to start or assist another one involves suffering, sacrifices and joys. Once we have forged tight bonds among ourselves, it is sometimes difficult to convince the members of the community of the merits of the project, of the graces that come with giving life to another community or in supporting another community. Resistance is normal. It is very understandable, and we need time and patience to overcome it. It also requires time and assistance: to find and raise awareness in a new parish to the evangelical presence of the weakest, to find an interim coordinator, to establish the first coordinating team... Often, this is truly arduous. Nevertheless, when the new group meets for the first time, we forget all the suffering, in the joy of birth.

A new community can also be born at the insistence of one person who opens the way. Marie-Agnès, an adult with Down syndrome, was a faithful and passionate member of her community. When her family moved, she did not rest until there was a new community in her new parish. She personally went to visit the pastor, and pestered her parents to get involved in the project, although they thought it was preferable to give their daughter freedom to act on her own. Marie-Agnès talked about the project everywhere, announced it during Sunday Mass, inviting the parishioners to meet afterwards for more information. This community sails on today many years later.

In another case, it was the loneliness of a young mother coming from Argentina and of her very little daughter with profound disabilities, found in the street, that was the origin of another group.

Likewise I think of one young priest, recently named to a parish, who decided that his first project would be to create a Faith and Light community. It would be the sign of evangelical priority. "We need to take Jesus' word literally when he says to invite the poor to the feast."

To give and to receive life

The community is not a cloister, it is connected with many other communities in a mutual exchange of life: with the parish in which it is rooted, with the contemplative community with which it is paired, and with the international family of which it is a basic unit. It loves to take the road: on pilgrimage, to a weekend retreat, to a summer camp...

Inclusion in the parish and in the Church was one of the priorities of Faith and Light at its birth, and it continues to be so. Inclusion has been strongly encouraged by the successive popes and by more and more bishops. Certainly, Faith and Light has encountered a lack of encouragement in some dioceses or parishes. Our community is proud to be a shoot coming from the first Parisian community, to whom the pastor[1] opened the parish and his heart. This happened even before Cardinal Lustiger declared: "Persons with disabilities are not brought into the heart of the Church as if they were outside. On the contrary, they show us where its heart is."

Today, in Paris, all twenty communities have their chaplains, most of whom are parish priests. In our community, the chaplain

---

1. Father Adolphe Hardy, pastor of St. Francis Xavier Parish, who later became bishop of Beauvais

is the vicar of the parish and he established the link with the parish. The parish Sunday bulletin announces our monthly meetings. When we participate in the Sunday Mass, it is announced in the parish newsletter and the priest warmly mentions our presence. Some members of our community serve at Mass; others are invited to participate in the offertory procession.

A pastor in a rural area, who agreed to be the chaplain of a community, remarked: "In the eyes of many, welcoming the poorest is truly foolish, but it is the choice that Christ made. Persons with disabilities, by participating visibly and concretely in the parish Mass, and as much as possible, in other parochial activities, find themselves included in the Body of Christ, his Church. There they receive the living waters with which Jesus wants to fill us."

Like many others, our community is paired with a contemplative community. For us, it is a Carmelite community. This is an unexpected gift, a mutual gift. We receive their prayers. Work, family responsibilities, conflicts on all sides frequently push us to the edge of asphyxiation. It's as if the nuns supply us with an oxygen tank. They affirm: "You give flesh to our prayers; your visit revives them." At the beginning of our community gatherings each year we spend a day at the monastery, which includes a significant time with the sisters. We sing, we pray together. We entrust all to them. They tell us about the important events in their life, very regulated but centered on the gift of prayer. During the year, we keep connected through the Guidelines. We give them a phone call when something difficult happens. This gives us peace.

Retreat for everybody!

Some countries or regions organize weekends and retreats around the Word of God and prayer. It is a very privileged time to deepen spiritual life. Over the course of two or three days, or more, we step away from the world. We are frequently welcomed by a Foyer de Charité[1], in a semi-silent environment, a place that promotes a life of communion with Jesus. About thirty persons, half of them with a disability, and the other half consisting of friends and family members, gather to listen to the Word and for the sharing that follows, exchanges in small groups, workshops by themes, celebrations, time to relax. Paired two-by-two, we do not know anymore who accompanies whom; sometimes it is one, sometimes the other. Anyway, each of us discovers ourselves, before all else, as a seeker of God.

Maria Cecília was paired with Carlos, whose vocabulary was limited to about twenty words. When prayer time arrived, Maria Cecília was embarrassed: what would she do? How to help him pray? Carlos knew very well. After a moment of silence, he took her hand and pointed with the other to the tabernacle. "Jesus". Later, "Jesus loves me." After another little moment, taking her hand again: "Love you". Silence again. Finally, he places one arm around her shoulder: "We love."

For those who have not yet received the sacraments of Confirmation and Eucharist, some preparation can be offered to them. In Paris, Father Jacques Cuche, a parish priest who accompanies several communities, was naturally led to prepare persons with disabilities sometimes for Baptism, and more frequently for Confirmation and Eucharist. Those who participated cannot forget the joy recently, of celebrating the Confirmation of fourteen young persons with intellectual disabilities by Cardinal

---

1. Foyers of Charity - communities of men and women who live together following the example of the first Christians, sharing what they have: wealth, gifts and charisms. Its principal mission is to lead silent spiritual retreats. It was founded by Marthe Robin and Father Georges Finet. See: foyerofcharity. com - Translator Note

André Vingt-Trois. What a joyful outpouring of the Holy Spirit they radiate to all those around them!

Taking the road

Born and confirmed during pilgrimages, this activity is inscribed in the genes of Faith and Light. For two or three days, the community breaks with its habits and routines[1]. We place our hand in the hand of the weak person who leads us on a whole interior journey. Many communities pick up the "pilgrim's staff" every year. Some are included in their diocesan pilgrimage and sometimes are even invited by their bishop.

And then there are the summer camps that are frequently initiated by the young friends and sustained by the desire of the families. In certain countries, especially in those where there are very few activities available to persons with disabilities, there has been, and still are, many summer camps, for instance in Italy, Lebanon, Egypt, Poland... Today we might find summer camps everywhere.

When we form a small community that lives together for a few days, there are amazing fruits. I have an extraordinary memory of a summer camp in Abruzzo,[2] in Italy, where I participated for three or four days. I carry the memory of little Pablo, five or six years old, with a profound disability. He was little in my arms with his look of trust, tenderness, abandonment. Presence of God...

Finally, there is the "international family". The community does not sail off alone (I love very much the image of the boat to describe what we are). It is part of a fleet of several boats that

---

1. Pilgrimages can be organized by communities, provinces, countries...
2. A region in central Italy – Translator note

travel together, accompanied and supported by a leader. And this leader is linked to a provincial coordinating team that organizes meetings, formation sessions, pilgrimages, etc., building up in this way an extended family with whom we have direct contacts.

"Up Sails!" the international newsletter[1], was born in 2009 after the changes in our structures and the beginning of a new team. A new wind was blowing; the little Faith and Light boat put up its sails and set a course out into the deep! Renewal was palpable. From West to East, from North to South we had a thirst to know what was going on in the world.

Ghislain and Corinne[2] launched the first issue. It was an immediate success. The seven communities on tiny Rodrigues Island, or the one lost in the middle of the fields of Scotland found themselves reconnected with the world. From everywhere, we were able to discover a little about the communities in Madagascar, Korea, Taiwan or the Democratic Republic of Georgia. Even more, when a serious event occurs in the world, many messages pour in to ask about our brothers and sisters in that part of the world. "Were our friends in Japan directly touched by the tsunami? How could we help them?" Yes, Faith and Light International is more than ever a united family!

Very importantly, the "Announcing and Sharing Day" invites each community to carry the burdens of the others, not only in our hearts, but also by our financial contribution.

As I come to the end of this chapter, I am afraid that I have given a kind of idyllic vision of the community. As in all groups, all families, there are ups and downs. There are moments where everything goes well (with the risk of getting too comfortable).

---

1. Published in French, English and Spanish and online at www.faithandlight. org - Translator note
2. Ghislain du Chéné was the International Coordinator and Corinne Chatain was the General Secretary for Faith and Light at the time. – Translator note

There are moments of weariness, of discouragement or tensions that can degenerate into conflicts. However these can also become a step in truthfulness and of growth.

With its shadows and light, the community is made of all these connections, of these countless treasures: persons with disabilities, families, friends, the interlinked communities all over the world. It is impressive to see how activities that are really so simple and that give life (welcoming, reflecting on the Word and sharing, prayer, a meal, celebration) move us to go out to meet others. They give us the grace to receive as much and more than we have given (love, listening, concern for the other, peace…).

CHAPTER 10

Going out into the Deep (since 1981)

We never planned the growth of Faith and Light in the world. We have never told ourselves: why don't we keep an eye on this or that country where the movement already exists, or why don't we invest our efforts in this or that part of the world? However, Jean-Jacques, a member of my community, with Down syndrome and a serious visual disability, regularly asked me about the growth of Faith and Light in the world. The movement had transformed his life and he was obsessed with its expansion. Each week I had a phone call:

"Does Faith and Light exist in Greenland?"

"No, Jean-Jacques.

"Then, Marie-Hélène, I believe that you must begin it there."

The following week, it could be Chile or another country that he had heard people talking about on TV. His missionary zeal and his exhortations touched me.

Certainly, like him, since the first pilgrimage, we have deeply desired that Faith and Light grow, but we wanted to let ourselves be guided by God, who would continue to speak to us through events and meetings.

In the first years, this ardent desire to continue, without a pre-established plan, led to an increase in the number of members in communities, but not in the number of communities. Some were born, but others died. This led to stagnation. During the first ten years we stayed around three hundred communities. This is an estimate, because at the time we had not yet specified exactly what a Faith and Light community was and all the communities were not clearly identified[1].

A mysterious fruitfulness

Subsequently, in order to calculate Faith and Light's expansion, as a "measuring line" we used the data collected every ten years at the time of the big international pilgrimages. We tracked the number of communities and the number of countries. Here are some numbers. In 1981 there were three hundred communities in twenty-seven countries. From 1981 to 1991, there were one thousand communities in sixty countries (this means seven hundred new communities and thirty-three new countries in ten years). From 1991 to 2001, the growth continued, but at a slower pace. We reached one thousand and four hundred communities in seventy-three countries. In 2011, we counted one thousand and six hundred communities situated in eighty countries. After a pause in the quantitative expansion of Faith and Light, the movement is living a new "springtime" thanks to the application of its new constitution, bringing important renewal to its leadership teams. I will come back to this later on.

Parallel to the history of Faith and Light, it would be very interesting and useful to have an overview of the history of society and of the Church, with its social, political, economical, cultural, moral and religious aspects. It would also be interesting to see the gains and losses in the area of services for persons with disabilities and the evolution of how society views them. In all of this there

---

1. The first international directory was made in 1983.

are considerable differences depending on the different continents and countries.

Faith and Light is not outside the world. As any other movement, it benefits from any progress and suffers the consequences of whatever deteriorates or goes wrong. For example, in Haiti, the political problems, the violence and the natural cataclysms strongly shaped the life of our communities that were very alive until 2005. It is one of the poorest countries in the world, and the one that touched me the most by its capacity to break down barriers, including the one around race. When I was there, I was told that Faith and Light was the only association where this happened quite naturally. Nowhere else had I seen so much joy, simplicity and a spontaneous integration of Faith and Light into the culture. More recently, the political and social upheaval in Egypt and in Jordan made it necessary to cancel a big pilgrimage. In Sudan, the creation of two countries caused almost all the communities in the North to emigrate. Their members became scattered throughout South Sudan. In such a poor country, so turbulent, yet so determined, the movement must still be reconfigured. It is necessary to sow seeds again in North Sudan.

If the numbers describing the expansion of Faith and Light are sometimes instructive, they do not speak at all about the essential. Because it is not the number of communities, or the number of countries that is important, but the quality of what is lived: love, and growing in compassion. Saint John of the Cross said: "The smallest movement of pure love is more helpful to the Church than all words combined[1]." A very loving community even if very shaky, but truly desiring to be close to the fragile person, to grow in love, to meet one heart at a time, is more useful than many communities stuck in their routine. At the same time,

---

1. *Spiritual Canticles.*

certainly what God desires is many communities burning with life and charity.

A question that we often ask ourselves is, "How has the movement come in contact with new countries and continues to do so?" In the recent past, the words of Jean Vanier, spoken during retreats or in a series of conferences, have frequently moved a person or a team to act. It also happens that assistants from l'Arche, coming back to their own countries after an internship of some months or even just one week in a l'Arche community, have often had the desire to introduce at home what they have seen, heard and lived.

In other cases, it was the Faith and Light Welcome Center in Lourdes that inspired the movement to start, for example in Gibraltar, Burundi and Rwanda. And then, of course, there is word of mouth and those unpredictable meetings that can happen in a parish, during a retreat or on a pilgrimage.

Some persons have worked extraordinarily for the birth and growth of Faith and Light in a part of the world where their call to commit themselves was manifested in a very providential way. The history of Faith and Light is, in large part, the history of these pioneers who dared one day, sometimes contrary to all reason, to risk reaching out to families isolated because of the disability of their child. Though believing that they had come to give and to help, they discovered that they received a hundred times more by simply learning what love means... Having found a treasure, they have taken up their pilgrim staff to carry this treasure to others. Let us note that, even if they were the trailblazers, their first concern, as that of the pioneers of today, has always been to immediately set up a team.

I have already spoken of Mariangela and Francesco, but there have been many others, so many other wonderful persons, parents, friends, priests or religious persons, inspired by persons with disabilities, who have given themselves wholeheartedly so that Faith and Light might live and grow all over the world. It would be necessary to write a whole book about them... Their names are already written in the heart of God. May our names also be there!

Pioneer amid the bombs in Lebanon and in the Middle East

In Lebanon and in the Middle East everything started with Roland Tamraz, at the time a young student of economics. In 1977-1978, he spent eighteen months as an assistant in l'Arche in France. Before returning to his country, he confided to Jean Vanier his desire to begin l'Arche, and perhaps Faith and Light. Jean encouraged him. In 1981, in collaboration with Father Atallah and Father Labaki, he invited Jean and me for ten intense days of conferences and visits. A very moving stay. Lebanon was at war. Beirut was split in two, in the east the Christians, in the west the Muslims. We lived in the perpetual boom of cannons and rattle of automatic weapons fire. The beltway that made it possible to go from one side of the city to the other was one of the most dangerous places. Forced to take our chances and risk danger, we only met one other car there. The economic situation was very difficult. For Roland, there were "other risks": life sinking in despair, for young people and for families, especially for those who had a child with disabilities. All those we met had a thirst for spiritual renewal, for a meeting with Jesus. They longed for peace and the restoration of relationships between Christians and Muslims. In this desert, Faith and Light communities rose up as an extraordinary answer. As there was no special catechesis, it was the members of Faith and Light who very frequently prepared young people for the sacraments celebrated in their parish community.

Their bursting forth was exceptional. Three years after our visit, there were fifteen communities, filled with life and enthusiasm. There were great numbers of youth, as well as families, all very committed. The persons with disabilities blossomed in all their beauty. During the violent bombardments in the city of Zahlé, Jacqueline, the regional coordinator, was crying for two of her students who had been killed. Nadine, a young woman with disabilities, told her: "Do not cry, Jacqueline... We need to pray for those who bomb us."

It seemed as if nothing could stop Roland's dynamism. Since the Beirut airport had been shut down, the only possible way to go to Europe was by sea, with a night trip to Cyprus, then a one-day wait before taking the airplane. But for Roland, no time was wasted: on each trip, he multiplied contacts. Mary Kaatsolioudis had eight brothers and sisters, four of them with disabilities. Very quickly she worked for the creation of two communities. Roland's missionary spirit took him to Egypt (1981), Syria (1982), which was enemy territory[1] and also led him to Jordan and to Greece (1987). The communities were symbols of unity, not only in Lebanon, but also throughout the tumultuous Middle East. They served as symbols of unity among the Christian traditions, between Roman Catholics and Eastern Catholics. Some Muslims, at least in Lebanon, joined a community looking for a place of peace, joy and unity for their children and for their families.

At the international meeting in Wetherby, in England, in 1982, Roland was accompanied by Joseph, a Syrian and a father of a child with disabilities. They stayed together in one of the little cells that served as bedrooms. They were inseparable. It was a call to each one of us to be an artisan of peace in all the little acts that make up daily life, the only ones that can build universal peace!

---

1. Lebanon and Syria were at war – Translator note

Pioneer in the heart of materialism
in Poland and Eastern Europe

Of all the countries behind the "iron curtain," Poland was the first where Faith and Light was born. This is not surprising, since it was the only communist country where Catholics were able to go to the West and establish contacts with their brothers and sisters in faith.

Marcin Przeciszewski, a student, made a hitchhiking trip through France in the summer of 1978. His meeting with persons with intellectual disabilities, during his stay at l'Arche in Trosly-Breuil was a shock. He says that he underwent a type of inner healing. For the first time, he experienced friendship as a very powerful spiritual reality.

Upon returning to Warsaw, he started the first Faith and Light communities with some friends. They met in people's homes. Marcin relates:

"One day, while we were meeting, a van belonging to the Militia stopped in front of the house where we had gathered, probably following an anonymous report of an illegal meeting. The armed police burst into the room and asked for our identity cards. We, the 'normal persons,' panicked, while a boy with intellectual disabilities approached an officer and asked him: 'What is your name?' And then: 'Do you want to be my friend?' Hania threw herself on the neck of a policeman and asked him if he would come back to our meetings. The police were completely at a loss. The officer then gave the signal to leave. In an instant we were alone. A resounding 'alleluia' expressed our relief and our joy."

Six months later, in May 1978, two Faith and Light communities were born in Wroclaw, founded by Teresa Breza, mother of Josia, a young woman with intellectual disabilities. Teresa looked all over the city for a priest who would prepare her daughter for First Communion. All refused, arguing that these children did not understand anything about its meaning, and that it was necessary to submit to the requirements of the Church. Desperate, Teresa borrowed money and bought a plane ticket to France to look for examples of specialized catechisms in order to take them to Polish priests. In Paris, her path crossed mine. Besides catechesis, I talked to her about Faith and Light. She was won over, because the movement involved both families and young people. This is how Faith and Light communities were born in Wroclaw with families, and in Warsaw with young people. Teresa and Marcin met at the pilgrimage to Lourdes in 1981.

During the first Faith and Light pilgrimage in Poland to Czestochowa in 1983, Jean Vanier, in front of the miraculous icon of the Black Virgin, expressed the desire that "Faith and Light communities be born in Moscow". The Polish thought that Jean was an affable dreamer. However, three years later, Marcin, in contact with a young philosopher from Moscow, a former Marxist converted to Orthodox Christianity, was invited to go to Russia. On learning this, Jean Vanier asked Marcin to survey the possibility of a retreat that he could give in Moscow. When the idea became reality, Jean talked about fragile persons, poor and persecuted, who had a very particular mission in the world. Some weeks after this retreat the first community in Moscow was born.

At the same time, there were contacts in Czechoslovakia. Marcin described to us the meetings at the Polish-Czechoslovakian border at Sniezka, the highest point in the Sudetes Mountains: "The border was very heavily monitored, but there was one stretch of road, three kilometers long, that allowed tourists, as well as Poles and Czechs to meet. When the border guards turned away from us, we exchanged our backpacks. In the backpack I gave to the Czech friends were books by Jean Vanier, copies of *Ombres et Lumière* and other documents about Faith and Light." All of this was a source of inspiration for those who were starting up the movement in Prague or in Bratislava.

Pioneers all the way into the shantytowns in Latin America

In 1975 Maria Cecília de Freitas Cardoso, twenty years old, was a special education teacher in Brazil. When, by chance, she heard Jean Vanier talk about Faith and Light to a youth group (not the one that she belonged to), the idea immediately captivated her. Her job put her in touch with persons with intellectual disabilities and their families.

It took two years to lay the foundation for a community, born in May 1977 in Rio de Janeiro, with seven members with disabilities, two mothers and four young friends. With a gathering every two weeks, they alternated a meeting at the parish and an outing in the community such as visiting a museum, going to the beach, meeting at the home of a member... All this would always finish with a good time of prayer.

In June 1977 Maria Cecília came to France. She stayed a month and a half at l'Arche, then participated in a Faith and Light summer camp organized by the community of Grenoble in July-August. After this, Jean asked her to be the National Coordinator for Brazil, even if there was only one community. In fact, unknown to her, a second community was being formed in São Paulo.

Zilda Furtado from São Paulo, whose journey was very similar to Maria Cecília's, met Jean Vanier in Brazil in 1975. That year, when Jean visited her country, she was a catechist at a school for boys with intellectual disabilities. She was enthusiastic about the idea of getting parents involved in the preparation of their children for First Communion.

Nothing happened immediately, but Faith and Light remained in Zilda's heart. She spent one year at the *École de la Foi¹* in Fribourg (Switzerland), went to visit l'Arche and participated in several Faith and Light gatherings in France. When she went back to São Paulo in 1977 she began to lay the foundation for the community in São Paulo, with the support of Cardinal Arns.

When Maria Cecília and Zilda finally met, their friendship generated the very rapid growth of Faith and Light in Brazil. I visited their country several times. It was a joy to work with them, to give talks in the parishes, to meet the families. I admired Maria Cecília and Zilda for their trust and their love. Confirmed in their plan, they created communities in rich neighborhoods as well as in poor ones, and even in the favelas. Maria Cecília found a way to be invited everywhere, and talked about Faith and Light to youth groups, Teams of Our Lady², in seminaries, at wedding receptions. Her word particularly touched young people.

In 1983 she left Brazil to work on a doctorate in Special Education in the United States. Zilda was nominated Coordinator for Latin America and the Caribbean, thereby participating in the International Council. Zilda still vibrates with excitement when she remembers the extraordinary experience she lived: "We were thirteen persons, with Jean and Marie-Hélène, like a family. During a whole week every year, we lived all the unfolding of Faith and Light around the world. Unimaginable! What is Faith and Light for you? For me? Faith and Light is my life!"

Returning to Brazil in 1987, Maria Cecília was entrusted with national and international responsibilities. In 1996 she

1. *School of the Faith* – a Catholic program begun in 1969 to prepare people, through biblical studies, spirituality and community life, to spread the Gospel – Translator note

2. Teams of Our Lady: an international Catholic/Christian movement offering married couples mutual support and a way to live the gospel as a couple and as a family – Translator note

married Tim Buckley, who had lived six years in l'Arche. At their wedding, there was much joy, especially among the two hundred guests from Faith and Light and l'Arche. Tim and Maria Cecília made professional choices that made it possible for them to dedicate the better part of their time to Faith and Light. They were the first coordinators for the Continent of the Americas and members of the international formation team. Today, Maria Cecília summarizes her story in Faith and Light as a love story:

"For me, it was very easy to come to Faith and Light. It was a strong, very clear call from God, when I heard Jean's words in 1975. It was also very simple: some persons with certain disabilities and often very rejected, did not have any friends. They had the right to have friends! I said: 'Here I am, I want to be one of these friends. Jesus is there and leads us by the hand.' I have now been in Faith and Light for thirty-four years, a whole lifetime, and fifteen of those years with Tim. There has been an abundance of joy and certainly also difficult times, and conflicts. Sometimes we have lived them well, at other times we have made mistakes, but we keep each person in our hearts and we give thanks for this very abundant life. Magnificat!"

Pioneer even in the prisons of the Philippines and in Asia

Jean Vanier went to the Philippines for the first time in May 1984, invited by a young Filipino man, Chris, who had stayed several months as an assistant in l'Arche in Liverpool, England and who hoped to prepare the foundations for a l'Arche community in his country. At the end of his visit, Jean suggested that Chris start with Faith and Light instead.

Bella Feliciano, a young psychologist, mother of four children, led a prayer group, which included some Little Sisters of Jesus.

Her group was very touched by the words of Chris, whose life was transformed by his experience in l'Arche. Bella was particularly touched by the story of Eric, a young man with disabilities. "As I listened," said Bella, "my heart burned with the words of Isaiah: 'It is by his wounds that we are healed.'" As the whole group was very touched and interested, Chris explained that becoming friends with all the "Erics" in their neighborhood could be done very simply through a Faith and Light community. For six months the group had been praying to know what their mission might be. When Chris asked who wanted to participate in the launching of the first community, all gave their names.

Chris made it clear that it was necessary to have a "national correspondent," simply to write reports and to send them in. This would not take more than three hours each month! Bella accepted this role. She expanded it to a whole other dimension since, three years later, six communities had been born. It was at this moment that I went to the Philippines, in June 1987, for the Asia-Pacific Zone Meeting, "the impossible zone", as we called it at the time. It was so large, so spread out, so diverse but so beautiful. The leaders of India, Hong-Kong, Mauritius, Australia, New Zealand, Philippines, Japan and South Korea were invited. Their primary goal was to choose a coordinator for the zone. It was Bella who was elected.

Two priorities were entrusted to her: to accompany the older countries and see to the formation that they had not yet had and to help the younger countries, because the beginnings are very important to assure proper growth. Six years later, the zone had discovered its identity and a great cohesiveness. Two communities were born in Taiwan; Australia and New Zealand were ready to form another zone.

During our stay in Manila for a zone meeting, I was very touched by our experience in the large national prison, in the high security block reserved for those prisoners accused of the most serious crimes. Among them was Nonoy, condemned to death by a military tribunal, who had already been in prison for eight years. His wife Nellie was part of a Faith and Light community and of Bella's prayer group. With the help of the Little Sisters of Jesus, Nonoy organized Bible-sharing groups in the prison who carried in their prayer the Faith and Light community in Manila and the start of a new community, born within the prison itself. They heard that a zone meeting was going to take place in Manila and saw an opportunity to have a Faith and Light meeting in the high security block. The director of the prison accepted.

This was an unimaginable moment. We arrived, with heavy hearts, in front of this enormous building with massive doors. Two guards were waiting for us; one of them carried an impressive collection of keys. Each one of us had his or her personal "pass" that we had to show many, many times to the guards whose faces lit up at our arrival! Finally we arrived at the heart of the prison, a courtyard guarded in its four corners by heavily armed soldiers. There, a dozen prisoners waited for us, in their bright orange uniforms, ready for the meeting. They had helped to prepare and decorate the courtyard. Together, we enjoyed drinks and little sandwiches, which we also shared with the guards. We lived the meeting as we usually do. It is always incredible to see with what strength the charism of persons with disabilities makes all barriers fall. There were lots of songs and dances, including the bamboo dance, where Filipinos show their surprising agility. It was touching to see these prisoners moving harmoniously. Freedom, friendship and joy for a few hours. What a grace for us: this moment lived with men considered the lowest of the low and the worst in the eyes of the world, and in whose hearts the child with disabilities awoke the desire to welcome Faith and Light in their midst.

Pioneer feeling his way in Zimbabwe and southern Africa

Father David Harold Barry, an Irish Jesuit, welcomed Jean Vanier in Zimbabwe in November 1982. Father David knew him through l'Arche. But, as soon as he stepped into the village of Bulawayo, Jean started to talk about Faith and Light. In Harare, the capital, a first meeting took place at the home of Rem and Ann Fernandez who became the pillars from the beginning. "At the end of the meeting," Father David said, "we looked at each other with astonishment about what we had just discovered... It was literally like a treasure hidden in the field." Two communities were born, one in Bulawayo, the other in Harare. A small team went out to the villages to spread the message. The film of the pilgrimage, even more than words, was an extraordinary medium to "explain" Faith and Light. Teresa de Bertodano, the correspondent for the English-speaking communities of Africa, went more than once to support and accompany the group on its travels. She was so strong in her fragility. It was also astonishing to see her at the international meetings, when she appeared, very small, surrounded by three enormous African leaders from different countries in southern African.

In those years, before 1990, the movement grew considerably, all the way to Zambia. Links were created with Botswana where two communities were born thanks to Sister Elizabeth. Lesotho saw the birth of the beginnings of a community. In 1990 the work of Father David took him to Lubumbashi (in the Democratic Republic of Congo), where communities popped up like mushrooms, reaching a total of eighteen. At the meetings of that time, there were representatives of thirty to forty communities in a zone that stretched from Lubumbashi all the way to Cape Town. In 2002 there was a memorable pilgrimage in Zimbabwe: it was a historical landmark, its highpoint.

"In fact, in 2003", writes Father David, "when Jean came to visit us for the last time, there were warning signs of what was about to happen. In Zimbabwe and in the neighboring countries the honeymoon was over. A combination of economic difficulties, political uncertainty, and perhaps also lack of understanding in the communities resulted in a profound loss of commitment. There was a general collapse in Zambia. Repeated efforts to maintain the communities in Botswana failed and the contact with the Democratic Republic of Congo practically ceased, even if the communities continued to meet."

Meanwhile, during this very shadowy period, a small nucleus remained faithful and kept a light burning in South Africa and in Zimbabwe. It was a daily struggle. Since 2010, we can see some signs of rebirth. Contacts have been established with Zambia and in Zimbabwe; a small group of persons goes throughout the countries to remobilize older communities and to remind all of the values of Faith and Light. This has made possible the restarting of several communities and the arrival of new friends. Urged on by many who were able to participate in an international formation session in Alexandria (May 2010), a national session could be organized in Zimbabwe in spite of the huge difficulties that the country experiences. "Perhaps," said Father David, "the time has come for a second birth and we sustain ourselves with this message: 'Proclaim the Word urgently, in season and out of season[1].'"

Surrounded by faithful and very committed friends, Artkin, a zone coordinator from 1998 to 2007, wrote: "Faith and Light, is my life! The movement propelled me on a path of spiritual growth that I would never have known otherwise. The persons with disabilities have taught me what true love is. Today, I am happy in my community with Lillian, my wife, and our five sons."

Embers for tomorrow?

---

1. 2 Timothy 4: 1

Pioneer in post-communist Ukraine

Born in Canada, of Ukrainian immigrant parents, Zenia Kushpeta grew up among the diaspora of Toronto who had always dreamed of a free Ukraine. In the beginning of the 1980s, having an artistic temperament, she threw herself into a musical career. A teacher and a concert pianist, she gave the impression of being an accomplished person. In reality, Zenia was searching for the place where she could find meaning for her life. She pictured herself traveling far away as part of an international association, but found herself within the l'Arche community, Daybreak, close to Toronto, for a year. Meeting Rosie turned her life, in a radical way, upside down. Rosie had just joined l'Arche after spending many years in an institution. Most of the time she had been imprisoned on a little cot under a mosquito net found in the combination "living room-dormitory" that she shared with a dozen other children. She did not talk, she did not walk, she could not eat by herself and she continually cried out in pain.

One day, seeing Rosie sitting in the garden, Zenia came and sat down near her. Rosie seemed to be in a world of her own, unreachable. Little by little, a bond was formed between the two young women and Zenia discovered Rosie's courage as she bore her sufferings. Zenia was deeply touched by the authenticity and interior freedom of the young woman. They became friends. Rosie was the origin of Zenia's commitment with l'Arche, which lasted many years.

In 1991, with the fall of the Soviet Union, Ukraine gained independence. For the first time, Zenia was able to visit the country of her roots to try to contribute to its reconstruction after centuries of domination and more than seventy years of communist rule. Arriving in Lviv, Zenia was a shocked and grieved witness to the intolerable situation in which all the people lived – particularly persons with disabilities. The living conditions in the psychiatric hospitals and institutions were disastrous and tragic. Immediately Zenia knew that she had found her land and that she was called to share with the Ukrainian people what she had learned from Rosie during her years in l'Arche. The nearly destitute conditions in which she lived did not matter much to her. And, in January 1992, she was "missioned" by l'Arche-Daybreak to found the first Faith and Light communities in Ukraine.

The first years were filled with challenges. Persons with disabilities were relegated to the bottom of the social ladder: despised, ignored, rejected. If community life was to be possible, the people needed to learn to trust others, to live without fear, to accept responsibility...

With a group of young people, Zenia began to visit families. The first was Myron's family. Myron was a young man, twenty-five years old, who practically did not talk and who refused to look anyone in the eye. People had mocked him mercilessly! His family was invited, along with many others, to a parish for the first Faith and Light meeting. They could not understand the interest that was being shown to them. In the community, Myron began to smile, relax and make friends. He shared his love of music and dance with them. His simplicity, his transparency, and his big heart won over all who approached him.

Little by little, Faith and Light is developing in Ukraine. Today there are over thirty communities growing in more than fourteen cities. And, Faith and Light has prepared the soil for other initiatives. In 1993, Zenia created a specialized center for children with disabilities. In 2001, in the heart of the Catholic Ukrainian University, she launched a little Christian Office for Persons with Disabilities to promote a new way of seeing persons with disabilities in society and to provide management to five sheltered workshops for adults with intellectual disabilities. In 2008, these workshops became the foundation for the first l'Arche community in Ukraine.

When, in 2007, I was invited for the celebration of the anniversary of the movement, I was astounded by the vitality of the Faith and Light communities. I have never seen as many young people, so dynamic and so close to the persons with disabilities; parents amazed and delighted to see the new abilities of their child stimulated by all these friends. An unimaginable joy! We spent four days together on an old military base in an immense forest near Lviv. The commanding officer, a father of a child with disabilities, put the whole base and all its staff at our disposal._Everything seemed good to them, the meals based around potatoes, beets, cabbage, etc., and the large dormitories holding sixty people. Revealing extraordinary talents, a grand spectacle regrouped the five hundred participants into three military divisions. Instead of arriving with their aircraft carriers, their submarines or their tanks, each division presented its banner: love, peace, joy. Prophets for a new world, our brothers and sisters with disabilities were jubilant. "From their swords they have forged plowshares and from their spears, sickles. One nation will not draw their sword on another, nor will they train for war any more.[1]"

An unlikely pioneer in Argentina

Father Osvaldo Napoli deeply desired the birth of Faith and Light in Argentina, but he was very busy coordinating special catechesis and was not able to do more. Everything happened thanks to a priest who did not want to even hear about persons with intellectual disabilities!

Father Alberto Bochatey, a young Argentinian priest, had received permission from his religious congregation, the

---

1. Isaiah 2: 4

Augustinians, to do graduate studies in Moral Theology in Rome[1]. A few weeks after he arrived, the Father Prior of the house where he was lodging spoke to him about a group that was looking for a chaplain. They only had two meetings a month. Father Alberto was unenthusiastic, but still he was open to accept this request. When he learned that it was a group of persons with intellectual disabilities, he was overwhelmed.

He had come to Rome to meet wise and intelligent people and not to waste his time with little "imbeciles," as he told his Prior in no uncertain terms. So, without much tact, he gave a rather ambiguous and reticent response to Maria and Enrica (community coordinator and a friend in the community respectively), hoping, after all, that this would eventually discourage them. But they gently persisted in inviting him until the day when, both worn down and a bit ashamed, he responded that he would come just to celebrate Mass, but that he would leave immediately after because he needed to get back to his studies.

God waited for him in the persons of Marina, Raffaele, Roberta, Massimo, Cristina, and many others! They responded with smiles to his rather frozen face, and their hands caressed him with a simplicity that only children and siblings freely allow themselves. "I, the student and the professor, discovered myself simply as poor Alberto who did not understand anything, who had a 'disability'."

Father Alberto was not able to read the most hidden and most important page of his life: to discover this profound secret that God had entrusted to the "little ones", a secret that only they can reveal to us and that they have revealed to me.

During the Mass and the meeting, in which he finally participated, a light went on inside him: we cannot come to Faith and Light without loving littleness and simplicity. Lowliness and

---

1. In the early 1990s – Translator note

evangelical humility were needed. "In the same way that Peter denied the Lord three times, for fear of being identified as a disciple of Jesus, I denied Him for fear of abandoning competition and the world of the wise."

Being chaplain of the community for two years left such a mark on him that on his return to Argentina he had only one certitude: to bring Faith and Light and to sow the seed in the parish in Mendoza that had been entrusted to him. Everything started with Sergio and his family, who lived about a hundred meters from the rectory. Two years later, there were three communities in the city, then a dozen in the country, when he became the national chaplain.

"Today, I cannot re-read my life without my 'special friends.' The spirituality of littleness, of friendship and of celebration has been a constant source, as much in my priestly life as in my academic life. Jean told me one day: 'Do not forget to include persons with disabilities in your studies and in your writings.' This is what I do."

Today Father Alberto Bochatey is the rector of the Augustinian International College in Rome. He is a professor of Moral Theology, a specialist in Bioethics, and a member of the Pontifical Academy for Life. He is still chaplain of a Faith and Light community in Rome.

Planned for Burundi, born in Rwanda

Not all Faith and Light communities are born from the initiative of pioneers. In many countries they are born according to the unexpected will of God and his Providence. I experienced this particularly in Burundi[1]. Candide and her husband, an

---

1. This was in the 1980s – Translator note

employee of UNESCO, had seven children, and the second to last had a severe disability. The family lived on the outskirts of Paris. Candide frequently came to ask me for advice about the education of her little boy. She wanted very much to create "something" in her country. On the occasion of Air France inaugurating a flight Bujumbura-Paris, her husband received three free plane tickets. He was not able to travel at this time, but Candide could. She invited me to accompany her with a third person for this flight in the first class cabin. "Come with me, we will spend just a week there, then two or three days in the neighboring country, Rwanda." Marie-Vincente, General Secretary of Faith and Light, whom I invited to be the third person, was delighted. In Bujumbura, the welcome was excellent and we had opportunities to see the Bishop, visit centers, have conferences, meet with families interested in Faith and Light and in the creation of a little school.

At the end of the day, set for departure to Rwanda, we were at the airport. Candide was delayed by police procedures: "Get on the plane," she said, "I will join you." A small plane with ten seats, not very reassuring. We settled in our seats. The engines started. The propellers turned. No Candide. Suddenly we saw her running on the landing strip, followed by four police officers. She climbed the steps, entered the plane, and sat in her place. But not for long. The police pulled her up and removed her from the plane. We wanted to follow her. "Don't even think of it," she shouted. "You need to go, God watches." And we took off. "God watches" is very beautiful, but we had no address, no contact. On our arrival in Kigali, night fell. The police questioned us: we had no vaccine certificates against yellow fever and, most importantly, we had no address of a place to stay. "You will spend the night in the police station at the airport, and tomorrow morning you will be sent back to Bujumbura." I was not very happy with the situation. "Wait," I told him, "I do not remember, but if you give me the telephone directory, I believe I can find the name and the address." And this was done. I looked for a Christian community and I called the first on the list, Caritas Christi. A warm male voice answered. I explained our situation. It was a Jesuit. "I will be at the airport in ten minutes, I will settle things, I'm on my way." Father Jean Gasenge arrived, greeted the airport personnel, including the police, in a friendly manner and assured them that he expected us, that our rooms were ready. Caritas Christi was a retreat house with small rooms, very simple and pleasant, overlooking a magnificent park. It felt like we were in Paradise!

For forty-eight hours Father Jean devoted himself to us, putting aside all his regular tasks. There were visits of all sorts, especially to a big center in Gatagara for children with physical disabilities. This center was run by a team of priests, with extraordinary availability and tenderness for each of the children. Father Jean was strongly interested in Faith and Light and thought that the movement, if introduced in Rwanda, would do marvelously. He would talk with several families and would get back in touch with us.

After many months without news, I wrote to him. No answer. Despite the silence, I regularly sent him all mail addressed to the national coordinators. We trusted. After four years, Father Jean finally contacted us. He had never stopped thinking about Faith and Light, but he never found the ideal person to coordinate the movement in Rwanda. And now, there she was: Josefa, secretary to the Dean of the Catholic University.

Josefa had a child with profound disabilities, Pacifique, and she was prepared to commit herself. Everything was ready to go. Marie-Vincente would return there three more times. I was also there for two formation sessions. The movement was growing and full of life until the horrible tragedy of the genocide that decimated the country, including Faith and Light. No parish, no family was spared.

When I went back, in 1996, I was deeply shaken by the terrible signs left by so many abominations, so many open wounds. I was also touched by the will to forgive, impossible from a human point of view. And there were also the heroic acts of those who risked their lives to save others.

Pacifique's father told me how his son had saved his life. Soldiers, armed to the teeth, broke into their house. They had heard that Josefa, the mother, was hidden. In fact, she lived for several months between a board and the ceiling, surviving thanks to the care and vigilance of her husband. The soldiers shouted: "We are going to kill you!" Pacifique threw himself toward his father, sheltering him with his body, to protect him, crying with pain. The soldiers hesitated a moment, then they put down their arms and left. Pacifique did not have the instinctive movement to run away, hide, or save his life. On the contrary, he risked his life for love of his father.

The need for peace and love that the person with disabilities has, was and continues to be, a powerful motivator to ask God to give everyone the strength to realize small steps on the way toward reconciliation. Today Rwanda has twelve communities… As far as the team in Burundi, they first chose to maintain a small school that, after many years of effort, proved to be unsustainable. With support from Father Guillaume Ndaéyishimiye, a Jesuit, this team dedicated itself to the launching of Faith and Light; today four communities grow there.

CHAPTER 11

To Maintain Unity and be Re-energized

To continue to grow in fidelity to its vocation, a movement such as ours needs to continuously work to consolidate its unity, by returning to its roots and renewing its missionary spirit. In Faith and Light we made the choice to keep alive our unity and fervor by relying on three fundamental pillars: fidelity to international and local pilgrimages, a closely-knit international team and regular meetings all over the world.

The foundational pillar: world pilgrimages every ten years

We cannot separate the deepening and the expansion of the movement from the three big international pilgrimages to Lourdes that initiated the last three decades (1981, 1991 and 2001[1]). Each one allowed Faith and Light to grow, to raise awareness and mobilize new countries, to generate new communities, in particular those with children, and to give new breath to those already in existence.

---

1. There was no single, fourth pilgrimage to Lourdes because the decision taken was to launch numerous pilgrimages in 2011-2012 to "set the earth on fire".

These gatherings were very different from the founding pilgrimage, the one in 1971, when everything needed to be invented: the formation of communities, the spiritual preparation, the conception of adapted liturgies, the practical organization to the smallest detail if we wanted to avoid a monstrous mess. All that was now established. The way was ready. We knew the general outline of what needed to be done, what needed to be avoided, in the movement as well as in the sanctuaries and in the city of Lourdes.

There were also many points in common: first of all, each one started its work taking into account the requests from the countries and from the persons with disabilities and their insistence: "Well, when are we going back to Lourdes?" Next, the time of preparation in the community was considered as important as the event itself. An international pilgrimage needs to map out its plan two years before the event. On the spiritual plane, we must count on at least one year with guidelines that serve as framework and nourishment for the monthly community meetings.

And then, when in Lourdes, there are other constants: the warm welcome by the local bishop on the esplanade; liturgical celebrations marked by beauty, simplicity and adaptations authorized by the Church so that they are accessible to all. Other important moments: the washing of the feet and the Way of the Cross by community, the morning of reconciliation on Holy Saturday with the joy of receiving the sacrament of pardoning, the big celebration across the river on Easter afternoon in white or colored ponchos, a prefiguring of the eternal banquet where Jesus will dry all tears from our eyes, the emotions stirred by the Pope's messages read during the Easter Vigil, the journalists' wholehearted plunge into the event: "Who can describe the amazing things – this faith so truly incredible - that took place these days ?" wrote one of them.

The community that meets becomes, for four days, a community that lives together. The friends then discover the heavy daily burden of the parents. They want to do everything to lighten the parents' load. The parents wonder at the availability of the young friends, with their commitment to their children, when they could have taken four days of vacation with other friends. The persons with disabilities repeat nonstop "Alleluia"...

For each pilgrimage, we were aware of the risk of falling into routine. This pitfall was avoided. The treasures of the past permitted new initiatives to spring up. Just as the morning that dawns is new when we trust the Holy Spirit.

Now a few words about the originality of each one of these three events.

1981: Pilgrimage of Thanksgiving

"We need to go back to Lourdes to be polite. Ten years ago the Holy Mother gave us Faith and Light, we need to say thank you." These were the words of Jacques, a young man with disabilities. It matched the counsel of Marthe Robin, seven years before, when she reminded me of this filial duty of gratitude.

The 1981 pilgrimage was not the extraordinary explosion that 1971 was; it was more the peaceful joy of an immense family. Delegates from three hundred communities, including many French (seventeen) and foreign bishops, came from twenty-seven countries. Remembering the previous pilgrimage, the hotel owners opened their big hearts and doors, and joyful pilgrims appreciated gathering at the hotels just like anyone else. The pain that Camille and Gérard had experienced there with Loïc and Thaddée seemed so distant!

The United Nations declared 1981 to be an "International Year of Persons with Disabilities". Rémi Montagne, Secretary of State for Social Affairs, who had the occasion to spend one evening at l'Arche, was touched and immediately accepted our invitation to the pilgrimage. In his address to the pilgrims, he stressed the interest of the initiative of the UN and assured: "It was necessary that a spiritual summit bring to this material effort the breath of the Spirit, and, by the Spirit, give a common soul that inspires and transfigures our actions."

To obey the words of Jesus, "Wash one another's feet", celebrated by the washing of the feet during Mass on Holy Thursday, we wanted to live it in community in the places of lodging also: the hotels, the boarding houses, the hospitals.

This original ritual was introduced at l'Arche in Liverpool, then in the one in Trosly. From there, this tradition had spread to all the homes of l'Arche. 1981 was the first time that we in Faith and Light dared to live it. Three days before the pilgrimage, during an informational meeting in which more than a hundred hotel owners participated, we shared with them our plan and asked them for their collaboration. We needed water jugs, basins, and a place for each group. Sensing the truth and the beauty of this gesture, with great eagerness they set about looking for these uncommon objects. In a few hours they had raided all the stores in Lourdes and the surrounding area…

For this "paraliturgy" of washing of the feet, we sat in a circle. After having heard the account from the Gospel of Saint John[1], one after the other, we washed the feet of our neighbor and then we let our feet be washed. We softly sang *Ubi Caritas* or another refrain that celebrates the love that is given.

During the 1981 pilgrimage, it was beautiful to see a mother wash the feet of her son with disabilities, and even more touching to see a young girl with intellectual disabilities and psychological difficulties, wash the feet of her father. Usually aggressive, she

---

1. John 13: 1-17 – Translator note

carried out this gesture with much tenderness. In the evaluations of the pilgrimage, the washing of the feet was among the most important moments. It awakens a simple joy. Jesus told us: "Happy are you if you do this."

The celebration of the Passion of the Lord, on Good Friday, in the Basilica Saint Pius X, was preceded by a dramatic representation, brought to life by about sixty persons from the l'Arche community. I passed by to see them in the sacristy, where they were gathered for a final preparation. I thought I would find agitation and excitement. However, there was a great stillness, everyone praying, asking Jesus to help all the faithful to relive what really happened two thousand years ago.

"It will not be a comedy," one of them told me. It is true; the one who represented Jesus seemed to carry Christ's sufferings in his very being. He carried our rejection of the other and our divisions, to transform us into new women and men.

1991: Pilgrimage for Unity

The theme of the pilgrimage, "toward unity", signaled from the beginning the profound desire of our Protestant and Orthodox brothers and sisters to fully have their place. We had worked extensively together, especially on the ecumenical commission. The call for unity continued to echo in Lourdes with the song: "Father, make us one, that the world may believe in your love." And we made this concrete by our unity around the littlest ones.

However, the first ecumenical meeting on the morning of Good Friday was not without difficulties: five hundred people attended, instead of the two hundred expected, and it was impossible to translate in all the languages. These obstacles did not impede the flow of grace. A Russian Orthodox man, sitting on the floor as most of the participants, shared about his emotion during the singing of the Our Father. He gave his left hand to a Lutheran and his right to a Catholic: "During that time, I felt how much what brings us together, our baptism, our love of Jesus Savior, present in the littlest ones, the Bible that is our common nourishment, was stronger than all that separates us."

Frances Young, mother of Arthur, a young man with profound disabilities, is a Methodist Pastor from England. She also told how she had lived this pilgrimage. The liturgical commission had entrusted to her a number of services that she accepted to carry out in "the spirit of obedience". This is how, on Good Friday, during the celebration, she was invited to hold the cross that hundreds of persons with disabilities and others came to touch, venerate, kiss with ardent faith and tenderness. It would have been impossible for her to be on the other side and venerate the cross, but there, she held it to make it possible for others to manifest, by some sign, their love for Jesus. That same evening she was among a group of parents who gathered to share their suffering, to pray, listen to witnesses, sing a refrain from Taizé: "Stay with me, watch and pray." As many mothers who were present, not to mention fathers, she could not hold back her tears.

The next morning, a young man with disabilities, James, a frequent visitor to Lourdes, took her by the hand to guide her to the Grotto. Together, they touched and kissed the damp rock and she then felt that there was something important in the simple act of touching, especially for persons who had challenges in elaborating concepts. Together, in silence in front of this spring of pure water, they recognized its beauty and its mystery. Then they went to the fountains and James washed her face. Water purified her tears. In her turn, she washed James's face, and together, they drank from their cupped hands. She relates:

"Monday morning at the Grotto, I finally could repent of my arrogance and I gave thanks for the obedience that I demonstrated this week. I found myself saying the Methodist covenant prayer

'Fill me, empty me' and I was aware of the emptiness at work within me. I returned to the fountains and I washed my hands and face, receiving then the purification after repentance. Then I quickly climbed the stairs to the upper Basilica. I entered. Suddenly, it was warm and welcoming. The white statue of the Virgin shined through the halo of my steamed up glasses and peace slowly began to invade my heart."

An ecumenical celebration brought closure to the pilgrimage on Easter Monday. On the esplanade there was a scene inspired by the Gospel of Saint John[1] in front of perhaps more than fifteen thousand persons. It was the meeting of Mary Magdalene with the risen Jesus on Easter morning. Jesus, represented by a man with disabilities, tells her: "Go find my brothers." The young woman playing Mary Magdalene approached, one by one, a female Methodist Pastor, then an Anglican Bishop, then a Cardinal, then an Orthodox Bishop, then finally a Catholic Bishop and brought them to Jesus. They knelt in front of him, before he helped them up and hugged them with these words: "Love one another as I have loved you." Then they hugged each other and gave the crowd this invitation: "Share the peace of Jesus risen." In a continuous wave, this peace was shared neighbor to neighbor.

The bold surge of pilgrims from the East

After years of persecution, repression, imprisonment, surveillance, Eastern Christians rediscovered the joy of freedom. They were filled with enthusiasm and came in large numbers. More than a thousand Poles, one hundred and fifty Hungarians, as many Yugoslavians, sixty-eight Russians, fifty Czechs, twenty-three Lithuanians, ten Romanians. The iron curtain having

---

1. John 20: 11-18 - Translator note

fallen, they dared to face a long and difficult trip. The desire to come to pray at the base of the Grotto with a multitude of brothers and sisters, and to express their faith and their hope with complete freedom, gave them the necessary boldness. To limit transportation costs, the Polish pilgrims traveled by bus, busses often dilapidated and breaking down, four days to come and the same to go back. They carried their own food, baked potatoes. During the trip, they slept on the floor in parishes or convents. It was a relief for the parents and friends, who were apprehensive about the difficulties of the return trip, to hear their brothers and sisters with disabilities demonstrating their joy at going back in the same conditions. They did not see the discomfort, the exhaustion, only the happiness of living together this exceptional time.

Families with young children

By the end of the 1980s, communities with small children were developing. We wanted to mark their importance in the movement by a special invitation to the pilgrimage. Many parents responded and formed a community to go to Lourdes. Their presence prompted us to make some adaptations: a day care center for the little ones, activities for the children a bit older and for the adolescents, animated by the young people. A large number of the youth came from Chemin Neuf[1].

Many of these families gave witness that they had found peace again, intimacy, and a trust that the birth of their little one had obscured or broken. On the part of the rest of the pilgrims, "How to name it?" extra gentleness, tenderness, simplicity reigned ...

---

1. A Catholic apostolic community, with Ignatian spirituality and an ecumenical vocation; a fruit of the Charismatic Renewal.

"Let the little children come to me[1]". Ghislain du Chené, who later became international coordinator, participated with his family in a community with young children. He has often given witness to the essential importance of this step for him and for each one in his family.

2001: Pilgrimage to "drink at the source"

Easter 2001. The theme of the pilgrimage "Come, drink at the source" brought us back to our very roots, when we had heard the invitation of the Virgin Mary to persons with intellectual disabilities and their families who had hardly any place in the city.

In 1854, Mary showed Bernadette a spring that had previously been unknown. After Bernadette dug out the weeds and the dirt, a small spring of water trickled out, very clear water that purified and healed. We are to come and to drink. Mary revealed it to the world to help us to discover another spring, which itself was also hidden very deep in our heart: the presence of Jesus and of his Father. But this source is frequently buried under the mud and the stones that are our guilt, our anguish, our rebellion; our desire always to be number one. Jesus calls us: "Let the one who is thirsty come to me and rivers of living water will gush from their hearts.[2]" We rediscovered in this way how much our brothers and sisters with disabilities are a source of living water for us.

During the preceding pilgrimages, Jean Vanier and I had taken a major role in the overall organization. When the decision of having this fourth pilgrimage was taken, we shared our choice not to have direct responsibilities. It was necessary to put together a team that would take on this responsibility. Yet it was difficult

---

1. Luke 18: 16 – Translator note
2. John 4: 13-14 – Translator note

to recruit anyone. It was necessary to find someone who would have both competence and knowledge from personal experience of what Faith and Light was: "Something that does not seem like anything else," as the people from the Touring Club observed before, during and after the first pilgrimage.

We turned to l'Arche, and specifically to Alain Saint-Macary, who had had responsibilities at the highest levels, first in the community in Trosly, then eventually with l'Arche international, where he had been vice-president.

He accepted the challenge along with Bernard Bataille. Sharing the responsibility equally, they formed new teams.

Among the many members of l'Arche who have helped us, I would like to mention Cariosa Kilcommons, who assembled and conducted a small international orchestra and composed a special song for the pilgrimage. We remember the joy with which she accomplished her mission during the 2001 pilgrimage, as she had already done, and would do again in Faith and Light international meetings.

In this year of 2001 we received a providential sign of unity through the liturgical calendar. The Orthodox celebrated Easter on the same day as the other Christian denominations. Encouragement for ecumenism at the beginning of the millenium! Again, the ecumenical commission worked very hard so that this aspect might be lived in great harmony respecting the rules of each tradition. At the beginning of the Easter Vigil, representatives of the different denominations were gathered around the altar of the underground basilica during the liturgy of the Word. Before beginning the liturgy of the Eucharist presided over by Cardinal Stafford, head of the Pontifical Council for the Laity, he explained that each Christian denomination was now called to celebrate according to its own rite. A difficult parting that reminded us of the incompleteness of our unity and that spurs us to desire it even more fervently.

The two hundred Orthodox pilgrims celebrated the Vigil until daybreak. "Christ is risen!" one would proclaim, and another would respond, "Yes, He is truly risen!" They continuously passed on these shouts of joy to all they met throughout that Sunday. There is no need to speak the same language to invite your neighbor to share this announcement of Easter joy everywhere. (How beautiful it would be if this Orthodox tradition spread to the other traditions, replacing our plain "Happy Easter!")

On Easter morning, twenty-eight liturgies were celebrated by six denominations in fourteen languages. Orthodox, Greco-Catholic and Anglican Eucharists, Lutheran Liturgies, the Lord's Supper, witnessing the diversity of our traditions and our desire to move forward on the way toward unity.

This pilgrimage of 2001 had some organizational difficulties: it brought together more than sixteen thousand pilgrims instead of the twelve thousand planned for, therefore there were inevitable malfunctions. Because of this, even more than for the other pilgrimages, life in the places of lodging had a critical role. We could see a real maturity compared with the previous pilgrimages. When we spend several days in community, we see everything, we share everything, the little joys of family intimacy as well as the usually hidden misery that no one suspects: this large son with autism clung to his mother from morning to night; this couple that takes turns, meal after meal, to nourish their nine year old daughter, one small spoonful at a time; and also this young friend who offered to stay awake during the night so that the parents could sleep. In community, when we live four days together, we laugh with those who laugh, we cry with those who cry.

As Maureen, international coordinator at the time, said so well: "When God raised up Faith and Light, he did not give us a business, a school or an organization, but a family. In our Faith and Light families there are frequently grains of sand in the gears. When things go badly, it is necessary to dare to talk with each other with the help of God, to ask forgiveness and to give ours." What was the most touching in those days were the thousand little gestures of kindness, of solidarity that bonded each community more deeply.

2011-2012: A fire on earth

In February 2011, in Lourdes, was the sending off of the forty provincial pilgrimages that would take place over the course of two years while looking forward to the international meeting in 2013 to celebrate the end of the Jubilee and to launch a new stage: "Now, everything begins."

The pillar of unity: a closely-knit international team

The more Faith and Light saw the number of its branches grow, the more it exposed itself to diversity: diversity of languages, cultures, mentalities, traditions, political and economic situations. This was, and continues to be, one of the essential roles of the international council. It is the guardian of the deep roots that ensure the unity of the movement, lived at the base especially by persons with disabilities.

Beginning in 1969, the international council was composed of a Bureau (the international coordinator, the international chaplain, the founders) and the zone coordinators. It was enlarged with the creation of each new zone, from six members in 1972 to around twenty in 2006. In 2008, the new Constitution provided a reduction that brought the number of the international team to twelve persons.

Relationships among members of the council were not always idyllic. First of all, they were complicated due to the diversity of languages (English, French and Spanish are our three official languages). Simultaneous translation, already tricky for professional interpreters, was really difficult for the volunteers that we recruited from within the movement, having the good fortune to benefit from their admirable personal involvement. It was also painful for those who do not know any of the three official languages and who needed to rely on a translation whispered by a participant whose French, English or Spanish were sometimes approximate! Certainly, this brought mistranslations and misunderstandings. Happily, among the members of the council, several were bilingual, able to notice a mistake and rectify it immediately. On the other hand, differences of sensitivity and opinion between North and South, West and East could create the risk of dissension. But, at the same time, we had the obligation to hear the point of view of the other, to understand and dialogue until we could arrive at a consensus. We avoided voting, except for the nomination of leaders. When we had vigorous disagreements, the meals, the evenings, the prayer together helped us to rediscover, if not union in the points of view, at least a communion of hearts.

In September 1981 we welcomed Marie-Vincente Puiseux, who was called in subsequent years to accomplish an important mission in the movement. After finishing her studies in philosophy, she looked for a position serving persons with disabilities. First she committed herself for a year in l'Arche, then at OCH, and finally with Faith and Light. In 1984 she was named General Secretary, a central role in the movement, because it is the only person having a full-time office at this level. Marie-Vincente fulfilled this role for twelve years: organization and coordination of the secretariat team, administrative and financial tasks, contacts and links with the different countries...Little by little she also took up missions for the African continent, about ten countries, from Ghana to Botswana, passing through Rwanda and Burkina Faso. She supported the new seeds, organized specific formation sessions. Her international mission continued until 2000, when she assumed the role of editor for the magazine, *Ombres et Lumière*.

To be in tune with the world, reflect and innovate

The international council was a bit like the community coordinating team for the whole world. It would meet for a short week either at la Ferme[1], or in another area of the world.

One essential part of our work together was dedicated to the presentation of reports by each zone. We would immerse ourselves in the different parts of the world, each with its joys, its growth, its successes, its difficulties, its crises, its internal conflicts, its dramas. All was shared in a climate of trust, without fear of judgment. Everywhere, mysteriously, those that were the weakest, where one small flickering hope remained burning, found new life again through our prayer. It could be a country from which we no longer received news due to conflicts or wars, such as Ghana or Sierra Leone, or others, victims of natural disasters, as in Mexico[2], where Lupita Mendez Gracida, unshakeable, had begun one community that remained alone for about ten years before there was a remarkable flourishing of new life.

One equally important aspect of our mission was to reflect together on the essential needs to which we would try to respond. Because of this, for example, we worked toward the formation

---

1. At the heart of Trosly-Breuil, la Ferme (the farm) is a community of welcome and of prayer founded by Father Thomas Philippe. A team of about twelve laypeople organizes and facilitates spiritual weekends and retreats, which are well known to communities and leaders of Faith and Light. La Ferme de Trosly, 23 rue d'Orleans, 60350 Trosly-Breuil. Email: laferme@ lafermedetrosly.com

2. In 1985, a magnitude 8.1 earthquake struck Mexico, causing massive loss and destruction – Translator note

of leaders, which they themselves felt was a necessity. We ran three, nine-day international formation sessions. François and Marie-Noëlle Bal, a very committed couple who had had various responsibilities over the years including as vice-international coordinators, were key persons behind this huge project. After this we created a formation commission, which published a number of booklets[1] (*Retreats in Faith and Light, Summer Camps,* etc.)

On another front, we reflected on ecumenism and initiated an international commission led by Roy Moussalli[2] and made up of priests, pastors and laypeople belonging to different Christian traditions. This commission also published some brochures addressed to interdenominational communities and to those that are rooted in a single denomination, because all of us, without exception, are concerned with the breakage in the Body of the Church and are so happy to verify that the person who is weak and with disabilities could be a bond of unity and a source of communion.

Questions about finances weigh on our shoulders. Tackling them is always a delicate time in the agenda because we came to Faith and Light to be friends with persons with disabilities and their families, so we are taken aback to hear talk about money. It is a subject that we do not need to be worried about, but one with which it is indispensable that we concern ourselves.

The communities and the countries said to be "rich" were able to cover their expenses. But there were many other expenses: the visits of the international leaders, formation sessions, meetings of the various teams, as well as the functioning of the international Secretariat, no matter how minimal this cost is. Finally, and above all, two thirds of the countries that joined us were in great economic difficulties. It was absolutely necessary to organize

---

1. See appendices
2. A dedicated Faith and Light leader from Syria – Translator note

international solidarity, most often based on the help from the countries in the North to those in the South, giving priority for linking according to language. For example, France supported many French-speaking countries in Africa. Everybody agreed in principle. But we were all a bit tense at the international council as well as in the zone councils, when it was time to deal with this topic, particularly concerning the financial participation of each member. It was good then to remember the irreplaceable contribution from the countries in the South through their simplicity, their joy, their poverty, the ease with which they give the little that they have. In the same way we remembered the contribution of the countries in the East, through their exceptional courage in facing difficulties and adversities, and their energy to launch Faith and Light.

When we became lost in our discussions, we were helped by the four keywords of Jean concerning finances: trust, transparency, competence, generosity.

An issue frequently came up, from some leaders in the zones where Faith and Light existed since the 1970s. They were concerned with the future of certain communities whose members were aging.

In all families – and Faith and Light is a family – we are concerned with the members that grow older. Aging is not some type of failure; it is the opening up of a new stage of life. But what to do? These discussions were happening everywhere. Would it be necessary to sustain the life of communities that no longer met? Abandon them? To send them young members, even when the community was not able to integrate them? In fact, each situation is different. It is necessary to accept that some communities disappear, but also to support a community that is very weak but where the members faithfully continue to meet from time to time and at a slower pace. If the persons with disabilities find some measure of friendship, there is no reason to extinguish a flame that still seems to want to burn. And then, we can suggest to a community that has decided to stop their activities to carry, through prayer, the birth of a new community that would carry on for them. Many have carried in their hearts a community with small children, a place of hope for parents, their children, friends and the entire movement.

Even if the agenda of the international council was packed, there were always moments of genuine relaxation. I remember this particular evening, animated by Jean Evariste, a retired Belgian Air Force Colonel, and Jacinta Torres, a Social Worker from the Dominican Republic. They welcomed us very seriously, a mock seriousness. "They had become aware," they told us, "that the founders had never actually been elected. It was extremely urgent that we make up for this injustice." The evening then was dedicated to a process of discernment that defied all the very strict rules for discernment that we had put in place. A lot of laughter until the final vote where Jean and I were elected unanimously! Justice was restored and celebrated until late in the night with sparkling wine and specialties brought from the four corners of the world.

We multiply the ports of call!

The international council took on a different tone according to the countries in which we met, the type of living quarters and the welcome that we received.

Over the course of a few days we lived as citizens of that country, trying to understand and appreciate everything. We always planned a meeting, a meal and an evening with the national coordinating team and a good time of sharing and of celebration with one or several communities from the surrounding area. A precious time for all: for the national team, it was an opportunity to become aware of the international dimension of the movement, and of the specific place that it had. From the "international" side, it was an opportunity to understand and to own the joys and difficulties of the host country, to see their points of strength, their weak points (or even better, "their areas of growth," as we love to say). To restore trust, to confirm, comfort and challenge according to their strengths at the moment, when the first enthusiasm seemed to be fading

For example, in Sweden, in 1984, we came at the invitation of Marianne Abrahamsson, coordinator for the North Europe Zone, which encompassed the British Isles and Scandinavian countries. Choosing the city of Göteborg for our meeting was a sign that we gave as much importance to the countries where only one community existed as to those that had dozens. It was also a sign of our desire to see Faith and Light born in a predominantly Protestant country. One evening a priest came to speak to us about Sweden. He mentioned that there were eight million inhabitants in the country and only about twenty thousand of them were Catholic. And about 80% of these were immigrants. The tiny interdenominational Faith and Light community in Sweden had twelve members, strongly united and welcoming. On another day, we welcomed the coordinator of Norway, Tonia Berit, and the coordinator of Denmark, Erik Achen. They lived a similar situation with the same conviction and the same hope.

When faced with countries that seemed to stagnate with only one community and which had a tendency to become discouraged and to blame themselves, Jean Vanier loved to remind us of the *bacuri,* a Brazilian fruit. It is said to be delicious, but you need to wait forty years between the time you plant its seed and the appearance of the first fruit. Some communities resemble a *bacuri,* which requires so much patience and hope. Other communities are more similar to tomato plants, which bear fruit quickly and in great numbers.

Do not let the *bacuris* disturb us too much; it is the work of God. Always do the little that is ours to do, our five loaves and two fish. The multiplication is God's business. The essential is that each community, the only one if no other community exists, be a place of love and of growth.

Another recollection: in 1992, we met in France, at Issy-les-Moulineaux, and I have a very moving personal memory. At this meeting, one of our joys was to welcome two new members, Greta de Arispe of Peru, new coordinator for South America, and Désirée Kong, of Mauritius, new coordinator for Asia.

On the morning of July 22nd, I received an urgent call about my mother, who was gravely ill. "If we truly form an international family, even if we delay our work, we need to be there for the wake and funeral and surround Marie-Hélène and all her loved ones," the international council decided. They rented a bus to take them to a village in the center of France. It was both emotional and consoling for me to welcome this very loving entourage, truly my other family. "Today," Monsignor Marcel Gauillière, national chaplain for France, assured me, "your mother can see her posterity extend to the farthest corners of the earth." I give thanks for her and for my father for their unwavering support of my mission, not to mention that of all my brothers and sisters.

A third memory of the meetings of the international council is of the one in Syria in September 2004. Its exceptional preparation was the work of Roy, our vice-international-coordinator, with all of his team, of course. His journey is worth retelling.

Roy came to Faith and Light, as if by mistake. He did not feel any particular attraction to persons with intellectual disabilities, nor did he recognize in himself any aptitude to help them either. The community in Damascus, at that time, was very fragile and filled with tensions. Everything began for Roy in his meeting and his friendship with Issa, a person with disabilities. "She transformed me," he said. At a given moment, he sensed that if both of them would enter a community together, even if it was weak and fragile, it would help Issa grow and would deepen their friendship. Roy, himself, stayed very anchored in his decision not to accept any responsibilities. God had other plans...

When I first met Roy, he had become national coordinator for Syria and had immediately given a big boost to the movement there. In 1997 we gathered in Cyprus for a meeting of the Middle-East zone, which was comprised of Lebanon, Egypt, Syria, Iran, Cyprus and Greece. I was the person from the international team accompanying the zone and was present to lead the process to elect its new coordinator. Roy's name was mentioned by all the participants. Having the responsibility to reflect with him and to come to know his feelings about the eventuality of his nomination, I felt him torn. This call corresponded with his heart and with his abilities, but he found himself weighing this against his love for his wife, Zouka, who did not want him to take on more commitments. What if he telephoned her and presented the situation to her? If he was able to reach her by phone, which was not obvious at that time since no one had cellphones, and if she gave her "go ahead," would he be able to consider this as the sign for which he was looking? This is what he did. Zouka sensed that Roy was acting on a call from God and his "Yes" amazed me.

If I dare to bring up this occurrence, it is to express how much gratitude Faith and Light has for the spouse who agrees to participate in the life of the movement like this, with real sacrifice, in a humble and hidden but very fruitful way. The couple strives to carry the mission together, one holding an official role, the other more by listening, prayer, trust, offering.

Subsequently, while serving as vice-international coordinator, Roy was asked to accompany the international ecumenical commission. Here he accomplished extraordinary work, encouraging the birth of communities, rooted in different Christian traditions, establishing and strengthening their relationship with their leaders. "Roy," wrote Viviane Le Polain, who worked very closely with him," is a man of dialogue and of peace. I remember the soundness of his judgment, his precision, his ability to dedicate himself to the essential. He was remarkable for his concern for the formation and growth of each person, his openness to the Holy Spirit, his interior freedom and his boldness, even in difficult situations or when conflicts arose. Deeply touched by the gift of the littlest ones, by the mission of Faith and Light and by the vision of Jean Vanier, he let himself be on fire for the mission."

After this detour, let us return to the international council meeting about thirty kilometers from Damascus, on the edge of the desert. The population of Syria is composed of 90 % Muslims and 10 % Christians, Orthodox and Catholic. In this country there are about forty communities, incredibly alive, full of joy, of wisdom… and of young people. Two Christian traditions are very present in them. Four Catholic and Orthodox bishops, who accompanied the movement, joined us at our "hermitage" for a very cordial sharing, followed by dinner and a celebration with the communities of Damascus.

It is good to work and to reflect in a house away from the world. As in each of the meetings of the council, a pilgrimage was planned. Roy took us to the monastery of Mar Moussa, in the middle of the desert. After a rough hike on a mountain track of loose gravel and stones, we came out on a magnificent area. Not far from this place, there is a grotto where, it is said, God came to encounter the prophet Elijah. We also felt the presence of God in the joy of finding there a monastic community that prays and works for the unity of Christians and in the dialogue with Muslims, a very different vocation than ours, but we were happy to sense that we were close to one another.

It brought to my mind the reflection of Bishop Theotonius Gomes, archbishop of Dacca and national chaplain for Faith and

Light in Bangladesh: "One of the great legacies of the twentieth century will have been that we have become aware of the needs of the person with intellectual disabilities and have drawn our attention toward the weakest. The next step will be this spirit of communion among religions and among human beings."

The pillar of the mission: international meetings

International meetings are gatherings of all the family that happen regularly. Initially we had them every year. The time between each meeting has increased as the movement grew.

Beginning in 1982 in Wetherby (England), the meetings were held every two years. In 1986, in Santo Domingo (Dominican Republic), we decided on an interval of four years. Afterwards, in 2008, in Lourdes, it was extended to five years.

On D Day, at the welcoming, they are all there: national or provincial coordinators with the international council. There is an identical scenario in all details: the same strange disparity of members, the same obstacles overcome in order to arrive from distant places... Identical yet radically new, due to the sparkle of the opening ceremony. Like snow in sunshine, the weariness melts away, as does the memory of worries left at home when the unifying song bursts forth, "Friends, let's sing all our joy, all the countries are together again."

What are we going to live together? A celebration of thanksgiving for all that is going on in each country, a prayer of intercession for so much suffering everywhere, a reflection on the will of God for us and on human expectations, and a return to the source, a new energy for tomorrow.

Workshops for formation are planned, as are liturgies and times of celebration. We set aside a large block of time for the reports of the international leaders and of finances, and finally for the election of the international coordinator and the members of the Board of Directors.

These meetings, held regularly since 1971, have shaped and deepened the history of Faith and Light. They, particularly the meeting in Wetherby in 1982, have resulted in a Charter and a Constitution.

For each of those that followed, I would like to simply take up two or three particularly striking points.

Rome in 1984:
At the heart of the Universal Church

Nine years after the pilgrimage of reconciliation, we met again at the heart of the Universal Church. What a journey in those nine years! The movement had grown and had put structures in place. In Rome, about one hundred leaders represented about thirty countries, six of them new: South Africa, Greece, India, Iraq, Kenya, Yugoslavia.

A highlight of this meeting was the audience with the Holy Father, Pope John Paul II. At his entrance, breaking all protocol, the participants sang a stirring Magnificat, which was welcomed by his amused and tender smile.

"There are still questions," he told us in his message, "touching, for instance, on your status in the Catholic Church, the requirements of an authentic ecumenism that is founded on the true insertion of each one in his or her own church. In your relations with the Holy See, the Pontifical Council for the Laity will be able to guide you[1]. You are aware that is necessary to cooperate with the other associations in the Church and in society

---

1. The following year, the Holy Father nominated me as a member of this Council. The links became natural.

that work in the same line. And you remain willing to participate in the Church's activities, particularly within the framework of parochial, diocesan and national pilgrimages. Because it is necessary to include persons with disabilities and those close to them, as much as possible, in the whole Body of the Church, where they must fully take their place."

As the greatest sign of his affection, the Pope then took time to greet each delegate personally.

Before leaving Rome, the Italians had prepared a surprise for us. In the morning, in groups of twelve, we joined a Faith and Light community in the city to share the morning and a noon meal before we all met together to celebrate the Eucharist and the fiesta, and finally an evening of prayer, centered on Saint Francis with a remarkable mime of his life. We were touched to see how close we felt to the *Poverello*[1], with his love for persons who are weak, with his joy. Yes, a very good guide for us.

Dominican Republic in 1986: Welcomed by the poorest

In 1986, many asked why the international council chose the Dominican Republic as the setting for an international meeting. We were a hundred and ten delegates, coming from thirty-seven countries. For the first time, we would cross the Atlantic and deliberately pitch our tent in a poor country where all infrastructures were very unstable. But we knew that Jacinta Torres, the young national coordinator of the country, was very determined and efficient. She invested all her enthusiasm and competence in the preparation of the meeting. It would not keep

---

1. The little poor one, an affectionate nickname for St. Francis of Assisi – Translator note

us, we knew, from having a risky adventure. For example, to obtain visas for the country was a nearly impossible mission. A dozen delegates arrived without visas and Jacinta had to spend hours going from place to place, negotiating authorization for entrance. When we arrived at night on a magnificent hill where we would hold the meeting, we discovered that the water system was broken and the facilities were very minimal. It allowed us to share, even if just a little, the conditions of so many poor people.

One of the most moving days was the one we spent in a destitute neighborhood. Simplicity, joy, fervor for the Sunday Eucharist, with so many large families! On every corner, children were trying to sell roasted peanuts or green limes, the buses were extremely overcrowded, we crossed large tracts of wasteland bordered by block shacks topped with a roof. The hot, humid weather exhausted us. The water from the heavy rains had made puddles everywhere.

When we arrived at the door of a poor hut, a small girl cried out with joy and went to fetch triumphantly a pitiful, badly fitting pink dress. It was her only dress, the one she wore to the community meetings. She did not speak. This was her way of telling us that she belonged to the Faith and Light family. A little further away all the community was gathered in front of Elena's home. We sang: "Fiesta, fiesta, fiesta de Fe; fiesta, fiesta, fiesta de Luz" that became the favorite song of the meeting.

During the meeting, we had the responsibility to elect a new vice-international coordinator to succeed Francesco Gammarelli, who had just returned to the Lord. Pain of his absence, but assurance of his vigilant tenderness, were present during this whole meeting.

The person to replace him should be a father, bilingual, with a handicapped child, belonging to a continent other than Europe. All the persons nominated, one after the other, refused. Jean and I nominated Marcin Przeciszewski, who was unknown to the council members. He did not match any of the criteria mentioned, but the council were won over to the idea of asking him if he could see himself carrying this responsibility. In fact, after he started Faith and Light in Poland, fifty-three communities were born. He had not been able to come to the international meeting. I went down into the city at lunchtime to try to reach him by phone. Very little chance of success! It was very difficult to communicate with Europe and nearly impossible with Poland. Miraculously, I stumbled upon Marcin at home on a one-day leave during his military service. I passed on to him the request from the council. He answered me with three very serious objections, almost prohibitive. Our conversation became more and more difficult to hear, and I said: "Marcin, finally, I only have one question for you: do you accept that we vote on your name?" I was stunned to hear him say: "Yes, yes, this is very good," and the connection cut off.

After deliberation, he was elected unanimously. But it was impossible to reach him. It was a Polish delegate who, on his return to Warsaw, brought him the news. Very aggressive, Marcin wrote me a vehement letter, not understanding what had happened. I didn't either. The misunderstanding came from the fact that the connection was so bad that, in my last question, Marcin had understood that I was asking news of his uncle! How Providence can use surprising ways! Marcin carried out his mission over the course of several years. He worked for the birth of Faith and Light in Eastern Europe, bringing to the international council this Slavic spirit and vision that were foreign to us but so essential[1].

One year later, when Father David Wilson asked to resign as international chaplain, Bishop Fernand Lacroix, who had just turned seventy-five and had left his office as Bishop of Edmunston (Canada), joyfully accepted to succeed Father Wilson under the

---

1. Today, Marcin is director of a communication agency of the Polish Bishops.

condition, he said with humor, that we would give up working during meals.

Listening, wisdom, simplicity, humor, it was good to work with him, who never spared his effort or his time until his death in 1994. This left a great emptiness for the movement. Having traveled to Canada for his funeral, I landed in a blizzard. In spite of the weather, Faith and Light members from everywhere made every effort to come to tell him, one last time on earth, of their affection, their sorrow, their deep gratitude and their hope for tomorrow.

Edinburgh in 1990:
Passing on the torch

We were nearly two hundred coming from fifty-six countries, from all corners of the world in Scotland for this third international meeting. We welcomed delegates from sixteen new countries. There were now eight hundred and fifty communities around the world. I remember the terrible time that our Lebanese friends were living, but they gave this witness: "Faith and Light gives us the hope to live in this tragic world of war. Everybody leaves the country. But we have discovered, thanks to our brothers and sisters with disabilities, a reason to stay. Their voice, for us, is the voice of Jesus."

There was an incident in Edinburgh that was an opportunity for a new level of reflection. Three Protestant delegates from Australia asked to meet Jean and me. One of them was in tears: "You say and you write that Faith and Light is an ecumenical movement. Well, since the beginning of this meeting, we feel that all celebrations and liturgies are strictly Catholic. You welcome us very nicely, but as guests, not as full members. We feel like fish out of water." The next morning we talked with the international council who decided to entrust a group with the task of overseeing the ecumenical aspects of the pilgrimage for 1991. Very soon we were able to see the improved quality of the fruits harvested. From this group was born the international ecumenical commission that oversaw the editing of several brochures for reflection on, and practical orientations for, living ecumenism well in Faith and Light.

During the meeting in Edinburgh in 1990, since my mandate as international coordinator was finishing, we needed to choose a new leader. Maureen O'Reilly was elected. Of Irish origins, she was second in a family of nine children. She had come to know Faith and Light in Detroit, in the United States of America, thanks to her brother Bob, who had intellectual and psychological difficulties. Thanks to him also, she worked for the Archdiocese of Detroit in the Office for Persons with Disabilities. After having been elected national coordinator for the United States in 1986, Maureen participated in one of the nine-day international formation sessions. That was her first immersion into the international dimension of the movement. This allowed about twenty or so participants from several countries to get to know her, to appreciate her, and to be able to nominate her. She fully embraced her task, having an extraordinary trust in all her team, making efforts to speak in French, acknowledging her mistakes, sacrificing her vacations to visit countries and to work for peace and reconciliation wherever she went. She had a marvelous sense of humor that put her listeners at ease, led people to move forward, making herself understood by all and engaging her enormous creativity. She always considered the other, whatever their origin or disabilities, as superior to herself. She told me: "I pray everyday for the members of the international council, and from time to time for the leaders of the countries. I simply present them to God, naming them one by one, and asking Him to bless them." From 1990 to 2002, she directed the movement with gentleness, wisdom and love.

Warsaw in 1994:
Where Faith and Light "breathes with two lungs[1] "

Faith and Light had grown: there were, at the time, a thousand two hundred communities in the world. We were three hundred persons, from seventy countries, lodging in an immense seminary, and we walked kilometers of corridors each day to go from one place to the other. The heat was stifling. To quench our thirst, they served us lukewarm cherry juice … We felt anew the poverty of this country that was emerging from endless years of oppression.

One of the significant events was the election of our new international chaplain, Father Joseph Larsen[2]. He was returning from the Philippines, where he had been national chaplain. As a missionary, he lived in the slums for twenty-four years. On his return, he lived on the barge-chapel *Je sers*[3], docked on the River Seine on the outskirts of Paris. The barge welcomed all types of poverty. Over the years, our friendship grew as well as our communion in Jesus. He would no longer be Father Larsen, but Father Joseph. He traveled through different countries giving Faith and Light retreats. His word, so profound and alive, immediately touched persons with disabilities and, with them, all those who listened to him.

---

1. An expression used by John Paul II even before the wall fell. He greatly desired that Europe would find its unity and breathe again with two lungs, Western Europe and Eastern Europe.

2. A priest who belonged to a missionary order from the Netherlands -Translator note

3. French for "I serve" - Translator note

Each month he wrote a letter to many of his friends in Faith and Light. Sharing from a personal experience that could seem very ordinary but that he contemplated with his profound spiritual sense, these little stories from life, these *fioretti*[1], immersed their readers in wonder and invited them to deepen the spirituality of Faith and Light. This spirituality is not limited to the hours of the monthly meeting, but is meant to impregnate all our daily life, on the bus, in the supermarket, on the phone, at work or in the kitchen... The essential, the only truly important thing, is to love. Not to talk about love, but to be love. To let others become important to us, as important as they are to our Father in Heaven. These letters, gathered together in a small booklet called: *Faith and Light in everyday life*, comprise the treasures of his heart drawn from the Gospel.

Father Guy Vanhoomissen succeeded him in 2005. Belgian, Jesuit, superior of a religious community, professor at the Institut Lumen Vitae[2], he had also spent fifteen years in India and kept an unreserved love for this country and its people.

He discovered Faith and Light in 1984 in Lourdes during a Belgian pilgrimage and became chaplain of a community. "I was far from imagining at that time that Faith and Light would occupy such a place in my life." His first words as international chaplain were: "Be joyful with those who rejoice, weep with those who are weeping. Be of one heart among yourselves. Do not have a taste for great things, but let yourselves be drawn to

---

1. This word comes from the disciples of Saint Francis of Assisi, the Franciscans, who, after his death, began to tell the most significant stories from his life to transmit them to future generations. These stories were put together in a small book called *The Fioretti of Saint Francis of Assisi*.

2. An international institute founded by the Jesuits in Brussels, Belgium that offers formation in the areas of catechesis, pastoral ministry and social development with intercultural experience to church leaders - Translator note

what is simple[1]." It is really what he lived. In 2006, at the end of his first mandate, he was called by his congregation to other responsibilities.

Quebec in 1998:
Invited to the home of the Governor General

On an extraordinarily beautiful campus in Cap Rouge, a place with a magnificent view of the whole bay, four hundred delegates arrived from seventy-five countries: Catholics of several rites, Anglicans, Orthodox and Protestants from different churches.

During the evening of reconciliation, five "ways of the cross" converged on the one Cross, close to which we asked God and our brothers and sisters for forgiveness. There was a Byzantine Liturgy with the akathist hymn to Mary, Mother of God [2], prepared and celebrated with fervor by two Orthodox priests, two Greco-Catholic priests and a Catholic priest. And there was the celebration of the Washing of the Feet in more than thirty small groups, into which were welcomed Bishop Maurice Couture, Archbishop of Quebec, Bishop Paul Marchand, Auxiliary Bishop of Ottawa, Reverend Martin Sadler of the United Church of Canada, Father Georges Chehwaro, Orthodox priest of Syria, and Father Joseph Larsen.

It was a moment of profound unity around Jean Vanier, when we met at the Citadelle, the summer residence of the Governor General of Canada, where Jean's parents had often stayed. They now rest together in peace in a small chapel there. Many

---

1. Romans 12: 15-16

2. A well-loved Orthodox devotional service expressing praise and gratitude to the Mother of God. The hymn, with more than 20 verses, is chanted while standing - Translator note

remembered Mrs. Vanier who came to live in Trosly in 1969, in the home "des Marronniers¹", until her unexpected death in 1991, when we were making the final preparations for the 1991 pilgrimage. It was a shock. She was so welcoming, so attentive to each person and to each event. At the Citadelle, our international family praised and thanked God for the parents of Jean and for Jean himself.

A little later, Mr. Roméo Leblanc, Governor General of Canada, welcomed us in the sumptuous halls of the Citadelle, with all the solemnity that he would have with dignitaries. He was visibly touched by the simplicity with which persons with disabilities lived this marvelous moment and came to thank him. A delightful reception awaited us, with an orchestra. Then, we started to dance! It was certainly the first time that a ball like that was improvised in those halls! Christine said to René: "It seemed like we were in the movies", and René answered: "Or in a dream!" Or maybe on the mountain that Isaiah spoke about "where the Lord will give a feast, a feast of rich meats and fine wines for all peoples, even if they have no money²".

Castel Gondolfo in 2002:
Welcomed by a Pope with disabilities

Two hundred and thirty participants from seventy-three countries were welcomed at the magnificent house of Castel Gandolfo, which is the summer residence of the Popes.

Pope John Paul II, in spite of his illness and his disabilities, gave us a private audience. Because of his state of health, there was uncertainty until the last moment if he would be able to keep

---

1. "The chestnut trees" - a home connected with L'Arche - Translator note
2. Isaiah 25: 6-12; 55: 1-3

this meeting. Waiting for him, we were deeply touched. Eighteen years before, the Holy Father had welcomed us in Rome. Then, he was "God's athlete". Now he arrived, bent over his cane. His face disfigured, his luminous smile had disappeared. His body moved stiffly. We were touched that he let himself be seen in his weakness and his powerlessness, even more touched than when he had appeared before, in full possession of his intellectual power and with his radiant bearing. Today, it was the face of Jesus and Jesus' body nailed to the cross that we seemed to see through his body, to tell us of his love in his extreme deprivation. In him, we also saw the face of our brothers and sisters with the most severe disabilities. In their all-encompassing littleness, they call us to join them through the communion of hearts. The Holy Father tried to read his message to us. Despite his efforts, his speech became less and less audible, and finally it was his secretary who finished the reading.

"In welcoming all these 'little ones' marked by their intellectual disability, you have recognized them as special witnesses to the tenderness of God. We have much to learn from them, who have a specific place to take in the heart of the Church... I also think of their parents who, thanks to you, find themselves supported in their suffering and who see their pain change into hope so that they might welcome, with humanity and in faith, their children with disabilities."

It was in Castel Gondolfo that Viviane Le Polain was elected international coordinator; it was the first time that this role was filled by a mom. All her great competence never took away her motherly heart, which connected so well with wounded hearts. Viviane was a student in Brussels when, in 1972 – at 18 years old – she let herself "embark," at the invitation of a Belgian Jesuit, Father Roberti, on a pilgrimage to Lourdes with persons with intellectual disabilities in the spirit of the 1971 Faith and Light pilgrimage. The farthest thing from her mind was that one day she would become a mother of a child with multiple disabilities. "Later on," she said, "I understood that the Lord was gently preparing my heart for the journey that would follow."

After her marriage with Didier and the birth of her two older sons, the birth of Laurent in 1980 was perilous. She almost lost her life, but she was certain that the Holy Virgin would watch over, and would help make it possible for Laurent to share his smile, his joy to live, in spite of his severe disabilities.

In 1983, Father Roberti came to ask her to start a Faith and Light community in Tournai in Belgium, where the small family had come to live. "How could I refuse this call that matched my desire to share with other families a little light of hope in the midst of their suffering. I had the desire that other parents could feel that they were surrounded, supported by true friends, and that they might be able to discover the gift of their different child." For Viviane, this was the beginning of a strong commitment in service and responsibility at different levels. To dedicate herself to this, she chose to leave her profession of teaching Philosophy and Religion, which she very much enjoyed. Before becoming our international coordinator, Viviane had ten years of experience behind her. She had been Maureen's right hand and Maureen had completely entrusted to her the accompaniment of the International Secretariat in Paris. She had an amazing mastery of documents and did not leave anything to chance. Her total investment in the task at hand, her acuity and her struggle to achieve the determined goals were exceptional. She was ready.

The following year she found, in Corinne Chatain, the General Secretary that she so much sought. When she was eighteen, Corinne did not like persons with disabilities. A person had to be somewhat deranged, she thought, to find joy in being close to them, as some young people affirmed. Arriving at the

Foyer de Charité in Châteauneuf-de-Galaure to make a retreat, she saw an issue of *Ombres et Lumière* among the magazines available to those making a retreat. She was captivated by the witness of parents, particularly one by a mother who described how much she suffered with the way people looked at her son Christophe, who had severe disabilities. This way of looking, "is mine", Corinne thought. She collected all the issues of the magazine that she could find and started to read everything, the witnesses, the editorials, the meditations, etc. She discovered the answer to her simple question: how can we love wounded persons? By loving them. This is how, when she left Châteauneuf, Corinne chose to work in their service. She offered her services to Faith and Light, to the OCH. There was only one vacancy, as a clerk. Why not? When, one year later, there was an opening in the editing of *Ombres et Lumière*, she was able to step right in. At the same time, she and her husband Thierry began a Faith and Light community. She became its coordinator, then coordinator of a region, of a province, and of a zone, until the day when, in 2003, she was called to be the General Secretary of the movement with a small team of three salaried persons.

Filled with creativity and imagination, with a sense of organization and great precision, Corinne was passionate for each aspect of her mission.

On her desk, there used to be a picture with the words of Therese of the Child Jesus: "It is because I am small and weak that I am pleasing to God." And another one, from Saint Paul: "My grace is enough, my power is manifested in weakness.[1]"

---

1. 2 Corinthians 12: 9

Madrid in 2006:
A pause to renew

Thirty-five years after the birth of the movement, the international meeting was held at Escorial, close to Madrid, and had as its theme "Enlarge the space of your tent" (Isaiah 54: 2), words that call us to a new opening. There were four hundred and twenty delegates from seventy-nine countries. The local team prepared a terrific welcome for us. In the middle of the gardens, an immense Bedouin tent had been pitched by our Syrian and Lebanese friends to be the space for our prayer, celebrations, evening programs. The environment was joyful with multiple opportunities to meet one another again in this celebratory atmosphere so characteristic of the Spaniards, to the rhythm of castanets.

A serious question arose, concerning the general assembly, and it was faced head-on. Viviane Le Polain and Roy Moussalli finished their international mandates that they had taken with as much faith and love as competence. With them, all the international council had become aware that the structures no longer matched the size of the movement and its needs. They had become too heavy and too complicated. The international leaders were staggering under the weight. It was very difficult to find nominees willing and able to take on the breadth and the diversity of the mission without being crushed by the burden. It was necessary to simplify.

It was necessary to sit down, reflect, have the courage to postpone the election of coordinators and take a break. We proceeded to appoint a temporary Board entrusted for two years to a small group. Henri Major, the husband of Louise Sauriol who had been coordinator for the zone North America for many years, accepted to take the presidency in collaboration with Philippe de Lachapelle, the director for OCH and Father Guy

Vanhoomissen, our international chaplain. Corinne Chatain took on the continuity of tasks and served as a link among everyone. The life and the accompaniment of the movement were assured by the continental, zone and country coordinators. In this way, the most important was safeguarded: the life and the support of the communities. The persons with disabilities kept us faithful and hopeful.

During this time, a study group was given responsibility to consult the different levels of our structure, inviting them to reflect on the essential of our identity and our mission, and to receive from them suggestions for the future.

All this gave shape to the international meeting two years later. An essential part of which was to propose to the members of the general assembly a new and simpler structure with a better distribution of responsibilities. After this, we proceeded to the discernment and election of the leaders.

Lourdes in 2008:
A "constitution" for today

In October 2008, there was this exceptional meeting in Lourdes at the Cité Saint-Pierre, where the Secours Catholique always welcomes us warmly. The two hundred leaders and chaplains coming from seventy countries met to adopt the new Constitution and elect a team of international leaders to enact it. The assembly elected Henri Major president of the Board of Directors. He is a lawyer in Canada and we had gotten to know him at the international meeting in Quebec because he had accepted to help with its organization. Ghislain du Chené was elected international coordinator.

The birth of Julie, who has Down syndrome, had greatly shaken Ghislain and his family. A short while later, Ghislain, an engineer, "fell in love" with Faith and Light! Member of the community "Mustard Seeds" with his wife Isabelle and their five children since 1990, he very quickly placed himself at the service of the movement and took on various responsibilities. What certainly marked him the most was his accompaniment of the countries in Africa. If Ghislain loves this continent unreservedly ("the most beautiful," according to him), its inhabitants love him in return: his kindness, his patience and his white hair made him a wise man, loved and heeded.

Since his election, and especially after his retirement, Ghislain, always with the support of Isabelle, is the Faith and Light "globe-trotter". Courageous, tireless, enthusiastic, he travels the world to participate in provincial assemblies, pilgrimages, formation sessions… The hours on the plane or the endless trips by train or bus, the stopovers in out-of-the-way villages in farthest Romania or Togo, for example, do not frighten him: he accompanies, he witnesses, he teaches, he re-shapes according to the needs. The expression of Saint Thomas Aquinas: *suaviter et fortitier*[1] defines him perfectly.

At the same time, Father Isaac Martinez, General Animator for the Congregation of the Missionaries of the Holy Apostles, relieved Father Vanhoomissen. Father Martinez was the first international chaplain coming from the south: Peru. He entered Faith and Light in 1983. His young brother had cerebral palsy. It was very natural that he became chaplain of a community.

Father Isaac has his home base in Montréal, the headquarters of his congregation. His numerous missionary travels also benefit Faith and Light, to which he brings knowledge of poor countries, the sensitivity of a man from the South and the great quality of his listening.

---

1. With tenderness and strength.

During the meeting in Madrid, Jean Vanier and I announced our decisions to no longer be part of the structures, manifesting in this way our total trust in the leadership. Ghislain told me some time later that this decision confirmed him in the mission that he received and gave him wings. Certainly, Jean and I continue to be closely linked, forever in a communion of hearts, with Faith and Light, with our primary commitment: to be a member of our community, a friend of the weakest and we continue to be ready to serve.

A word of Bishop Jacques Perrier also touched us very much: "To be faithful to the roots of the founders does not mean to imitate them, but to be carried by the essence of their inspiration." He reminded us also how the international pilgrimages have changed spirits in Lourdes. "Faith and Light is now part of the DNA of Lourdes." To this, Ghislain answered: "And Lourdes is part of the DNA of Faith and Light."

When the time for departure came, we were encouraged by the message of Pope Benedict XVI, that Faith and Light, with its new crew, had set out to sea:

"The Pope rejoices that through Faith and Light, numerous families are helping one another and together give much-awaited witness about the infinite value of all human life, even that of the most fragile. May each one always be guided and supported by the conviction that disciples of Christ must, in their mission, express a love, which they have first of all drawn from the heart of the Savior.[1] This is how, by the gift of the Spirit, the one who is weak can say: 'I am strong.'"

---

1. John 4: 10

Lourdes in 2011:
The sending off of forty pilgrimages as "messengers of joy"

From January 28 to February 2, 2011, seventy-nine provincial coordinators (out of eighty) coming from all over the world, met in Lourdes. Most of them were newly elected leaders, many were younger people, and their expectations were great. The choice of the place, Lourdes, and of the date expressed the desire to remain faithful to our roots. The date, February 2 is the "Feast of Light," that was adopted by the movement and that is celebrated everywhere. This is the day when old Simeon[1] called the little baby Jesus the "light of the world who would enlighten all nations". He also announced that a sword would pierce Mary's heart, this sword that so many parents feel at the announcement of the disability of their child. Today, all wanted to respond to the great desire of Jesus, Light of our hearts: "I have come to bring fire to the earth and how greatly I desire that it were already blazing.[2]"

At the opening of the meeting, an enormous candle bearing the logo of Faith and Light was lit by Ghislain du Chené and Father Isaac. This flame shone until the end of the meeting. It continued to burn even longer, because the Cité Saint Pierre (Secours Catholique) that welcomed us, was in charge of lighting it again throughout each of the 40 pilgrimages.

On February 2, at the end of the Eucharist for Candlemas, the leaders lit the candles for their provinces from the flame of the big candle that celebrated our 40 years, so that its flame could be carried to the whole world.

During these days, we became aware of all the work that had been accomplished over the course of two years. The twinning of pilgrimages was in place, each province inviting another province

1. Luke 2: 25-35 - Translator note
2. Luke 12: 49 - Translator note

to participate in its pilgrimage and each province being invited by another. This sometimes resulted in unusual combinations, for instance Madagascar with France-East, or even Malaysia, Australia, New Zealand and Eastern United States.

The preparation teams worked for many months to prepare, take into account the material aspects and plan the spiritual dimension. Despite enormous difficulties, the unexpected, the setbacks that people ran into everywhere, fervor and enthusiasm were there, at the Grotto of Massabielle[1]. Everyone wanted to be an instrument of Jesus' heart on behalf of the weakest and those who accompany them, so that the fire of his love would spread. And may he make each one of us a messenger of his joy![2]

---

1. The grotto where the apparitions took place in Lourdes – Translator note
2. "Messengers of Joy" was the theme of the forty pilgrimages around the world to celebrate the forty years of Faith and Light – Translator note

Epilogue

How could this happen?

In 1990, I had a visit that troubled me deeply. The president of an association, which campaigned for the elimination of newborns with serious disabilities, wished to see me. As I was very intrigued and a bit startled by this request, I asked Pierre Caubel, a volunteer working for publicity and editing of *Ombres et Lumiere*, if he could be present for the interview. A general in the Air Force Reserves, he and his wife Suzon have a little girl named Marie who has a very rare kidney disease. In addition, they adopted Jerome, a young child with very severe disabilities, who came alive in an extraordinary way after he arrived in this family, which already had seven children.

Our visitor introduced herself: she was the mother of Michel, a young man, twenty years old, with an intellectual disability and psychiatric problems. She told the sad, extraordinary tale of her impossible life: abandoned by her husband, shunned by close friends, hostility from the neighborhood because of her son's cries night and day, her professional career ruined by her repeated absences, and the list of hardships she had experienced just went on and on... She ended with a cry of anger and despair: "Don't you think that it was a crime to allow a child like mine to live?" Pierre's inspired response was the following: "The crime, madam, was that you were left all alone in your suffering." There was a long silence. All of her aggressiveness fell away, as if she had been relieved of a colossal burden. We hadn't judged her, or condemned her; we had understood her. She said quietly, "Yes, that's true, I was left all alone with Michel."

We were able, then, to begin to speak. I mentioned Faith and Light. She listened, stunned and open-mouthed. Now and then she asked a question, and then she (referring to Faith and Light) murmured twice, "How could this happen?" Despite our invitation to keep in touch, we never saw her again, but neither Pierre nor I have forgotten her.

She had awoken two feelings in us: the first, a profound compassion for her, for Michel, and for all parents who are living with their children in intolerable situations. Her story reminded us of the monumental challenges the lives of persons with disabilities pose within the world.

In a number of countries, so many people with intellectual disabilities are still considered insane and are sometimes locked up in overcrowded institutions where violence is inevitable. Others are hidden within their family, regarded as a disgrace, a curse. Still others wander the streets or villages, especially in countries where poverty and misery reign, and where the majority of the population lacks everything: food, housing, clothing, medicine.

In other so-called "developed" countries, the value of persons with disabilities is recognized. Laws promise them equal rights and opportunities, participation and citizenship, demand their inclusion, promote their right for autonomy and independence. Immense progress has been made in areas such as equipment or financial assistance, but at the same time, in these same countries (as elsewhere), the suppression of the child with disabilities before birth is allowed, and even encouraged; prenatal testing of mothers has become systematic and it often has the goal of preventing the birth of a child who does not match the one dreamed of or who is not like everyone else.

This emphasis on autonomy and independence, as important as these may be, seems to ignore the essential need of persons with disabilities to be loved and to love, to live the joy of belonging to a community, where the person is encouraged to have an authentic spiritual life, where friendship and fidelity are fostered instead of superficial relationships that have no future; a place where one may discover the happiness of giving oneself and in serving the common good.

At the same time, the amazed wonder of Michel's mother about Faith and Light made us feel with a new intensity how astonishing the work of God through the littlest ones is. "This is impossible! How could this happen?" How can the most wounded persons be able to assemble such an immense multitude in Lourdes and make it into one family? How can disability, disease, objectively considered as something bad – be transformed into a way of love and even of joy?

What then is this great mystery of the person with intellectual disabilities into which we are called to enter?

It is partially unveiled in the Gospels, only partially because we cannot understand fully until heaven. God who chooses the weak to confound the strong, God who hides his mysteries from the wise and intellectuals and reveals them to little ones; God who assures us happiness when we invite the poor, persons with disabilities, to our meals and to our banquets. Jesus who goes so far as to identify himself with them: "Everything that you do to one of these little ones, you do it to me.[1]" Jesus powerless on the cross, who reveals himself in the child that cannot move and whose sufferings we cannot relieve.

In this way, when we help a person with disabilities to walk or to eat, when we go to visit, when we look at him or her with tenderness, it is Jesus that we help, we visit, we regard with

---

1. Matthew 25:40 – Translator note

tenderness. It is Jesus, as present as he is in the Eucharist. It is he, present in the most disturbing child, who is able to make burst forth moments of unexpected joy.

This is why the song of thanksgiving of Faith and Light rises up towards God, because He calls us to walk with those nearest to His heart.

With Mary, we would like to repeat the Magnificat:

> "He removes the powerful from their thrones,
> He lifts up the lowly,
> He fills the hungry with good things.[1]"

September 8, 2011.
On the Feast of the Nativity
of the Virgin Mary.

---

1. Luke 1: 52-53 – Translator note

The Faith and Light Prayer

Jesus, you came into our world
to reveal the Father to us, your Father and our Father.
You came to teach us to love one another.
Give us the Holy Spirit, according to your promise,
so that he will make us
instruments of peace and unity,
in this world of war and division.
Jesus you have called us to follow you
in a community of Faith and Light,
We want to say « yes » to you.
We want to live in a covenant of love
in this big family you have given us,
where we can share our sufferings and difficulties,
our joys and our hope.
Teach us to accept our wounds, our weakness
so that your power may be revealed.
Teach us to find you
in all our brothers and sisters
especially in those who are the weakest.
Teach us to follow you in the ways of the Gospel.
Jesus come and live in us and in our communities
as you first lived in Mary.
She was the first to welcome you.
Help us to be faithfully present, with her,
at the foot of the cross, near the crucified of the world.
Help us to live your Resurrection.
Amen.

Appendices

Contact

Faith and Light international

3 rue du Laos 75015 Paris, France

T. + 33.1.53.69.44.30 – foi.lumiere@wanadoo.fr

Publications

For community building

The Charter and Constitution

Guidelines for the first year

Sharing our responsibility in Faith and Light

You will shine in the world like bright stars

To nurture the meeting

Annual guidelines

"Up Sails!", the Faith and Light international quarterly letter sharing news from the five continents.

For deepening our life together

Deepening our spirituality in Faith and Light

Retreats in Faith and Light

Messages of the Churches to Faith and Light

Ecumenism in Faith and Light

Letters to my brothers and sisters, by Father Joseph Larsen

Websites

Faith and Light International www.faithandlight.org
L'Arche International www.larche.org/en/home

Faith and Light around the world

Faith and Light is present in the following countries:
Argentina. Armenia. Australia. Austria. Belgium. Benin. Brazil.
Burkina Faso. Burundi. Cameroon. Canada. Chile. Colombia.
Croatia. Cyprus. Czech Republic. D.R. Congo. Denmark.
Dominican Republic. Ecuador. Egypt. Estonia. France. French
Guiana. Galilee. Georgia. Germany. Gibraltar. Greece. Honduras.
Hong Kong. Hungary. India. Iran. Ireland. Italy. Ivory Coast.
Japan. Jordan. Kenya. Kuwait. Lebanon. Lithuania. Luxembourg.
Madagascar. Malaysia. Martinique. Mauritius. Mexico.
Netherlands. New Caledonia. New Zealand. Nicaragua. Nigeria.
Norway Pakistan. Paraguay. Peru. Philippines. Poland. Portugal.
Reunion. Romania. Russia. Rwanda. Serbia. Seychelles. Sierra
Leone. Singapore. Slovakia. Slovenia. South Africa. South Korea.
Spain. Sudan. South Sudan. Sweden. Switzerland. Syria. Taiwan.
Togo. Ukraine. United Kingdom. USA. Zambia. Zimbabwe

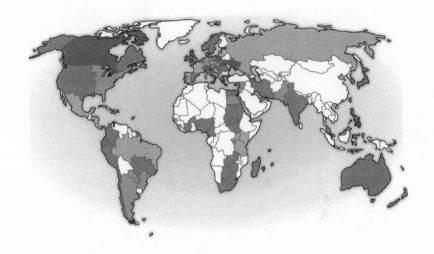

Made in the USA
Middletown, DE
29 November 2014